We Survived

KILOMETRES

MILES

We Survived

**Fourteen Histories
of the Hidden and Hunted in
Nazi Germany**

Revised and Updated

ERIC H. BOEHM

A Member of the Perseus Books Group

Copyright © 1985 by Eric H. Boehm, updated 2003

Westview Press books are available at special discounts for bulk purchases in the United States by corporations, institutions, and other organizations. For more information, please contact the Special Markets Department at the Perseus Books Group, 11 Cambridge Center, Cambridge MA 02142, or call (617) 252-5298 or (800) 255-1514 or email j.mccrary@perseusbooks.com.

Published in 2003 in the United States of America by Westview Press, 5500 Central Avenue, Boulder, Colorado 80301–2877 and in the United Kingdom by Westview Press, 12 Hid's Copse Road, Cumnor Hill, Oxford OX2 9JJ.

Hardcover edition published by Yale University Press, 1949; reprint edition, 1966 by Clio Press.

Material for Epilogue 1985 adapted with permission from "Comment: 'Prevention of Genocide,'" by Eric H. Boehm, in *Western Society after the Holocaust*, edited by Lyman H. Legters (Westview Press, 1983).

Find us on the World Wide Web at www.westviewpress.com

A Cataloging-in-Publication data record for this book is available from the Library of Congress.

ISBN 0-8133-4058-6 (pbk)

*Dedicated
to the
Survivors*

*In Memory of
the Countless Dead*

Contents

Introduction: In Retrospect

The Historical Setting of We Survived

JUST AS HUMAN EVIL IS REVEALED IN THIS BOOK, so is the human potential for good and the possibility of attendant salvation. Viktor Frankl, himself a survivor of Auschwitz, addresses the issues of good and evil in humankind and the attendant therapy he espouses in his famous book *Man's Search for Meaning*. He emphasizes in this searching book: "The rift dividing good from evil, which goes through all human beings , reaches into the lowest depths and becomes apparent even on the bottom of the abyss which is laid open by the concentration camp" (p. 87). The great Italian literary figure, Primo Levi, became one of the most sensitive observers in the Auschwitz extermination camp. He made this insightful observation: "Survival without renunciation of any part of one's moral worlds— apart from powerful and direct interventions by fortune—was conceded only to a very few superior individuals, made of the stuff of martyrs and saints."[1] The literature on survival and genocide has grown exponentially in the past decades—itself part of the huge evidence of our search for a meaningful interpretation of who we humans are and what we are capable of becoming—and seeing us always groping for answers.

In 2002, as these lines go to the publisher, we are again living in times of threats of wars. The relevance of the chapters in this book to issues of survival that confront us today is more acute than ever during this new era of weapons of mass destruction that were first developed in World War II. The chapters in this book hold up to us a mirror of humanity—at its worst and its best: evidence of both the horrible and the good of humanity runs through the pages of this book.

A longer historical perspective we try to convey below, with the help of the distinguished historian Arthur Schlesinger Jr.'s insightful article, provides reason for hope. Long-term survival is a function of good government, both on the national and world arenas. The United Nations Organization may not be all we wish it to be, but contrasted with the weakness of its predecessor, the League of Nations, the United Nations is a beacon of significance and strength. The issues that engaged our minds and hearts during the darkest and most threatening of times of the twentieth century led many contemporaries to believe in a "wave of the future" of totalitarian states—that in fact capitalized on acute human needs to treat human beings as pawns. In his overview of the twentieth century Arthur Schlesinger Jr. conveys that faith was justified in "the coming victory of democracy" (as we expressed our optimism in the darkest days of the twentieth century) and hence of governments that nurture the lives of their citizens. Here is his article on the twentieth century, both replete with realism and hope: "Totalitarianism collapsed before the superior power, energy and vitality of free societies."

Witness to the Century: The Glorious and the Damned
Arthur Schlesinger Jr.[2]

It's coming to an end at last, this disordered, disheveled, fantastic, path-breaking century, this crazy epoch of troubles and tragedies and triumphs. Our century has been glorious, and it has been damned. It has sent humanity through unprecedented horrors on the way to the stars. It has been, in the words of the English philosopher Isaiah Berlin, "the most terrible [century] in Western history." The world wars carried destruction to the far corners of the planet. The chronicles of human wreckage—the Holocaust and the gulag—haunt us still. At the same time, ours has been the century in which science and technology have opened dazzling new prospects for suffering humankind.

What will the future make of the 20th century? Five hundred years from now, our century will probably be remembered most of all as the century in which earthlings at last burst their terrestrial bonds and began the exploration of space. My generation was reared on the visionary imagination of Jules Verne and H.G. Wells. But space travel always seemed a romantic dream. I never thought that men would actually land on the moon in my lifetime. Yet it happened in 1969. To me it was the most exciting event in the century. The aftermath has been rather dilatory, almost as if Columbus had come to America in 1492 and no one had bothered to follow up. But the century ahead will surely see startling new developments in the grand adventure of space.

From the perspective of 2500, our century will also be remembered as the century that opened the Pandora's box of nuclear weapons. Henry Adams, the most brilliant of American historians, had earlier foreseen the possibility of ultimate catastrophe. "I firmly believe that before many centuries more, science will be the master of man," Adams wrote in 1862 while the *Monitor* and the Merrimack, two new ironclad vessels, were harrying each other around Newport News, VA. "Some day science shall have the existence of mankind in its power, and the human race will commit suicide by blowing up the world."

Precisely a century later, that day almost arrived. The Cuban missile crisis of 1962 was probably the most dangerous moment in human history. Never before did nations locked in mortal rivalry possess the technical capacity to destroy the Earth. Fortunately wise statesmanship averted disaster, and the superpowers never called forth their dread arsenals. Yet the threat continues into the century ahead. No problem is more urgent at the millennium than the need to stop the testing and proliferation of nuclear weapons.

The Cold War cast grim shadows over the Earth for nearly half our century. But men and women in centuries to come will very likely find the confrontation between the Soviet Union and the West almost as obscure and incomprehensible as we today find the Thirty Years' War—the terrible conflict that devastated so much of Europe in the first half of the 17th century. Looking back at the 20th century, our descendants will probably be astonished at the disproportion between the causes of the global civil war, which may seem trivial, and the possible consequences, which might have meant the veritable end of history.

The outcome of the Cold War did at least register the conditional triumph of democracy. The 20th had been a rough century for the democratic states, under siege from without by totalitarian dictatorships, bedeviled from within by poverty, racism, gross inequality and spiritual vacancy.

Our century began in an optimistic mood about the future of democracy. Then the Great War showed that democracy could not guarantee peace, and the Great Depression showed that democracy could not guarantee prosperity. Fanatical anti-democratic movements arose in the wake of the First World War—communism in Russia, fascism in Italy, Nazism in Germany, militarism in Japan. The economic collapse of the 1930's increased the appeal of totalitarian creeds. Despairing people concluded that democracy was hopeless, that capitalism was finished and that the dictators offered the best hope of salvation.

By 1941 only about a dozen democracies were left on the planet. The democratic faith had its back to the wall, fighting for its life. Totalitarianism appeared to be, in the title of Anne Morrow Lindbergh's best-selling tract, "the wave of the future." Yet, as the millennium descends upon us, democracy has triumphed over its two mortal enemies, fascism perishing with a bang, communism with a whimper.

But the conditional triumph of democracy does not solve our problems. The failures of democracy in the 20th century produced the totalitarian challenges. In the century ahead, if people are not once more to turn their backs on freedom, democracy must construct a humane, prosperous and peaceful world. It must deliver the goods.

"The problem of the 20th century," the black historian W.E.B. Du Bois wrote in 1900, "is the problem of the color line." That will be even more the problem of the century to come. Racial justice is an acute internal problem for the Western democracies. And it will be an even keener problem between the democracies and the Third World. The Second World War hastened the end of colonialism and newly independent states now struggle to define their identities, to modernize their societies, to keep heads above water in the globalized economy.

For if the 20th has been a century of destruction, it has also been a century of liberation and of creativity. Democracy has at last confronted some of its internal contradictions—the subordinate role, for example, that white males had so long allotted to the other sex and to other colors. The arts have flourished—literature, painting, music, sculpture, architecture, not to mention the 20th century's most distinctive and popular art, the movies.

Even more spectacular have been the metamorphoses wrought by science and technology. We have seen a revolution in medicine. Science has contained scourges of the past—smallpox, polio, diphtheria, malaria, tuberculosis—and has plumbed deeper than ever before into the human condition. Molecular biology thrusts forward into the very basis of life. The discovery of DNA leads on to genetic surgery, recombinant DNA, transplantation, cloning and heaven knows what. Cancer and AIDS still defy our scientists and present a bitter challenge to the 21st century.

And technology has revolutionized the way we live. The computer and the microchip are bringing about structural transformations as profound as those produced by the Industrial Revolution two centuries ago. The Industrial Revolution represented the shift from a farm-based to a factory-based economy. We are undergoing a comparable shift today from a factory-based to a computer-based economy. The Industrial Revolution was a time of strain. But it stretched over generations and allowed time for human and institutional adjustment. The Computer Revolution is far more compressed, far more dynamic—and in consequence far more traumatic.

The instantaneity of communication in the digital age has shrunk the planet and created the world market. Problems abound as a result. Globalization reduces the capacity of the nation-state to shape its economic destiny. It threatens labor and environmental standards painfully attained in developed countries. It plunges people into a vast anonymous arena beyond their comprehension and control. It thereby generates a backlash in the form of religious fundamentalism and ethnic tribalism. One great task for the century ahead is to come to terms with the global market. The way to tame the destructive consequences of globalization is to build and strengthen international institutions.

But do not despair. The victory of democracy over totalitarianism shows that free men are not the slaves of history. The totalitarian movements had presented themselves as the embodiment of inexorable historical forces. There was, they said, no resisting the wave of the future. History, they deeply believed, was on their side. Ideology provided assurance that victory was inevitable.

Yet totalitarianism collapsed before the superior power, energy and vitality of free societies. Where totalitarianism suppressed the individual, democracy empowers individuals, giving them the opportunity and the right to think and debate and invent and dream.

We know now that individuals can make a difference to history. Suppose Lenin had died of typhus when exiled to Siberia in 1897; suppose Hitler had been killed on the western front in 1916. Does anybody think that the 20th century would have been the same? And had Lenin and Hitler lived, would democracy have defeated totalitarianism without the leadership of Franklin D. Roosevelt and Winston Churchill?

In December 1931 Churchill, crossing Fifth Avenue in New York, was knocked down by an automobile—a moment, he later said, of a man aghast, a world aglare: "I do not understand why I was not broken like an eggshell." Fourteen months later Roosevelt, sitting in an open car in Miami, was fired on by an assassin; the man beside him fell dead. Suppose the automobile had killed Churchill and the bullet had killed Roosevelt, could Neville Chamberlain have rallied Britain in 1940? Could FDR's vice president, John N. Garner, have produced the New Deal and the Four Freedoms? For better or for worse, individual leadership can transform the course of history.

No leader brought out the best of the 20th century more effectively than Franklin D. Roosevelt. In striving for his objectives, FDR could be tricky, manipulative and tough. But these objectives amounted to the emancipation of humanity. He defined them best in 1941 when he set forth the Four Freedoms—Freedom of Speech and Expression, Freedom of Worship, Freedom from Want, Freedom from Fear. These remain humanity's vital purposes today.

As I have written elsewhere, our world at the end of the 20th century is manifestly not Hitler's world. His Thousand Year Reich had a brief and bloody run of a dozen years. It is manifestly not Lenin's world. That ghastly world self-destructed before our eyes. Nor is it Churchill's world. Empire and its glories have long since vanished into history. Our world today is the world of the Four Freedoms, Franklin Roosevelt's world, constructed on his terms, propelled by his hope and his vision.

The 21st century agenda is formidable. But the conditions for its fulfillment are within reach. FDR's Four Freedoms still offer the noblest goal for our troubled but yearning world—the world that we will soon quietly pass on to our children and grandchildren.

Notes

1. Primo Levi, *Survival in Auschwitz: The Nazi Assault on Humanity* (New York: Simon and Schuster, 1996), p. 92

2. Arthur Schlesinger Jr., "The Glorious and the Damned," reprinted with permission of *AARP Bulletin*, December 1999, pp. 14–16.

Introduction

By

ERIC H. BOEHM

IN SEPTEMBER of 1945 I drove through the Neukölln section of
Berlin. A peculiar odor still hung over the center of the city—
the odor from the corpses which lay in the canals, under the
ruins, and in the flooded sections of the subway. Everywhere was
the contrast of life and death. People were queued up in front of
a store located in the one remaining fragment of an apartment
house. In another building halved by a bomb, with a bathtub
hanging in mid-air, a woman was replacing a piece of cardboard
with a precious windowpane.

I detoured around impassable streets, crossed the bridge of the
Landwehrkanal, and stopped at the Thielschufer synagogue. It
was the day of Rosh Hashonoh 5906. I wanted once more to attend a Jewish service as I had known it in Germany as a boy—
and to take part in the first New Year in twelve years to be celebrated openly and freely by Jews in Germany.

As I saw the congregation praying I felt that there was poetic
justice in these of Hitler's and Himmler's intended victims being
alive while their murderers were dead. Yet the survivors were few
and the dead were many.

After the services I talked to several persons of the congregation. As mail connections had not yet been restored, some had not
been able to get in touch with their relatives abroad. They longed
to send word that they were alive, and I was happy to be the messenger of good tidings. The little they told of themselves and
what had happened to them during the war stirred me deeply. I
felt that their stories should reach more ears than mine.

As an interrogator of German prisoners during the war I
had gained in understanding of Nazi Germany and had become
acquainted with the activities of the opposition groups within the
country. When, after my discharge from the American Army I

took a job as press control officer with the Information Control
Division of Military Government, scrutinizing newspapers published in the American Zone of Germany, I learned how difficult
it was for the press control branch to establish papers and find
editors who had not compromised themselves with the Nazis.
More than once the trail of an anti-Nazi led to a concentration
camp and ended there.

Those who fought for human rights against Nazi injustice
came to call themselves "the illegals." Where injustice had become law, normal standards and values were reversed, and those
who stood for uprightness and humanity were lawbreakers in the
Nazi state.

It is not yet known exactly how many suffered at the hands of
the Nazis for their opposition. According to a Gestapo report of
April 10, 1939, those charged with political crimes in the first
six years under Hitler included 162,734 in "protective custody,"
the euphemism which usually meant concentration camp; 112,-
432 sentenced by trial; 27,369 awaiting trial. In one sample
month, May, 1938, 1,639 were executed after trial for political
offenses of all sorts. Before 1933 such trials or executions were
almost unknown. According to a secret report of the Gestapo for
1936, the year of the Olympic Games in Berlin, almost 12,000 persons were arrested in Germany for illegal propaganda; in addition there were 17,000 trials for sedition. Of the Wehrmacht
9,523 were executed on charges of mutiny and political work
against the Nazis even before the coup d'état of July 20, 1944,
with its toll of additional thousands. Over a period of twelve years
almost 3,000,000 Germans were in and out of concentration
camps and penitentiaries for political reasons—sometimes for as
little as a remark critical of the government. About 800,000 of
these had been arrested for overt anti-Nazi acts; only 300,000 of
them were still alive after the war—so that among the "illegals"
alone 500,000 gave their lives. As the war progressed and as Nazi
conquests extended, Central Europe became one vast prison in
which millions of people from all nations were behind barbed
wire.

Hitler's decision, made at the beginning of the war, to extermi-
nate German Jewry brought to a climax a persecution which

started in 1933 and increased steadily in ferocity. The Nuremberg Laws of September, 1935, decreed the systematic exclusion of "non-Aryans"—those with one or more Jewish grandparents—from social life and many phases of economic life. The signs "Jews not allowed" became commonplace, occasionally emended "Jews and dogs not permitted." In November, 1938, the assassination of vom Rath, third secretary in the German Embassy in Paris, by a young Polish Jew was made the occasion to carry out a well-laid plan which involved the arrest and detention in concentration camps for at least a few weeks of most Jewish males, from adolescents up; the demolition of Jewish homes and closing of Jewish businesses; the desecration of synagogues and graves; and the levy of a fine of a billion marks on German Jewry. The total exclusion of Jews from German economic life was almost achieved. After 1941 they literally became a marked people, having to wear on their outer garments the badge with the Star of David outlined in black on a yellow field. After that deportation to the death camps of eastern Europe started in earnest.

Some figures on the fate of the Jewish community of Berlin, which was by far the largest in Germany, are illuminating:

Jews by confession in Berlin in 1933	somewhat over 170,000
Emigrated during the Nazi period	70,000
Deported during the Nazi period	slightly under 100,000
Of mixed marriage, not deported	3,000
Liberated and returned from camps	1,900
Lived underground and survived	1,500
In Berlin in November, 1947	7,861

Of the 500,000 Jews in Germany, 281,900 had emigrated by July 31, 1940, as well as two-thirds of the 200,000 Austrian Jews. Only a handful of the remainder are living today. Jews in the rest of Europe suffered even larger losses because most were caught when the Wehrmacht conquered their countries. Five million European Jews in all were exterminated or died in camps of starvation and disease. Distributed over a period of a thousand days, from 1942, when the wholesale liquidation of Jews started, to 1945, this represents 5,000 murders a day. Such numbers defy our capacity to understand, but when there is just one person you know and love among them, the figures assume concrete meaning.

A cousin of my father's living in Berlin told me how her fiancé had saved her from deportation and death by hiding her in his apartment for two years, sharing with her his single food ration card. Her story suggested some of the ways the persecuted had managed to live in spite of all odds. With the help of various organizations, such as OdF—a society formed by the "Victims of Fascism"—and Jewish, Protestant, and Catholic churches, I came to know more than fifty persons who told me of their struggle for life and freedom.

Some of them speak in this book. Many types of experiences of the hidden and hunted are included. There are the Jews, such as Frau Jeanette Wolff who suffered both for her socialism and for being Jewish, and Rabbi Leo Baeck, once the spiritual head of the Jewish community in Germany. There are accounts from a wide range of political, religious, and moral opposition. Günther Weisenborn tells of one of the underground organizations most active against the Nazis. The young mechanic, Herbert Kosney, who might like his father have become a National Socialist, instead turned toward Communism and tells of his share in its resistance. Antiwar feeling, which influenced many of the younger generation in Europe, had a part in the anti-Nazi development of the young artist, Knud Christian Knudsen. Lagi Countess Ballestrem-Solf, daughter of a distinguished diplomat, opposed National Socialism from liberal convictions and on moral grounds. The story of the conspiracy of July 20, 1944, is told by the Protestant clergyman, Eugen Gerstenmaier, one of its leading participants and rare survivors.

Most of these people spent many evenings and week ends telling me of the lives the Nazis caused them to lead—as lawbreakers, plotters, deserters, fugitives, prisoners. Truth was many times stranger than fiction. Sometimes their good fortune seemed beyond belief, their ill fortune beyond endurance. I questioned and took voluminous notes. Some who were able and willing to write down their experiences I asked to do so. The stories as given here have been kept scrupulously close to the form and language of the informants. The accounts are confirmed by documentary evidence and great pains have been taken to be accurate. Dramatic as some of the happenings are, there is nothing fictitious except, of necessity, a few proper names. These are indicated as such in the index.

The material was not complete when I returned to the United States in September, 1947, to resume my graduate study. Frau Alice Stein-Landesmann, whose own story is among these, and Inge Pauli, who is now my wife, were my capable mediaries in Germany and ran down the answers to the innumerable questions which kept arising. Material for the stories of Leo Baeck and Heinrich Liebrecht was secured from them in the United States and that for the chapters of Eugen Gerstenmaier and Günther Weisenborn was obtained by correspondence after I had left Germany.

Words cannot convey the heartache the living feel for the loss of their dear ones. None of them wear it on their sleeve. They talk hesitantly too of events which reflected glory on them; often I first heard about these through third persons. But they are willing, or even anxious to speak, because they had promised themselves during the Nazi years that they would tell their story as a warning to posterity, or because they felt that their sufferings had made them better, or believed they owed it to the dead to try to prevent a recurrence of the Nazi disaster.

As life in a totalitarian dictatorship is so different from a democracy some words of explanation are called for. In the newsreel shots of Nazi pageantry we saw the masses marching and heiling their Führer. We read of 99 per cent plebiscites. But of course we saw no newsreels of anti-Nazi opposition, of concentration camps, of surreptitious distribution of leaflets, or of arrests at night by apparently harmless civilians—the Gestapo. Only the fanatic supporters and the masses giving their whole-hearted or conditional support were in evidence. We could conclude from the success of Nazi domestic policy that large sections of the German population followed their Führer, all the more readily because of the traditional German obedience and faith in the authority of the state. Millions of others had the apathy of those "not interested in politics."

The gradual increase of National Socialist power and en-
croachment upon individual liberties was so widely accepted as
necessary to overcome the economic crisis, and was so insidious,
that many Germans did not realize they had been placed in a
strait jacket until they tried to move. Then they found, as
Thomas Paine once said, that tyranny, like hell, is not easily conquered. Once in command the Nazis had at their disposal all the
powerful techniques of a modern state, against which the single
individual is almost helpless. They perfected their methods of
reward and punishment, providing great benefits for entering the
the fold and harsh penalties for the recalcitrant.

Nazi propaganda, like a nation-wide revival meeting, pre-
cluded rational thinking. Mass meetings, speeches, bands, pa-
rades were designed to arouse emotion, befog thinking, and intimidate opposition. The printed page, the radio, the cinema
were harnessed in one vast campaign, pounding out slogans day
in and day out and slyly perverting information. It took considerable strength of character and independence of spirit to remain
uncontaminated.

Meanwhile the police became an instrument of terror. They
took over and improved some old techniques, such as registration
of all changes of residence, a common custom in Europe. Identification cards, also known before 1933, increased in number and
significance. Informing, shadowing, wire tapping laid men's
minds bare to the all-seeing eye of the state. People used the war-
time slogan of the spy-fearing government, "Careful! The enemy
is listening!" to warn the incautious against making critical statements publicly. An honest word or a sympathetic deed might be
an act of heroism. The remark "I shall live to see the end of
Hitler's thousand-year Reich" was enough to send one to trial or
straight to concentration camp. And fear of the camp, of torture,
of death lay oppressive upon the nonconformer.

Even the normal instinct for self-preservation played into the
hands of the Nazis. Many Jews complied with deportation orders
because they had come to believe that obeying, as they had been
accustomed to since childhood, would help avoid worse disaster.
They wanted to believe that they heard the truth when told that
the transports were going to "relocation" or "labor" in the east.

Adjustment to the Nazi regime produced new techniques in everyday life. Codes were developed for freer communication by letter. Words took on new meanings. "He has gone on a trip" might convey "to concentration camp." A member of the family or a visiting friend gave an agreed number of knocks or rings at the door.

Before the war the anti-Nazis fought a losing battle within Germany, and fought it with little encouragement or understanding from the peoples of the democracies. During the war it was difficult for the outside enemies of the Nazis to realize that those dying for the cause of freedom on the "inner front" were joined in common cause with us. To those who survived—as well as to millions of others—Allied victory meant liberation. It was the break of day for which they had waited and worked and suffered, and it made their struggle through the Nazi nightmare meaningful. Yet today they are still suffering hunger, hardship, and disillusion . . .

The character of "civilized" man is revealed in these pages in extraordinary dimensions. As his capacity for evil is seen in large, so is his capacity for good. There are among our contemporaries those whose standards of humanity are as lofty as any in the great moral teachings of the Judaic-Christian tradition. While terror and fear ruled with a knout, righteousness continued to live. It lived underground, it was "illegal," submerged, imprisoned, evicted, and deported—but it survived. As these chapters show the weaknesses and the crimes of man, so they also testify to his strength and heroism. Let us draw our hope from that.

Acknowledgments

My thanks go first to the persons who have made this book possible through reliving their past for me. I spent many memorable hours with them and acquired friendships I shall always cherish.

It is difficult to conceive how this book would ever have been completed without my wife who began helping me as soon as the work was started. She aided me untiringly in gathering material. After I had returned to the United States she was the intermediary between the survivors and me. When we were reunited, she stood by me with counsel and suggestions from her rich store of knowledge about Germany. Finally, she alone shouldered the long, hard task of typing and retyping. When the work on the book, which I carried on alongside my studies, threatened to overwhelm me, it was she who stepped into the breach with encouragement and help. I can never express my thanks to her fully enough.

To Miss Roberta Yerkes of the Yale University Press goes my heartfelt gratitude for her skillful editing of the manuscript. By her searching questions she contributed greatly toward clarifying the book for an American audience. She was often able to bring insight and aptness of phrase that expressed the vigor and deep feeling of the original experiences. Her selfless work went far beyond anything I could reasonably have expected.

I should like to thank my friend Norvin Hein for his constant readiness to read and criticize the various manuscripts, over which he spent considerable time, and for his stimulating and valuable suggestions. I am also grateful for advice and assistance to John Derby, Ignatius Mattingly, Ernest Mylon, Hilde Oppenheimer, Mr. and Mrs. Maximilian Pauli, Paul Pickrel, and Alice and Claire Stein-Landesmann.

E.H.B.

We Survived

PROLOGUE TO CHAPTER I

The Strength of Two

ALICE STEIN-LANDESMANN is a novelist and playwright. Her play *Bahnwärterhaus* was produced in the 1920's in Germany, the Netherlands, and the United States and ran in Berlin for seventy-two performances.

Frau Landesmann sometimes recalls the peaceful and pleasant world before World War I and talks of people she knew in her youth and while her husband was alive: Gerhart Hauptmann, Hermann Sudermann, Joseph Kainz, Max Reinhardt. When she speaks of her recent past it is as if she talked of a different person and another world.

I

The Strength of Two

ALICE STEIN-LANDESMANN

IT IS a rainy October evening in 1942. I have never been in this part of the city before. Here in north Berlin I feel as if I were walking through a strange town. But that is reassuring: nobody knows me here. It is quite dark by now. Not a lamp throws light on the rain-swept streets. We cross a desolate backyard.

"Look out, two steps. Here we are. Don't make any noise." Claire unlocks the door. I step inside but hesitate. My being revolts against this enforced concealment. I feel a lump in my throat.

Claire puts down my little suitcase and switches on the light. She comes toward me, her serious, frank face showing that she understands my feelings. "Don't let it get you down. Believe me, you'll get used to it, everything will go well in a little while." She takes my hands in hers and smiles. It is that smile of hers that made me love and trust her at first sight.

I look at my surroundings. It is one of those one-room apartments which serves as kitchenette, bedroom, and living room. Dark velveteen curtains shut out the hostile world; books—scores of books—line the walls. There is a low tile table with tea glasses and flowers.

Claire takes my hat and coat. I am old enough to be her mother, but she looks after me as if I were a child. It seems incredible that this young woman should really wish to share her bed and ration card with me. I do not see how I can accept the sacrifice. I try to speak but my voice fails, I can only stammer, "I can't . . ." A wave of despair floods over me.

"Now stop it, you mustn't worry," says Claire. Her matter-of-fact manner is magically reassuring. "Remember you promised?

We'll have a cup of tea, and about eight o'clock my father will come to see me. I didn't like to call off his visit, but he won't ask awkward questions. That is not done in our family. You are here now, and nobody will be surprised."

An hour later I am engrossed in a game of checkers with her father, the shoemaker Franz Kochan, to whom Claire introduced me as "Frau Riebe." Claire is doing some mending. The old man rarely speaks. His finely moulded head is bald, his face looks haggard and drawn, he appears to be a sick man. Now and again he looks up from the board and scans my face.

"Frau Riebe thinks like us, Father—but I still think you'd better not talk politics," says Claire.

"I assume that any person I meet in your place is all right," the old man mutters. He sighs, and his thin white beard quivers.

For the first time I detect an expression of fear and sadness in Claire's eyes. I see her give her father a reassuring pat on the arm. Has my situation made me peculiarly sensitive? I cannot refrain from taking her hand: is there some secret trouble here, too?

"Everything is all right," she whispers.

Old Kochan pays no attention to her words. At last he moves one of the checkers, handling it carefully with his hard, gnarled fingers. No one speaks. The radio announcer introduces a song hit from a light opera.

I forget all about the game while my mind runs back over the hours since my first meeting with Claire.

Less than a week ago I climbed for the last time the four flights of stairs to the apartment of my old friend Hedwig Simon, to say farewell. This woman of seventy-three was to be called for next morning and shipped to Theresienstadt, the Jewish ghetto town in Czechoslovakia. All day long we packed and sorted her belongings. On a table by her bed lay a bundle of letters from which she read to me before handing them to me for burning. She had kept them for more than forty years. They told a story of tender love between herself and someone who had died long ago. In spite of her great self-control, Hedwig was suddenly overwhelmed by despair. I persuaded her to lie down and, exhausted, she slept. As I looked down at this woman, so full of grace and charm that

I loved her with all my heart, I bitterly regretted that it was not in my power to make her sleep of exhaustion end in merciful eternal rest.

The sound of the doorbell roused me. It was Claire Kochan, whom I had seen here several times before. She was a small person whose sturdy hands showed that she was accustomed to hard work. She had met Frau Simon through friends and knew her only slightly. But she had made it her duty to supply the old woman with foodstuffs that were officially denied to Jews, such as fruit, white bread, and other delicacies. Today she too had come to say good-by. We sat together for about an hour, waiting for Frau Simon to wake. I learned that only a year ago Claire had lost her closest friend, a young Jewish nurse who had been deported to Poland just as she was about to emigrate to the Argentine.

Claire told me that she had made up her mind to take a Jewess into her home. A year ago she had not been in a position to do so, but now she could offer another woman the shelter she had been unable to give her friend.

"Have you found a place to hide?" she asked me. I stared at this young woman who seemed so determined to assume this great burden. When I said that Hedwig Simon should be considered first, Claire shook her head. "To go into hiding under these conditions, you must have presence of mind and a certain adroitness in dealing with tricky situations, and you must be able to adapt yourself to new surroundings. She is too old to do that. I have a small place in Berlin-Wedding, one large room with cooking facilities. We can manage somehow, and you will find good books there."

"But you hardly know me, and living together so closely will mean that you must sacrifice a great deal!"

Her clear eyes met mine and she answered very seriously, "I have been ready and willing to do this for months. You are the person whom I can help. You would have to make up your mind to stay indoors, at least for the present, and to go out for a walk only after dark. It will not be an easy life for you, and you will have to do without many things you have been used to."

"But you are not thinking of the difficulties that will arise for *you!*" I managed to say.

The smile that lit up her face lent it great charm. "I'll take care of those," she said. "But let's talk about the most important thing. Of course we will have to manage on one ration card. Have you friends, by any chance, who could help you out with food now and then?"

I thought of my Gentile cousin Anna. She was a good person and would surely help.

"Fine. Now what about your things? I haven't much room to spare, but of course we will take everything into our home that is dear and important to you."

I told her that Anna would certainly store some of my things for me. Claire went on to speak of practical details. She was very matter of fact and efficient. She obviously came from humble surroundings, had been obliged to take care of herself for years, and had apparently worked hard to make a good home for herself. I wondered if she failed to see the danger involved in her proposal or was rashly disregarding it. But foolhardiness did not seem to be part of her character.

I suggested that we both think the matter over for a week. During the following days I was in a state of agitation. Did I dare to place such a burden on the shoulders of a kind-hearted woman? Should I endanger her life?

"Your move!" says Kochan. He turns again to Claire and looks at her sadly.

I try to concentrate on the game but I cannot help hearing him whisper, "You'll see, Claire, the boy will never get out again!" Claire gives him a reassuring answer, but I can feel that her optimism is only pretended. I lose the game.

Kochan rises to go. "Are you staying?" I feel myself blush.

"Frau Riebe is spending the night, Father."

"That is good. There's no sense running around the streets at night in this Egyptian darkness. First they start inventing electric street lamps. Then they go on to invent bombs, so that we can't use the lights! To hell with progress, if that is all it amounts to!" He leaves, and Claire sees him out.

For eleven hours every day I am by myself. At 7.30 A.M. Claire leaves for the office and she does not come back until 6.30. Being cooped up in this lonely room gives me much time for thought. I avoid showing myself at the window: this building has hundreds of eyes. Of course there is no actual danger if I am seen during the day; still, we do not wish to attract unnecessary attention. I dare not switch on the radio or use the typewriter. I read, write, do some mending, and find it hard to bear the monotonous routine of the day patiently.

For the present I have kept Claire's address secret from my friends. Once a week I market in my old neighborhood, as long as the woman who shares my former apartment goes on receiving ration cards for me. Nobody in that house is to know that I pay only occasional visits there.

And so each week I take the subway to western Berlin. I can use it only when I am not wearing the yellow Jewish star. On leaving the subway I hurry to some archway and change into a jacket adorned with that bit of yellow rag, so that I can do my shopping on the coupons allotted to me as a Jewess. Having completed my errands I change again in some corner, and once more look like a regular human being. I hasten down the steps to my train, always in mortal fear of meeting someone who knows me and may denounce me. By the time I get back to Claire's I am limp and exhausted with fear. But in order to get food I continued to inflict this torment on myself until the middle of December, 1942. Then I broke down completely, which meant that from that time on we had to do with less.

So now we have but one ration card between us. Once in a while Anna meets me in a small restaurant in Halensee and fills my market bag with food. Fortunately it grows dark early these days; that makes these meetings easier. In the streetcar I shrink into a corner, not daring to raise my head. At home I am startled whenever the bell rings. And at night voices, steps, shouts, quarrels, crying in my imagination are turned into sinister dangers threatening me.

Often after Herr Kochan's visits we would sit up late talking. It was natural that we should wish to compare our pasts, which had differed so widely. I felt ashamed when I realized how little I had known of lives devoted to nothing but work. In novels I had read of people who would walk two hours to save ten pfennig;

but Claire had actually bought almost every piece of furniture in her home from money saved that way. She told me casually about the years in which she was often either hungry or cold, because she had too little money to buy both food and fuel. She was so fanatically bent on being completely independent that her decision to let another person share her life seemed all the more surprising. But her naturalness helped to make intimacy easy for both of us. She was incredibly quick, and I, used only to working at my desk, was amazed at all she managed to do after a ten-hour day in the office.

Her mother had neglected her husband and small children and then left them. Claire told how her mother would lock her in the coal cellar at night, dressed only in a shirt, or would throw iron pots and pans at the children. Claire refused to look upon the woman as her mother and had severed all connection with her. Father Kochan divorced his wife after coming home from the war, in 1919, a sick man. He had devoted himself to his children so that they scarcely missed a mother's care. His only mistake was in not having them learn a proper trade. Three of his sons became bellboys in hotels; the eldest, Karl, went to work in a factory.

One son Bruno, was a fanatical Nazi, and Claire did not see him at all. The youngest boy, Richard, was the object of much loving anxiety on the part of his sister and father. An ambitious and gifted boy, he had early shown an inclination to live on false pretenses. Unlike his brother Karl, he spoke cultivated German and dressed very neatly. His craving for success had been stimulated when he worked as bellboy in a film actors' club. Later he worked in the clothing business for some time; then was unemployed for five years and did nothing but collect his weekly dole. Father Kochan provided him with cigarettes and stacks of books from circulating libraries. After that, by chance, Richard became a male nurse. He soon succeeded in obtaining a responsible position in a nursing home and was very adept at giving injections. His pleasant manners made him well liked and eventually he became the doctors' right-hand man. From that time on he associated almost exclusively with well-to-do patients, and his manner grew more and more snobbish. Claire watched this development with increasing anxiety. She seldom saw her brother; but he was always very faithful to his father and often took him out for a spree. The old man accepted these invitations with a mixture of pleasure and irony.

Richard had now been away from Berlin for two years and his family was in the dark about his occupation and his private life. He would turn up unexpectedly, invite his father to a sumptuous meal, and ask him to admire his well-tailored clothes. He would drop veiled hints about his activities and then disappear again. Claire was very depressed about all this and asked me never to mention Richard's name in her father's presence.

Claire herself had had various temporary jobs before she finally settled down. Kochan placed her in a baker's and confectioner's shop at the age of fifteen. After that she worked at a hairdresser's for a time. When she was old enough to realize that she was not suited for either type of work, she took a job as telephone operator in a big firm. She rose to the post of secretary to the personnel chief there, and thus in the course of nine years had acquired an excellent position.

Father Kochan had looked forward all his life to carefree days which never came. Now he was incurably ill and received a small pension as a war veteran. He would tell me now and then how hard he had tried to provide "decent clothes" for his children. "I wanted those kids of mine to look neat. And I wanted them to have fruit every day." He would smile, but it was a sad smile. "Believe me, it's no good—a man without a wife." He shook his head.

One evening late in January, 1943, old Kochan and I were once more playing checkers. The old man was bending over the board, his face as white as chalk. I noticed that he did not even see the pieces. And his pipe kept going out.

"It's true, they say, that many people are happy," I heard him mutter, "only I've never met any of them. Who promised us that we'd be happy anyway? And now, when I'm about to die, this rabble—these criminals—govern the country. There's no hope, Claire—" He suddenly turned toward her with a gesture of despair; his pipe dropped from his hand. I felt that this evening had new trouble in store for us. I stammered that I must go and get a newspaper, grabbed my coat, and ran into the street.

Outside it was pitch dark; the black-out seemed a terrible symbol of the conditions in which we were living. The pavement was slippery and I walked unsteadily, flakes of snow whirling around me.

Suddenly I felt my homelessness as a curse. In a dark corner of a doorway I took shelter and stood staring in front of me. Suddenly I began to tremble. The temptation was besetting me to put an end to it all, to stop being a burden to others, never again to wake up screaming.

But I mechanically retraced my steps to Claire's, thinking myself a coward. Claire was alone and in tears. She clung to me. I had never seen her so desperate. Finally she told me the story. The previous fall the Gestapo had forced their way into Kochan's flat to arrest Richard. The old man was mortally frightened, but fortunately the boy was not there; he was probably in Bavaria. When Richard turned up one day quite unconcerned, Kochan implored him to flee, but Richard felt sure of himself, called the whole thing a ridiculous mistake, and went immediately to the Gestapo to clear it up. He never returned.

Weeks later Kochan was informed that he could see his son in the prison in the Prinz Albrechtstrasse. He found Richard still confident and protesting his innocence.

Later his confinement became more strict. There was no trial in sight. Richard never broke his silence; he refused any help from his father. "I don't want interference of any kind. I don't need help!"

After Christmas Kochan heard that Richard had been taken to the Plötzensee prison, where he could see him but rarely. Richard had undergone a frightening change: he was seized with a fit of hectic activity. He implored his father to see various people who might help him. Kochan was unsuccessful; nobody had time, nobody was able or willing to interfere. Everywhere he was told, "Secret matter of the Reich, keep your hands off."

Weeks went by, and now the old man learned that Richard Kochan had been sentenced to death for high treason.

Claire and I huddled close together, our ice-cold hands clasped.

Claire reiterated her opinion that only Richard's desire to show off could have got him into this situation.

So Richard had already been in prison when Claire had taken me into her home! She must expect them to shadow her and to search her apartment.

"My being here increases the danger for you. I must leave!"

She shook her head. "There's only one thing . . ." She got up and fetched my papers from their hiding place. "What if we burn them? I don't know anybody we could trust them to."

I consented. We knelt in front of the stove and threw everything into the fire—all my identification papers, letters, photographs, and the affidavit for America which I had never used because the number assigning my turn at the consulate was so high. Now I was really nameless. And I would have to leave this place of refuge. I tried to convince Claire; we argued for hours. Neither of us thought of going to bed.

Events brought a decision sooner than we anticipated. Next evening the wife of Claire's brother Bruno came to the apartment unexpectedly. Claire had not kept in touch with her sister-in-law. She was a common, coarse woman; her elegant fur coat did not fit her vulgar face. Over the coat she wore a double blue-fox fur, and her fingers were loaded with valuable rings. The effect was grotesque, especially when she opened her mouth and began to speak in Berlin dialect. Claire murmured my name, and Frau Kochan looked at me with scarcely veiled curiosity.

"I've got something I want to tell you—but it's just between you and me—though you haven't taken much notice of me lately, and Bruno tells me that I'm to leave you alone. Still, I've got a heart, that I have." She gave a meaningful glance toward me.

"I was about to leave," I said, putting on my coat.

Claire showed great presence of mind. "You go on ahead, Frau Riebe, and tell Hanni that I will join you later."

Hanni Kruse was a girl in the office where Claire worked, and I had only recently made her acquaintance. She was the only one of Claire's friends who knew the truth about me. She was a very pious Catholic and led a secluded life. Her small apartment, which looked like a doll's house, was adorned with rosaries, statues of the Holy Virgin, pictures of saints, and an eternal lamp.

I had only a short way to go, but the big door of the apartment house was locked, as is the custom in Germany at night. I had to wait outside until a tenant came and let me in. Then I waited again quite a while before Hanni opened the door. She could hardly conceal her nervousness. I noticed that she did not take her eyes off the kitchen door as long as we were in the hallway. She didn't ask me to take off my coat and hat, but at last she invited me into the living room. I had the disagreeable feeling of being in the way.

"You are busy, aren't you?" I asked. "Claire intended to join me here, but maybe you'd rather we came another day?" I got up to go. Hanni, who had blushed violently, shook her head without speaking. At this moment Claire rang the bell and Hanni rushed to the door.

Claire sat down on the arm of my chair and put a protecting arm around my shoulders. "My sister-in-law has been to see Richard, and she says he asked her to tell me to be careful." She held me closer. "What can he mean?"

Hanni raised her head. "Frau Riebe can't possibly stay in your place," she said with sudden energy. "They will search the house, that's certain!"

"My darling child," I said, "there's nothing for you to do but to give up hiding me."

Claire took me in her arms, laughing softly. "Give you up? We haven't came to that yet, far from it—but let me be your child from now on."

Hanni sighed. She leaned forward and said with effort, "I am sure Claire expects me to take you in, Frau Riebe, and I would willingly do so—if it weren't that—that—I mean—there is somebody—I also have—" She smiled helplessly, with a gesture toward the kitchen.

Claire clapped her on the back. "Good for you, Hanni, you're a sport, though it's bad luck for us. Has this been going on long?" She did not wait for an answer. "We must get going. It's very late as it is." Hanni took us downstairs. It seemed that she had promised her guest not to let anybody in on the secret. She merely told us that the woman had been hiding in a coal cellar for the past three weeks, thanks to a kind-hearted janitor who let her slip in there. But the cellar was no longer safe, as the air raids were driving people to seek shelter in every basement.

The street seemed hostile: cold, bleak, dark, and silent. We walked in silence, each trying to conquer a gnawing anxiety. Claire suddenly stopped. "I have it—my brother! We must go to Karl. He won't ask questions if we offer him payment, and I'll tell him a good story." She turned about abruptly and headed for Karl's apartment in the Usedomerstrasse. I followed, half dazed. The streets were almost deserted, the feeling of isolation and the sound of our steps echoing on the pavement made this journey seem sinister.

The door was not locked, so we entered the huge tenement with its two backyards and several side wings. A noisy quarrel was going on inside a tavern in the main building. We climbed the five flights of stairs without speaking. Karl and his young wife were astonished to see us but received us pleasantly enough. They were as usual sitting in the kitchen, which was well heated. A basket that served as cradle for the baby was standing on the table. The mixed odor of cabbage and diapers pervaded the room.

"Well, well, are you favoring us too, Frau Riebe?"

I did my best to manage a smile.

While the young mother was telling me about the baby's digestive troubles I could hear Claire talking to Karl. According to her I had had a row with my landlady and could not spend another night in my apartment house, where a drunkard coming home late made sleep impossible. Could I stay with them for two or three weeks while I looked for suitable lodgings? Karl immediately agreed, evidently highly amused by the goings on in my apartment. He asked for details, which Claire readily invented for his benefit.

"The bed in the hall is free anyway," the young woman said.

"Would two marks a night be all right?" I suggested.

This side of the matter was treated airily. "We don't want to make money out of you—we can see about that later. I hope you won't mind my getting up at five o'clock. I'll creep past you on my stocking feet, and you needn't be afraid. Hope you won't start being jealous, eh, Trude?" Shouts of laughter. The baby woke up and started crying.

Claire seemed satisfied. She announced that I would bring around a few necessities the following morning. I would spend the days at her apartment, which would be convenient, as I did her marketing for her.

She pressed my hand reassuringly as she said good-by. "Try not to tell them anything about yourself," she whispered. I went to bed immediately, but I could not sleep. I felt stifled in this narrow hallway without windows, unaccustomed to my new bed, worried by the thought of the days to come.

Rather more often than seemed wise Claire and I risked staying in her room in the evenings, always haunted by the fear of being caught. Gradually our apprehensions diminished, and I stayed with her more and more frequently, going back to my bed at Karl's place late at night. Air raids were frequent and I was often obliged to go into the shelter with Karl's family. When bombs fell near by I trembled, thinking of Claire.

Once the rumor spread that a house on the corner of Lortzingstrasse, where Claire lived, had been hit. As soon as the all clear sounded I hurried out to find Claire, and met her coming to look for me. We clung to one another, unable to speak. Her house had not been damaged. We stumbled back to her room through the dark in silence. From then on I did not leave her. We had both realized that being together was our chief comfort.

Old Kochan was indefatigable in his endeavors to get help for Richard, but every evening he had the same sad news. No one would act. Claire talked with Richard's attorney, but there too the answer, given with a shrug of the shoulders, was "Secret matter of the Reich!"

Old Kochan grew more and more frail. In the middle of our checker game he would close his eyes as if he were trying to shut out the pictures his brain conjured up.

"I can't eat these days, everything seems to upset me. Only, I'd like to live long enough to see those curs die!" He muttered unintelligible words. Claire made tea for him and he warmed his shaking hands around the smooth hot glass.

The feeling of impending disaster drew Claire and me closer

together and we both felt fortified by the union. I had never had a daughter of my own, and had longed for one; Claire had never had a real mother. Now we each received at the hands of fate the priceless gift we had been yearning for.

A letter from the prison chaplain informed Father Kochan that Richard had been executed on March 17. The shock proved too much for the old man who died only a few days later.

At his funeral I met Claire's brother Bruno for the first time. He was wearing the Nazi official's yellowish uniform and cap with the state insignia. He cried heart-rendingly, and his wife, clad in furs and faultless mourning, spoke soothingly to him to console him. She made a point of not seeing me.

A heavily veiled woman seated in the first row of benches attracted notice by her uncontrolled sobs. When the clergyman mentioned the loving care the deceased had given his motherless children she heaved an audible sigh. "That is Father's wife!" Claire whispered in my ear. I could not help thinking what a strange family they were, and how unlike each other: Bruno and his wife who had enriched themselves from "confiscated" Jewish property, and Claire who was risking her life and safety for these same Jews. When the coffin was carried away the last bond that had united these brothers and sister was severed.

Just as animals instinctively blend into their surroundings, so I adapted myself to the district in which I lived. I wore no hat and no rings, went shopping wearing an apron, and fell into the habit of speaking carelessly. Here I was never regarded with suspicion. Apparently only a few Jews had lived in this part of the town, so nobody guessed the truth about me.

I had not seen my cousin Anna for some time. So one day in July I arranged quite daringly to meet her in the Tiergarten in plain daylight. Everything went smoothly. I hurried home and placed all Anna's gifts on the table for Claire to see: a whole loaf of bread, four ounces of butter, a little piece of sausage, a tin of sardines, peas, and various other things. Suddenly I heard Claire's rhythmic knock on the door. It was barely 2 P.M., not time for her yet. I hastened to unlock the door. Claire looked very different from the girl who had gone out a few hours before. Without speaking she emptied the contents of two briefcases on the table. All the little things she had kept in the office rolled out. I watched her, astonished and speechless.

"Don't be upset," she said at last. "I've been walking round and round for an hour now—I didn't want to come home and cause you such pain! But after all—" she stopped.

"Tell me all about it, darling." I clung to the one good thing of which I was sure: she was here with me and safe and sound.

"I was fired," she stammered and stared at me with a bewildered look. At last she told me what had happened. She had been summoned by her boss who told her that three girls in the office had denounced her for never saying "Heil Hitler" and for making derogatory remarks about the Nazi regime. No appeal was allowed. She must quit immediately. In due course a trial before the Gestapo would follow.

The chief of personnel had expressed his regret at losing her. He had been extremely satisfied with her work throughout the whole ten years of her employment. "But unfortunately . . ." He shrugged his shoulders.

We had no time to lose. Claire or her companions might be watched. I must leave at once. I crammed a few things into a small bag, determined to go to Berlin-Grunewald to find an old acquaintance of mine, Frau Marten. Just as I was about to leave Hanni came in. She offered to accompany me to Grunewald and report to Claire. It seemed wiser for Claire not to go out again. We said a hasty farewell. Once more I felt myself a prey to that hopelessness which so easily got hold of me when I had to leave Claire's soothing presence.

Frau Marten had a small ground-floor apartment opening directly on the front garden, in a building whose janitor was a dangerous and fanatical Jew hater. Hanni's request that she take me in—I could not bring myself to ask it—obviously worried her. However, my very inability to plead my cause and my helplessness seemed to impress her. She got the sofa in her sitting room ready for me. But the next morning she told me that much as she regretted it she could only let me stay two nights. I would understand—the janitor, his fatal inquisitiveness, the danger—

Claire came to see me at 9 A.M. We typed letters to her office and to the security officer. She intended to report at the labor office immediately and apply for a new position for fear of being suspected of sabotage. I told her in a whisper that I did not intend to accept Frau Marten's hospitality any longer; and she replied that last night Hanni had decided it would be better for me to come and stay with her, in spite of the other guest already living in her apartment. We would manage somehow. I felt much relieved.

The labor office at the Alexanderplatz was so crowded that it was impossible to get in that day, so we went to Hanni's, where I made the acquaintance of my new companion, Julie Hurwitz. She was an active woman of about sixty-five, with steady nerves. She had hidden in innumerable strange places before coming to this neat little home for which she was most grateful. Her brothers and sisters had been deported. Her only son had gotten away from the Germans in Iran and been interned by Australian troops. She was all alone.

We began what we called "noiseless family life." While Hanni was out we went around in slippers and did not draw water from the faucet. We braced ourselves for the ordeal of slipping out the door and going down half a flight of stairs to the toilet. The sudden opening of a door in the next apartment was enough to make our hearts jump. In this crowded building people were used to spying on one another. One day Hanni was warned that footsteps and voices had been heard in her apartment. She answered that her aunt and cousin had come to stay with her for a few days. Whereupon she was told, "Don't forget that you have to register them with the police within three days."

I made myself continue writing the novel I had begun. Julie sat beside me mending stockings. I would read bits of the story to her now and then and found her criticism very sound. When I expressed surprise at her confident judgments she told me that she had known a man who was obsessed with a love of writing. "He used to write and write, but he never found a publisher. I told him over and over again: forget it; nobody will want to read it as it is. God knows the poor man was his own worst enemy. Do you know that type of person? One day he ended by shooting himself. If he hadn't done it then, he would have had to do it now." She straightened up. "But *I* will not give in, not even if I have to sleep another eighteen nights in a coalbin with rats!"

Claire found work in a munitions plant, located at first in a huge underground garage in Wilmersdorf. She had of course been obliged to inform her new boss of the reason for her dismissal. To her surprise he was generous and kind. He even hinted that the company might intercede in her behalf. Claire's new work preyed on her mind, because she found herself now a cog in the terrible machinery of war. Her conscience revolted, but her sense of self-preservation told her that a position with a war plant might count in her favor in the trial.

Time seemed to creep by. Air raids occurred more and more frequently, though they had not yet reached our part of town. Hanni was obliged to appear in the shelter at night. Julie and I, of course, stayed in the apartment, huddled together, silent, struggling for composure. With each crash we felt as if we were on the eve of execution. If just our dead bodies were found after a raid, we would still have put Hanni in danger.

At last, in September, 1943, two months after Claire's dismissal, she was summoned to appear before the Gestapo for an interrogation. We both knew what that might mean. I waited near by, in a little restaurant in the Burgstrasse, with a book propped up—but I could not read. A cup of ersatz coffee in front of me grew cold. My eyes shifted between the clock and the door, which opened again and again. How strange, to see so many people who seemed to go about free of care and out of danger. The hands of the clock showed I had been waiting for more than four hours. Then the door swung open and Claire came in. She almost ran to me. I did not dare ask her questions; I just caught hold of her arm and we went out into the street. We walked silently for a while, in step.

At last she spoke. "Nothing has been decided yet." She pressed my fingers.

"Can you tell me?"

At first she had been made to wait. Then she was interrogated briefly and sent back to the hall again. When she was called in once more the interrogator's mood and voice were harsher. She was asked to repeat a third time the words of which she had been accused. She readily admitted that she had been in the habit of saying "Guten Tag" rather than "Heil Hitler" to her friends in the office, but she could not remember having criticized the government. When somebody called out at this, "You're a coward!" she said, "I am only trying to report exactly what I remember."

Finally she found herself facing a new official. "We are well aware of the fact that there is more than one enemy of the Fatherland in your family." Claire did not reply. She was cross-examined on Richard's crimes. Her declarations that she had no knowledge whatsoever of his doings were rejected with insults and threats. "Was he by any chance a Communist?" Claire said that she did not know. More questions. And then suddenly, "You can go now. You will hear from us."

So that was that. Not very reassuring. When would the trial take place?

Without wasting words we both decided that I would go back to live with Claire. It was a rash thing to do but we wanted to be together.

We had our first close air raid the night of November 22. We got up, dressed, and sat crouching at the back of the room, with our bags and rucksacks near us. Claire refused to go to the cellar without me. When the fourth bomb had crashed in a near-by house we both rushed to the door and down the stairs. All our usual caution vanished in this mortal fear. When we came out of the cellar after the all clear, many hours later, the street was a sea of flames. A strong wind was blowing sparks from burning houses onto our roof.

We stumbled along the glaring street over rafters, rubble, and glowing woodwork, while shrieks and wails mingled with the ripping of wood. The pavement was heaped with furniture, sewing machines, beds; and beside the piles weeping children were crouching. We had heard that a bomb had hit the block where Claire's brother Karl lived, but we could not get there because the police had closed the street. In the meantime Karl had succeeded in reaching our house by a roundabout way. We met him in our courtyard, which was strewn with broken glass and glowing tiles from the burning roofs.

Karl's own apartment was undamaged, but the adjoining house was on fire. Fortunately he had taken his wife and baby to the country. He hurried back to help his neighbors, and Claire began to help carry pails of water up to our roof to keep it wet. I sat in our room, shivering and dazed by the destruction I had seen. Our room too was pitiful to look at. The door and windows had been blown to pieces, the lamp had fallen from the ceiling, bits of mortar and plaster littered the floor. After collecting the glass we lay down to sleep on the couch at 5 A.M. Claire was soaked and chilled, her eyes inflamed by the smoke and her eyebrows singed by sparks. But we still had a home.

From that day on we no longer dared stay in our room during the raids. We crossed the backyard stealthily after all the other tenants had gone down to the air-raid shelter. Then we ran to the subway station or the nearest public shelter. There we used to stand in some corner or sit on our bags, exhausted and shivering. We kept this up for months.

Finally one day Claire said that this sort of life would wear out our last vestige of strength. She went down to the grocery in our building to do her marketing. The grocer was also our landlord and had known Claire ever since she was a child.

"It's rather a nuisance looking after old Aunt Riebe at night," she told him. "But she's frightened out of her wits by the air raids. You know she lives with my brother Karl, and he is often out of town for days on end. Between being scared and lonely she hardly dares close her eyes at night."

Grumpy old Klann listened to her tale attentively. "Oh, let her stay here if she wants to; as long as she's registered some place, she isn't in the way. Now would you like peas for your vegetable coupons?"

I hugged Claire in joy. To be able to go to our own air-raid shelter seemed sheer bliss. How one's conception of happiness varies with circumstances!

And so a new phase of our life began. The nights passed in the basement brought us into closer contact with some of the other tenants. "Aunt Riebe" was admitted into the community. Soon a tenant from the front part of the house began to visit us frequently. Lauterbach, a bank clerk, was a well-read man and an ardent enemy of the Nazis who had up to now managed to steer clear of the party. He was the only staff member at his bank who was not a Parteigenosse. Soon he made a habit of coming to our room after the all clear to hear the BBC news. Afterward we would have long discussions. We both found Lauterbach's intelligence and humor very stimulating. He would look at me in surprise when I spoke of contemporary literature and the theater or of knowing Gerhart Hauptmann, Sudermann, Schnitzler, or Max Reinhardt. In spite of my intention to be careful I could not always resist the temptation to speak of my youth, which had been so rich in pleasant experience. These memories were all I had. Yet I knew I could not live in the past; I must live in the present.

The hours in the air-raid shelter now gave me a certain feeling of safety. I had for so long felt excluded from any kind of community, and here I could meet some splendid people from a sphere of life hitherto unknown to me. Claire and I stayed in the little anteroom of the shelter, and the same people gathered there during every raid. Lauterbach always gave a critical commentary on the news that had been broadcast. At his side usually was Herr Wismar, the driver of a garbage truck. He was a tall, surprisingly well-groomed and good-looking man, who spoke little, but when he did speak it was worth listening to. Herr Ihme, a tailor, would lean against the cracked wall without moving. Every time the siren sounded he had to carry his wife, who had been paralyzed for eighteen years, down four flights of stairs. The old coachman Grimmel would help him. These four men fully understood each other's politics. Their common bond was a kind of stubborn resistance to Nazism and a conviction that the war was already lost. I only listened to these conversations, but Claire and Frau Wismar joined passionately in the discussion. I was astonished at the clear judgment with which this worker's wife would discuss political problems.

We spent every third Sunday in Köpenick near Berlin, where Claire's friends Inge and Gertrud Lindemann lived. In their tiny home set in its little garden one felt enveloped in heartfelt kindness and friendship. The Lindemanns insisted on giving us three meals, a rare treat for us. Often they would sacrifice one of their rabbits. In their garden we relaxed and were at peace. We always spoke of them as "the helpful sisters."

We had to go through all sorts of hardships for the sake of these pleasant visits. Generally, just as we were about to set out in the morning, the first "enemy" aircraft heading for Berlin were announced on the radio. "Can we get there before the raid?" we would wonder. Several times another alarm came while we were on the way. We would hurry along the road, scared by the bombers above our heads, and reach Inge's and Gertrud's home breathless. The big air-raid shelter was so far away that we stayed in the red-roofed little house, hoping for the best. None of us was a heroine by nature, but we had long since come to look upon the danger of those hours as commonplace.

One Sunday as we were having lunch we heard a commotion in the adjoining grounds. Inge looking out through the window recognized the men coming along the grassy path. "A police raid!" she called softly. "Get into the shed as fast as you can!" These police raids were fairly frequent because many foreign workers lived in the barracks close by.

We slipped out the back door and into the shed, which Gertrud locked after us. We stood there in the dark, paralyzed, hardly daring to breathe, straining our ears to hear steps and voices. "I hope the girls didn't forget to remove our plates," Claire whispered. We could hear the little terrier rush to and fro between the house and the shed, barking furiously. At last Inge seemed to have succeeded in getting it into the house. The time we had to wait seemed an eternity. No one tried the shed door, but it was two hours before the girls could let us out.

As 1943 drew to a close we began to hope that the Gestapo might have filed Claire's case away. We had enough worries without it. The number of air raids was steadily increasing; one could never feel safe. It was becoming more and more difficult to get along on one ration card, and we had no money for black-market purchases.

The war machine was still working at top speed. The speeches that were broadcast became more and more strained. Whoever took the trouble to listen carefully could gather from the hysterical babble that the confidence professed by Hitler and Goebbels was fake.

I had by now got so used to my new surroundings and my new name that I had to make an effort to look upon my former life as real.

In July, 1944, exactly one year after her dismissal, a date was set for Claire's trial. At the last moment it was postponed, which meant that we would have to bear the anxiety another twenty-one days. Both of us tried to conceal our fears, but we caught each other lying awake at night.

Early on the morning of July 26 we went to the court. Once more I sat in a restaurant waiting for Claire. The trial had obviously been late in starting, for an hour and a half passed before I saw her run down the steps. "Four months in prison!" she told me almost joyfully. Her lawyer was going to lodge an appeal. Our feeling of relief as we turned away from that bleak building was indescribable.

The judge had been on Claire's side from the start. He almost took her part and even dared criticize denunciation as such. The lawyer had emphasized the fact that nowadays everybody grumbles now and then without being politically unreliable. Several of her superiors had made statements that were very favorable to Claire. Of the three witnesses one withdrew all accusations, the other two began to waver when they saw the attitude of the court. Claire's lawyer thought that probation would certainly be granted. We were overjoyed.

Hanni Kruse and Lauterbach came that evening in order to celebrate with us. One nightmare had passed. Now we were grateful for every day that went by without our house being hit, and for every day that brought us nearer to the end of the war.

Once I was within a hair's breadth of having my identity discovered, and both our lives were in danger. One day, in the summer, Claire gave me five travel ration stamps which could be exchanged for eggs. A girl working with her at the factory had received them from a soldier in return for bread. She had asked Claire to do her a favor and turn them in for eggs at a certain grocery store in our neighborhood. I went there, stood in line, and when my turn finally came handed the grocer the stamps. He looked startled and called his wife. They whispered together and threw suspicious glances at me. Suddenly the grocer swung himself over the counter, grasped me by the arm, and shouted, "Get the police! Someone run for the police!"

The women in the store pushed closer to me, curious and eager for sensation. I had but one thought: I haven't a single identification card. My heart beat like a drum.

"What's the matter?" I stammered.

"Forged stamps," he screamed in anger. "Don't act so innocent. Those are forged stamps dropped by enemy aircraft. That calls for prison. We need a policeman for this!"

"That's treason against the people," his wife hissed.

A circle of menacing women closed in on me. "Where did she get those stamps? We want to know! Beat her up! People like that ought to be hanged!"

"There must be a mistake. A soldier gave me those stamps in return for bread. Please believe me! You can't think I'd come here with forged stamps. Please!"

This was followed by excited disputes. Some of the women took my side. I kept on defending myself. "It's shameful that a soldier should deceive one so. He begged me for bread, and I gave him 1,500 grams. How could I have expected this?"

I invented a moving story. Fortunately it and my tears finally pacified the grocer and I succeeded in convincing him that I myself was the victim. Other women asked to be waited on; they had lost interest in me. And so, controlling my tense feelings, I walked slowly out of the store, protesting all the way at the soldier's deceit. When I reached home I fell limply into Claire's arms.

About 6 A.M. on October 1 Claire had just got up and was going to wash when there was a loud knock on the door. I drew the blanket over my head and Claire threw another blanket across the bed.

"What is it?"

"Open at once. Police."

I held my breath and heard the heavy steps of two men and the following conversation:

"Are you Claire Kochan?"

"Yes, I am."

"Then we'll have to take you along."

"But for heaven's sake, why?"

"Orders. See here."

Silence—then Claire's voice once more. "I can't understand it. I don't know any reason—"

"Isn't it true that proceedings against you are pending?"

"Yes, that is true, but my lawyer has lodged an appeal."

"Well, in that case you'll be able to clear it up, but for the present you'll have to come with us to the police station."

Claire must have come close to the couch. I could hear her breathing hard. Then she said, "But please, I must dress first. Will you sit down?" I heard her draw up two chairs.

"All right, we'll look out of the window."

My heart pounded so I thought the policemen must hear it. After a long, long while I felt Claire's gentle pat of farewell on my blanket.

"Now I'm ready."

I heard noises that indicated they were leaving. The door closed, the key turned twice, and yet I had not the courage to move. When I finally threw off the blanket and looked around the clock said twelve minutes past six!

It was impossible to get hold of Claire's lawyer before nine o'clock. What should I do until then? What would be the quickest way to clear up this mistake? For it must be a mistake. I got up and dressed with automatic, mechanical movements. On a little table beside the door I noticed Claire's food ration cards. She had thought of slipping them underneath a book for me. Up to now I had managed to keep my feelings under control, but on seeing this I began to cry.

I put a piece of bread in my bag and then, unable to bear being alone any longer, went to find the daughter of Klann, our landlord. She knew of Claire's pending appeal, though not of my illegal life. There was nothing she could do, but I had to confide my sorrow to some compassionate soul.

After that I went to the Moabit district of Berlin and waited on the steps outside the lawyer's office. Frau Thomas, the kind office chief, came. She immediately rang up the public prosecutor's office. We learned that the file containing the appeal had been mislaid. However, they would do all they could to straighten out the matter.

"Probably your niece will be released before tonight." I breathed more freely.

The telephone rang. "For you, Frau Riebe, your niece wants to speak to you."

I heard Claire's voice: "Don't you worry, you dear old thing. I'm still at the police station, and I've been allowed to telephone from here. Whatever happened?"

I handed the receiver to Frau Thomas, who quickly explained the situation and promised to settle the matter as soon as possible. Claire was optimistic. "I am perfectly sure that we will see each other again very soon. But first I'll be sent to Barnimstrasse. Now, don't you worry."

I looked at Frau Thomas, waiting for an explanation. "Barnimstrasse?" She answered quietly, "Prison for women. But certainly not for long."

I waited for the lawyer. When he came, he was furious about the mess, which he said he would clear up immediately. I was to call up again next morning.

I walked home. To put off the moment of going back to our room I stepped into a telephone booth and rang up Anna, hoping that the kind soul would have time to meet me somewhere in town. I wanted to be comforted. But she was sick in bed, and I dared not set foot inside her house because the janitor knew that I was her Jewish cousin.

An interminable day and dreary evening. Lauterbach sat with me until midnight, but all his attempts to divert my thoughts were futile. At noon the following day I was told that since the July 20 attempt on Hitler's life there was no such thing as probation. A new application had to be handed in for a reprieve. This made it necessary to go through the whole case once more, and it would be days or even weeks before the matter could be settled. I might hasten matters, however, if I could persuade Claire's superiors in the armament plant as well as the head-quarters for armament production to send recommendations to the public prosecutor.

I tried for several days to get in touch by phone with the gentlemen in question. "My name is Riebe. My niece Claire Kochan . . ."

"The director is out of town." "The security officer is at a meeting." "The personnel chief is in a conference." "Call tomorrow." "Ring up again. I cannot disturb him now." "Call back in the afternoon." And so on and so forth.

Then I mustered up courage to visit the factory. After trying for four consecutive days I succeeded in speaking to the two chief men. They were very polite, wrote letters, discussed the matter, made phone calls. At last I was in possession of all the necessary documents. The only thing I still needed was a letter of recommendation from a certain captain in the headquarters for armament production. I went to see him twice. He was surprisingly sympathetic, listened to me patiently, and wrote the letter to the public prosecutor. The letters Claire's superiors had written evidently influenced him in her favor. He wished me success. Full of hope I hurried to the lawyer's office. He was optimistic.

I had delivered a letter for Claire at the door of the Barnim-strasse prison every morning. Warm stockings, handkerchiefs, and a wool jacket were not accepted, but I was ordered to hand over Claire's ration cards immediately. Each time the little wooden shutter opened and the severe eyes of the official in charge looked out at me coldly, I shivered, thinking what it must be like within those bleak walls. They never told me anything about Claire.

Anna and Hanni did their best to help me along, giving me bread and potatoes. However, I seldom did any cooking. Time seemed at a standstill. There was nothing for me to do now but wait. At last on October 15 I learned that Claire was to be released soon. The next morning found me waiting at the prison door at dawn. She did not come out. When after two long hours

I dared knock at the little window I was told that "nothing is known about a release here."

Back to the lawyer, more telephone calls, more waiting. Next morning I was again at the prison. This time I learned that Claire had been released a quarter of an hour ago. I rushed to the subway and hurried home. There she was.

For hours we sat together. The room seemed to have undergone a complete change, now that Claire was there to light it up. I had laid the table for a little celebration. We had real coffee, cake, sausage, even a little pat of butter, all presents from friends. Claire told me all her adventures. The day was not long enough, so we stayed awake half the night, while she told me what had happened.

She had received no letter or message of any kind from me.

She had had to hand over all papers, money, and jewelry; then undress and do ten knee bends to reveal any hidden money or cigarettes. After that she put on prison clothing: striped skirt, faded loose jacket, clogs, and woolen stockings that kept coming down because her garters had been taken away.

The wardress had unlocked the door of cell 218. A white-haired woman was sitting on the wooden cot. As the door clicked behind her Claire saw that the woman was handcuffed. Up to then she had not cried but now she felt as if she were being strangled. "Why?" was all she managed to say.

The woman pointed to two letters on the wall above her head: "T.K."

"What do those letters mean?"

The answer came quietly, with odd equanimity: "I was sentenced to death. The letters mean Todeskandidat. I belong to Jehovah's Witnesses."

Then they both cried.

The woman had been there for five weeks. Every Thursday afternoon the chaplain came to her. Whenever he visited one of the prisoners it meant that she would be handed next day the paper dress which they wear for execution. Consequently the woman had been expecting her execution every week.

Whenever the door was opened Claire had to rise and report,

"Cell No. 218, Prisoner Kochan, sentenced to four months in prison for sedition." She had ten minutes' quick march round the yard every day, always afraid of losing stockings and clogs. The old woman was excused from this because of heart disease and her sentence.

After three days a wardress marched Claire and nine other prisoners through the streets to the Alexanderplatz Station, while passers-by stared at their prison dress. They were taken to an optical factory at Rathenow. Here Claire worked at a machine ten hours a day, without sitting down for even two minutes. She lived in a dormitory for twenty-two women, political prisoners and others. A large tub in one corner served as a latrine. As the latest arrivals, Claire and a fellow prisoner had to clean the huge tub. Because the beds harbored swarms of bugs, Claire spent the first two nights on a chair. An overwhelming desire for sleep finally made her get into bed in spite of the disgust she felt. Often the food was spoiled peas or beans. Once there were bits of glass mixed with the peas, which had been salvaged from a bombed-out warehouse.

Early in the morning on October 17 Claire was ordered to get ready to leave, without being informed of the purpose of the journey. A wardress took her and two others to Berlin "on leave." In the Barnimstrasse prison she was made to change again. Then she was told that she had been granted six weeks' reprieve.

The six weeks would pass quickly. We must start a new action for reprieve at once. Would it be successful this time? Success depended on so many people and so many intangibles.

In spite of the fact that we ought to have been careful and sensible, we stayed together. The night air raids increased, and we began to have day raids as well. There was hardly any time when we felt safe, but the power of habit made us finish our daily tasks in spite of "enemy aircraft entering the country."

Late one evening Hanni and Julie Hurwitz came to see us. They wanted to discuss Julie's plan of moving into the suburbs, where she was to become manager of a branch drugstore and had been promised an attic to live in. Julie felt able to cope with the risks. Identification papers, ration cards, and so forth were to be procured. She could not tell us the details. Fanatical enemies of the Nazis were managing it for her. She actually succeeded in holding that job until the end of the war, acquiring the necessary knowledge of a business she had until then known nothing about. One of her best customers, who often dropped in for a chat, was the local policeman.

On December 1 Claire was granted a new reprieve. On January 1, 1945, another application was due. This time the captain in the headquarters for armament production himself filed an appeal for six months' reprieve. It was granted. We were much relieved.

But this blissful state soon came to an end. It was proposed to send Claire out of town as an antiaircraft assistant. We almost broke down under this new misfortune, and nobody could help us. We spent five days in great anxiety. I feared for Claire's life, and she worried over how I would live without her. Once more chance decided in our favor: Claire was told that she had been temporarily rejected.

We looked forward to the new year with mixed feelings. What more would have to be endured before the Hangman's regime collapsed? The nights in the air-raid shelter became like delirious dreams. Each of us hoped that his own few feet of roof might be spared, and yet we all looked for the complete annihilation of the city, because we knew that no uprising could come about before that.

"I am ready to sacrifice everything," said Claire; and she was taken at her word. On April 4, 1945, the part of the building above our room collapsed. Coming out of the cellar we found the entrance blocked with timbers and fragments of walls. Our room was a jumble of furniture and bricks, fragments of stove and lamps, pieces of glass. We looked at the scene without tears.

It was 4 A.M. We stumbled across the yard and through the rubble, each carrying a briefcase and between us the little suitcase which now contained everything we owned. We went to the nearest food office and waited there, shivering. People said we would receive bread and coffee. After two hours we went back to our landlord's and waited there till morning. In the clear light of day we saw a scene we will never forget. We learned that a neighbor was buried in her room. Evidently she had not heard the warning, and the bomb had hit immediately after it.

Claire was the first to pull herself together. "Come on, we must try to find a bed somewhere."

At last we were given permission to stay in the only room left in that section of the building, on the ground floor at the back, which had been miraculously spared. The door would not close, the window frames were gone, clouds of dust swept across the room, which was really no better than a corner of the street. Four stories lay piled upon it.

For twenty-five days we lived under this mountain of debris. Once more our friends helped us and provided pots, plates, and some linen. Some tenants who had not found refuge with relatives or friends were still living in the ruins. We took turns preparing our meals in the Klanns' kitchen. We spent most of the day in the air-raid shelter; aircraft and artillery bombardment forced us to go down there again and again. Claire no longer went to work; there was no transportation.

The last merciless fight was about to begin. Our puny individual lives had shrunk to insignificance. I had lost the last copies of my own books, my personal records of the work of a lifetime were gone. And the home that Claire had built penny by penny had vanished. But what did these mean when we were in danger of losing life itself? Every trip to the pump to queue up for water, every visit to the baker's involved risks. Screaming, pushing, and jostling each other, people dashed across streets or elbowed into hallways looking for shelter.

Barricades that would make a child laugh were built on street corners. What imbeciles were still thinking of defending Berlin? For days women had been trying to hide their men who without arms, without ammunition, were to form the People's Army. The Russians were already fighting in sectors of Berlin.

Sunday, April 29, seven Russian soldiers were using the ruins of our house as cover. A German ammunition carrier was parked in the hallway. Our street lay near the Brunnenstrasse, which led to the huge Humboldthain Bunker where the attack was now concentrating. The bombardment never stopped. Our building was hit and caught fire. There was not enough water to fight the fire. Suddenly Russians appeared on the scene bringing pails of water. More shooting. Everybody hastily left the building. The side wing of the house was beginning to burn too. Shouting, crying, frightened people crowded into the cellar, carrying their last treasures with them. As soon as there was a lull in the shooting the women risked going to the roofs to fight the fire. Again and again German soldiers forced their way into the buildings to look for men to help. "No, there are no men here!" Every one of us was ready to commit perjury. An hour later the ammunition carrier received orders to leave. The street emptied. We sighed with relief.

Two days later wild rumors spread in the excited crowd. A staunch Nazi waved a leaflet she had just got hold of. "People of Berlin, hold out! General Wenck's army is approaching!" Hostile silence met her. Suddenly a woman's hysterical voice screamed out of the dark in the air-raid shelter, "Hitler is dead!" A shout of relief was the answer. "Hitler is fighting at the head of the SS!" cried an old man who had just come in from the street.

Suddenly two Russians appeared on the stairs leading to the cellar, where we were standing to get a breath of fresh air. Two children came close to me, half shy and half inquisitive, and stared at the strangers expectantly. The elder soldier smiled and gave the smaller boy a mouth organ. Never in all my life will I forget how this simple gesture moved me. Up there, ten steps away, the "enemy nations" were fighting, and down here a Russian put out his hand to give joy to a German child.

In the afternoon we heard that the German Army had set fire to our whole block of houses. That meant that another two hundred men and women had lost their homes.

They were still building barricades. I had the impression that lunatics were at work. Suddenly our street was overrun by German soldiers. With loud shouts we were ordered to go down into the shelter. Half an hour later our next-door neighbors broke through the party wall and came into our cellar. Within a few minutes the whole place was full of smoke. People made their way up the narrow steps, screaming with terror and pushing each other aside. Flames broke out on all sides. Some brave men still dared to cross the yard to save their bedding. I called desperately after Claire who was also going back a second time to salvage things. We pushed our way across the hall, which was blocked by trunks and bundles. Continuous shooting greeted us in the street. Back of us were the burning houses and in front the street under fire. We were like hunted animals trying to get away but not knowing where to go.

At last someone instructed us to go to the AEG factory in the Brunnenstrasse. We would all be allowed to spend the night in the cellar there. We plodded ahead, too dazed by the noise and shooting to heed it much. Lauterbach was hit in the leg by a shell. We supported him. Klann, who had broken his ankle on the staircase a week before, hobbled along with the aid of two crutches. His wife and daughter pushed a small wheelbarrow full of food. Our eighty-year-old neighbor pressed a tiny bird cage containing her canary to her bosom. Weary, forlorn and desolate, we still obeyed the mysterious urge to live.

We spent the night crouching on wooden benches in the basement of the AEG factory. In the morning I discovered that my briefcase containing the manuscript of the novel I had been working on for three years was missing. It seemed too much to bear. Later I found that Lauterbach's son had taken it by mistake.

The next day we were told that we could not stay on here. Homeless, we took up our various burdens and filed out through the gate. Outside we halted. The shooting had ceased for the moment; no one knew where to turn. Even those who had friends or relatives who would take them in could not get to them.

One of our company suggested moving into a half-wrecked cellar under a ruin in our neighborhood. Eleven of us went there to live and sleep.

And finally the day came when white sheets were hung from the windows and we knew that the nightmare was over.

We stepped out into the daylight not daring to believe the good news, and raised our eyes as if expecting the long-desired freedom to shine upon us from the sky. We stood, a crowd of beggars in dirty rags, amid the chaos of a world that was breaking to pieces. Suddenly I remembered the scene in *Fidelio* when the prisoners slowly come out of the dungeon—and the low, hesitating chorus whose suppressed hope for release gradually increases to jubilation.

Claire took my hand in hers. Neither of us could speak. So much that could not be expressed in words made this moment an overwhelming experience for both of us.

EPILOGUE TO CHAPTER I

The Strength of Two

FRAU STEIN-LANDESMANN has legally adopted Claire as her daughter. They live in a happy complementary relationship, Claire taking care of the household and Frau Landesmann continuing her writing.

The novel, *Christiane,* which she wrote in hiding, was accepted, but its publication has been delayed by the shortage of newsprint and electricity. Another novel written since the war was serialized in a newspaper and will be published in book form. Frau Landesmann has also written many radio scripts, short stories, and dramas, and is acting as a consultant for a publishing house.

Although both she and Claire would be happy to emigrate, Frau Landesmann feels she must stay in Germany, where she can earn a living by her writing.

Their friend Hanni Kruse has married; Julie Hurwitz emigrated to the United States; and Inge and Gertrud Lindemann are in Berlin, one working as a seamstress, the other as a secretary.

PROLOGUE TO CHAPTER II

The Other Front

RAINER HILDEBRANDT, a student of Professor Albrecht Haushofer, asked me once if I would like to meet Herbert
Kosney, who was with Haushofer when he was murdered,
and who had "lived through death." This is the story that Kosney
told, speaking in a simple and modest way of his work against
the Nazis.

Albrecht Haushofer, son of the noted Nazi geopolitician, had
been a close friend of Rudolph Hess and worked on Ribben-
trop's and later on von Papen's staff. When the war started he
began to express his doubts of Nazi aims. His students at the
University of Berlin remember him for his brilliance and for his
allegorical criticisms of the Nazi state made by analogies from
antiquity. He took part in the Twentieth of July conspiracy
against Hitler and was arrested. The now famous *Moabit Sonnets*,
written in the prison of that name, were in his hand when his
brother found his body.

II

The Other Front

HERBERT KOSNEY

M Y FATHER was a butcher. His political views were close to those of the German Nationalist party and he became a convinced National Socialist. He wanted me to enter the Hitler Youth, and if possible attend one of the élite schools so that I would become a good National Socialist. He never failed to hang out the swastika flag when there was a party celebration.

If I had been exposed only to the political ideas of my father, I would probably have turned out to be an ardent Nazi. But my brother Kurt was just the opposite—a sturdy hater of fascism. He was a mechanic and realized early that capitalism exploited labor. He was seven years older than I and influenced all my political thinking. We were both members of a Communist Youth group which existed before 1933 and was later camouflaged as a sports group. Its main job was to open the eyes of young people to the dangers of the Hitler regime. We observed strict discipline and kept in touch with similar groups through two liaison men.

Our parents knew nothing of all this and we often had difficulty getting away from home to attend the secret meetings. We learned to keep silent at an early age—a useful discipline, as it turned out.

I was young and had no fears or doubts when ordered to become politically active. It was an adventure for a boy of seventeen or eighteen. Of course we were politically inexperienced, but our burning hatred of the regime made up for it. The concept of liberty intoxicated us and the danger increased the temptation.

In May, 1935, when I was eighteen, I was given the job of distributing leaflets. I was to make my first attempt at the Schlesischer station. There was much traveling; the stations were crowded, and foreigners were beginning to arrive to prepare for the Olympic Games in 1936. Filled with a fanatical desire to enlighten as many people as possible, I never thought of the risk I was taking. I imagined that I had a fairly good eye for people. I went up to a man who seemed to have come from the country, for he was looking around as if confused, and thrust a leaflet into his hand. He glanced at it in surprise and started reading it. I walked on and was just about to approach someone else when my man took me by the arm. As I tried to pull away he said quietly, "Keep still! Gestapo! Come along!" Five minutes later I was sitting in a patrol wagon. I was taken to the prison at the Prinz Albrechtstrasse where the first interrogations were usually held. For about thirty-six hours I was kept standing in a corridor with my face to the wall. During that time I was questioned once, for perhaps ten minutes. I said that I had gotten the leaflets from a man whom I did not know, and that I thought it great fun to distribute them. Questioned repeatedly, I always gave the same answer. Of course they did not believe me and I knew it. They beat me, but I stuck to my statement.

I was transferred to another prison and put in solitary confinement. There I had plenty of time to think over my situation. There were continual interrogations, and as I made no other statement I was always beaten. Occasionally I got something to do—always a sham. We had to carry sacks of peas or beans up the cellar stairs. Then we were shoved or struck, the peas rolled all over the steps, and we had to pick them up, which took hours. This sort of "work" was required every few weeks. Our "clumsiness" was another excuse for beating us. I don't know why they thought they needed a reason, for no one was fooled by it.

After I had been about six months in solitary confinement another prisoner was placed in my cell. I suspected that he was a stool pigeon and hardly talked to him.

Our so-called "recreation period" was one more ordeal. We were led out into the yard in companies for "calisthenics." That included two hundred knee bends. No one could stand that—so there was more punishment. At other times we had to march around the yard singing. Once I tried staying indoors, but they found me and dragged me out. I was ordered to run one hundred times around the huge yard. After the second time I collapsed. I was "revived" with rifle butts, collapsed again, and was again beaten. I was learning how much a man can bear.

I had no idea whether my family knew what had happened to me, so I was very glad when one of the SS guards named Gauschinski noticed me one day. He had been a storekeeper and an acquaintance of my brother's, and I hoped that he would tell Kurt where I was. He did, but it took another six months for my father to get me out. No matter how hard they made it for him he kept on trying, and in August, 1936, they released me. As a good Nazi my father was allowed to give surety for me. Before I was discharged I was ordered to sign three slips of paper stating that I would never talk about my time in prison—or I would be charged with spreading atrocity stories—and that I had never been mistreated. I had no choice and signed. After fifteen months' imprisonment I went home.

Before long I got a job as a mechanic with the Mauser Works in Wittenau, a northern suburb of Berlin. I was quite sure that I was still under surveillance. Naturally my hatred of the Hitler regime had multiplied, but I had learned one important lesson: to be careful. I spent almost every evening with my brother who was considered harmless. I lived quietly, and no one guessed what we planned and talked about in Kurt's apartment.

Early in 1937 I was inducted into the Labor Service and when that was over I performed harvest service duties. Eventually the Mauser Works asked for my transfer to them as armaments mechanic and I went back to work with them. My father died not long after that, believing to the end in the cause of Hitler.

On August 27, 1939, at 1 A.M., I received my army induction notice. I was to report at corps headquarters at six in the morning and was assigned to Camp Tibor, about ten kilometers from Schwiebus in eastern Germany. Most of the barracks were full of engineers and border troops. I got my basic training there.

Just before Christmas I was transferred to the motor pool in Rathenow (west of Berlin) where I worked as motorcycle mechanic. While I was stationed there, in April, 1940, my fiancée Hedwig and I got married. In the summer of 1940 I managed to be recalled to the Mauser Works, this time to work as a welder.

It was good to be in touch with my brother again. My wife and I shared an apartment with Kurt and his wife in the Hagenauerstrasse in northern Berlin. We were able to listen to foreign broadcasts and to gather our "five" and "eight" groups late in the evening. We were organized in these small groups for safety, so that only a few would be caught if there was treason. We also mimeographed copies of a "News Sheet for the Army." It was camouflaged as sports news and gave the men in the field the information that we got over the British radio. Soldiers who were going to the front took these leaflets along and passed them on. The "sports sheet" was widely distributed.

Then great changes took place for us. Kurt was working in the Windler factory for surgical instruments. He was evacuated with it from Berlin to Neutomischel in eastern Germany where the plant was reasonably safe from air raids. There he got in touch with Polish and French workers and joined a Polish resistance group. He was later inducted into the army but he had only one hundred days as a soldier. He managed to play sick and be discharged.

I could no longer be deferred from military service, for an unexpected difficulty arose. A fellow worker took it upon himself to report to the head of the Mauser Works that I was a Bolshevik, and the Gestapo became interested in me. Although they could not determine anything definite, my deferment was discontinued. I was first assigned to Riga and soon transferred to the reserve of the 93rd Infantry Division at Leningrad.

About this time I heard that eighty men of the resistance groups that met in Berlin had been arrested. We never found out who the traitor was. Fortunately my brother was still away. Soon after this our reserve was assigned to the "Feldherrnhalle" SA Battalion to replenish their very heavy losses. With this so-called "élite" unit watered down with ordinary infantry units, a few of us whose political ideas were anti-Nazi tried hard to work on the SA men. We had to go about it warily, for the danger was great, but that only gave us more incentive. My corporal Neizke and I tried cautiously to influence the soldiers. We had to feel our way to see if we could trust the men we talked to. Gradually small groups evolved among us which held together with an iron will. We were at the front at that time and often in contact with the enemy. I proposed that we should go over to the Russians. Ten of us had made up our minds to do so, but when the moment came the firing was so heavy that we abandoned the idea.

In 1942 I was assigned to the ordnance section. It gave me a wonderful chance to do sabotage, which I often used.

After a while I was offered the "opportunity" to sign up as a regular member of the Feldherrnhalle, a tempting offer, for it meant being put in a motorized unit and trained in Germany; but I refused.

By getting trench fever I finally escaped the constant pep talks urging us to join the SA. After four weeks in the Narwa Recuperation Home I was discharged and sent back to my old outfit. It took three weeks to locate it—at Kolm, where it had been transferred.

The German troops started having a bad time. There were constant fights with Russian partisans. For each dead Russian we received a premium of twelve Juno cigarettes. Lives got to be very cheap. I always shot into the air. They had no sure way of knowing that you did.

At the end of 1942 I got twenty-one days' furlough. On the way home we had a serious train wreck and a number of men were killed. It was ascertained that Russian partisans had changed a signal so that our train collided with an oncoming freight train. After we had helped clean up the wreckage we were transported to an army camp at the German border and granted an additional ten days' leave to recuperate before starting our twenty-one days' furlough at home.

I was anxious to see my wife and year-old son, and so I used the first opportunity to take a train to Berlin. We all received a Führer package, given to all soldiers coming from Russia, which contained additional foodstuffs such as fat, bacon, meat, and coffee, and was intended to make our meals at home on furlough better than we might have received on the civilian rations.

I thought a great deal about the train accident. So many common soldiers like me had no wish but to go home. The Russian partisans caused this wreck which killed and wounded many.

Who knows how many opponents of the war and antifascists were among the victims? They had gotten on the train full of hope to go home and now this—

Under the constant barrage of Nazi hate propaganda it was often hard to keep from being confused and to remember that the real enemy was the Nazi government.

My furlough was over December 12, but I was determined not to go back and had already made plans with my brother. I did not tell my wife about them, so that she would be innocent if she were questioned. I said good-by to my family and started for the station with Kurt. It was a dark winter evening, when one might easily fall on the street. I had had a plan while still in Russia: a comrade was to shoot me through the right arm, but he refused. But I could count on my brother. We stopped in the deserted ruin of a house. Kurt gave my left forearm a heavy blow with the butt of my rifle. He did a good job and I had a nasty fracture. Then he took me to the nearest army hospital where the "facts" were confirmed: "Accidental fall on the dark road to the station, and fracture of the left arm."

Next morning I went to headquarters to report the accident, and was assigned to the Hindenburg Hospital in Zehlendorf. I managed to draw out my treatment there for five months by the most insolent swindling. There were doctors and nurses by then who understood and sympathized with a soldier who did not want to fight. I had very good luck since I might easily have happened on the wrong person. But a day came when further delay was impossible and I was assigned to a reserve group in Potsdam. I was sent on to Spandau and then to Güterfelde near Berlin.

While assigned in Güterfelde I could live at home and go for treatment to a Dr. Olbertz. Meeting this man was a decisive event for me. His kindness and active energy stamped him as an extraordinary person. He knew after a few visits what my attitude was. His watchword was let's gain time. After three months during which I had massages and exercises, he promised to get me six months of home service in Germany and he succeeded.

During this time I was able to accomplish a good deal for our cause. I "procured" all sorts of weapons from the ordnance section: some antitank rockets, six machine guns and ammunition.

Every week end I met Kurt at some station and gave him arms—
even if it was only rifles and pistols. Our group learned at home
how to operate the weapons.

At night we would go into the orderly room and set the pins
on the maps of the front where we thought they should really be.
No one found out who had done it, but at least some of the soldiers started wondering about the army reports.

In our apartment house lived a functionary of the illegal Communist party named Herrlein, who worked for a big electrical
firm. He often got us radio parts that we needed. I installed
radios in some of the rooms in the barracks, and the number of
opponents of the war increased when they could hear how things
looked from the other side. We made real progress in enlisting
the help of earnest and active antifascists.

Dr. Olbertz was involved in many secret activities. He was
brimming with energy. His right-hand man was Blochwitz, a
first-aid man; he found out who among the wounded belonged to
"us" and could be definitely depended on. Such persons could be
sure that if it was possible to prevent it they would not be sent
to the front. Dr. Olbertz wrote them down as unfit for service
even though they had long been well enough to be sent back.
Five hundred men must thus owe their lives to the doctor. He
took great risks and knew no personal fear. Often he asked me
to do small jobs for him like repairing his radio, and we gradually
got to know each other better.

One day I received travel orders assigning me to Elbing in
East Prussia. I showed them to Dr. Olbertz. He gave me a medical
examination, noted fever, and put me to bed at once on suspicion of jaundice. Some time was gained in that way. He told
me I must acquiesce if attached to the SA division but that I
should under no circumstances volunteer for membership. I was
attached. It had a single advantage: wearing a brown uniform
gave me more freedom to move about.

Dr. Olbertz occasionally spoke of there being plans afoot. In
the spring of 1944 he asked me if I knew eight men who would
be absolutely trustworthy. I said I did and brought eight soldiers
to him.

We came secretly, of course, and late in the evening. There were other persons living with Dr. Olbertz, among them his friend Kleist who was to take over the supply stores in Potsdam when the decisive moment came. Exact plans were prepared, and nights were spent making the secret arrangements.

We knew no details beyond our own assignment, but it was apparent that Dr. Olbertz was participating in really big action against Hitler. We waited anxiously until it happened on July 20; then with the news came the terrible realization that the attempt had failed. Now we knew that everyone who was in any way connected with the plot was in danger. I learned that a Gestapo official had overheard Dr. Olbertz say to a friend in a restaurant, "Someone revealed it." The doctor was repeatedly ordered to the Gestapo office at Berlin-Weissensee for interrogation. He was heavily compromised through his connections, and we all feared for him.

Something else happened at the same time. Dr. Probst, a senior doctor, had requested me as car washer. He soon tried to question me about Dr. Olbertz. I knew nothing at all. Although a medical officer himself, Probst was always very friendly with the soldiers and seemed to have little contact with officers. I had doubts about this strange person from the beginning. They were confirmed one day when I was cleaning his car and found a pass showing that he was an SS leader and member of the Security Service or Counterintelligence. I hurried to warn my friends of this alarming discovery, but it was already too late for some of the chief people. What we most feared was that Probst had been spying on the doctor and Blochwitz.

In early August Dr. Olbertz was again ordered to appear in Weissensee. His chauffeur Zander drove him there. After a while Zander was told to go back to the barracks and wait for a phone call—which never came. When he reported to the orderly room Dr. Probst was already in charge. Zander was restricted to quarters and arrested shortly afterward. We never heard from Dr. Olbertz again. I found out later that he had been helping his friend Nebe, head of the Reich Criminal Police, who was among the disaffected Nazis who participated in the coup against Hitler.

There was a rumor later that Dr. Olbertz had committed suicide. His wife did not believe it because his hands and feet were known to have been tied.

Now I had to live in the barracks again. During the night after Dr. Olbertz' arrest Probst had me waked and several Storm Troop leaders questioned me about the doctor. I denied any personal connection and maintained that I knew him only as a physician, as he had treated me for a long time. They ordered me to turn on the radio and set the dial for "England." When I declared quietly that I could not do that, they got very rough and threatened me—but finally I was sent back to the barrack.

I knew now that only a miracle could save me. But I wanted to do everything I could to contribute to it. I remembered that Dr. Olbertz had once told me that an eye malady is very difficult to diagnose. I had had an eye operation as a boy. I reported to Dr. Probst claiming that I could not see very well. Probst sent me to the Westend Hospital where they specialized in the treatment of diseases of the eye. Two doctors took me in hand. They injected atropine and examined me.

An air raid interrupted us and I stumbled down to the cellar.

I was examined for several days running. They obviously suspected me of faking. A third young doctor shouted at me, "If you can't read now, you'll get ten years in prison!" I answered meekly, "Please, if that is good for my eyes." The head doctor gave me a letter in an open envelope and discharged me. I sensed that they were watching me, and stopping at the staircase I opened the envelope next to a large window. I tried to read, holding the envelope close to my eyes, and shook my head impatiently. Then I felt my way down by the banisters. One thing at least I had achieved: because of "greatly reduced strength of vision" I was not sent away.

On August 24 the Wehrmacht soldiers in the garrison were restricted to quarters. It was my birthday and I wanted above all to visit my family. I was wondering how I could arrange it when I heard that Blochwitz had been taken away for interrogation. That looked bad.

This was a time when being attached to the Storm Troops

would help me. I went to Blochwitz' closet where my brown uniform was hanging and put it on. In that I could leave, for the restriction applied only to soldiers in Wehrmacht units. I found some papers of Dr. Olbertz' in the closet, which I took with me. On the way to division headquarters in Berlin to warn my friends about Blochwitz I ran smack into Dr. Probst. He asked where I was going. I said that I wanted to inform Frau Blochwitz. "You keep out of this!" he shouted.

I went home in spite of the risk. My wife was expecting a baby in the next few days and I wanted badly to see her. (On September 3 we had a little daughter.) I could not delude myself about the unfavorable situation: Probst was a shrewd and merciless opponent. I felt his suspicion and hatred but could think of no way out.

When I got home I found my brother there on a short furlough. I told him the story at once. I hid my pistol in the sofa and the holster in my son's crib. Fate caught up with me in a matter of hours: a ridiculously large number of cars stopped before the house, lighting the front up brightly. There were Wehrmacht cars and Gestapo cars, criss-crossing the street so that no one could get away. When my brother opened the door in response to the furious ringing, they wanted at first to arrest him. I corrected the mistake. Lying would not help here.

A quarrel developed between the Wehrmacht and the Gestapo as to who should have me. The Gestapo won. They shoved me down the stairs into a car. A Gestapo official, Petereit, struck me in the face and explained tenderly, "I couldn't do it in front of your wife." Then he let himself go, and when I climbed out in the Wörthstrasse I had been beaten bloody.

The interrogations about the Twentieth of July were being held in a school building. I found others there that I knew: Olbertz' friend Kleist, the chauffeur Zander, Blochwitz, and a Herr Neubauer. We were questioned for hours. At night I was taken to the Lehrterstrasse prison where I had to lie on the ground. More interrogations, beatings, interrogations. But they learned nothing from us.

After almost a week they started new charges: membership in an illegal group. The Communist Herrlein had lost his nerve and admitted everything: clandestine radios, theft of arms, and so forth.

I was handcuffed and transferred to another prison. They bound me to a chair by one hand and one foot, hit me in the face, and questioned me. Gestapo Kriminalrat Habecker (known as Haase) led the interrogation. He confronted me with Herrlein, telling me, "You can admit everything, nothing will happen to you!" I continued to deny everything. They showed me an anti-tank rocket and asked if I recognized it as one I had stolen. I denied it. Then they sicked Habecker's dog on me; but strangely enough the animal went after its own master! They took me to the cellar and tied my hands to my legs and beat me with an iron bar.

Unfortunately they found a "pass" in my uniform which I had once received from a Russian major who was a prisoner of war and worked as carpenter in the labor unit at our barracks. It said, "Comrade Kosney is antifascist and may pass."

Herrlein spoke up and said that the Russian carpenter had given me the pass. I was put in solitary confinement with my hands tied behind my back. The interrogations and the beatings seemed to have no end. In March, 1945, they finally removed the shackles from my legs.

There were eight of us up for trial. Of these, seven, among them Herrlein, were condemned to death. But I could not be tried before a civil court. I must either go before a military court or be declared "unworthy to serve." That looked like my salvation, for it would take a while, and everything seemed to indicate that the war would be over in a few weeks.

The requests for pardons were rejected, and the seven men were executed on April 18.

My trial was scheduled for the 21st. That morning the handcuffs were taken off and I was driven to the Special Court. I waited there from nine to eleven o'clock. Then we heard that the judges had run away from the approaching Russians. So I was taken back to the old cell in the Lehrterstrasse. A shell hit the cellar that night and caused indescribable confusion. Prisoners were being released but entirely at random.

While I was cleaning out a bucket in the yard I ran across my

brother. He had been arrested in the fall of 1944 and taken to
Camp Conin. The inmates were liberated by the Russians in
January, 1945. He had made his way back to Berlin and hid in
our apartment in the Hagenauerstrasse. When the house was
searched he was found and arrested again. He claimed that he
was on furlough but as he had no papers they brought him to
the Lehrterstrasse on suspicion.

In these days of confusion some prisoners were free to visit
others. Doors were open occasionally. Former customs officers,
no longer needed at the borders, were being used as guards. Only
six SS men remained, and they kept dashing off to get news.

Albrecht Haushofer, son of the Nazi geopolitician, had been
arrested for participation in the Twentieth of July and was in
the Lehrterstrasse. He enjoyed some liberty and visited my
brother's cell a few times to listen to a primitive little radio Kurt
had built. A very kind warden, one of the customs officers,
brought us bread and cigarettes from our home and better
material for the radio.

Another Russian shell hit the building, and everyone fled to
the cellar. The names of a lot of prisoners were called and they
received their personal things. Among them were Kurt and
Heinz Haushofer, Albrecht's brother. The Russians were already
in eastern Berlin.

A little after midnight sixteen names were called out, among
them Haushofer's and mine. We went back to our cells and got
our things. It looked as if our martyrdom were over. We were too
much overjoyed to doubt.

The sixteen of us were taken up to the yard where we received
our personal belongings and papers, for which we had to sign a
receipt. Then we were sent through a narrow, pitch-dark hallway. My instinct warned me, but there was no way out. I felt my
way to one side, and touched someone. A flashlight was turned
on and I saw that on both sides of the passage SS men, wearing
steel helmets, were standing, heavily armed, their machine pistols
trained on us. We ran out onto the street between these living,
threatening walls. Then we were told, "You are being transferred to another prison. You'll be shot if you try to escape!"

It was a dismal night. The constant noise of the rain hitting the pavement was punctuated by artillery fire. This helpless little group, surrounded by SS murderers, sensed what was to come. The thought that I might have to die within an inch of freedom paralyzed me.

We were told to throw on a truck the belongings we had just received back—that we were going to the Potsdamer station. We walked flanked by about thirty-five SS men, a ring of murderers drawn tight around us.

I don't remember what went through my mind in those awful moments, whether I thought of my family or of escape or what I clutched at. We stumbled along in disconsolate silence. We were like cattle being marched to slaughter. The sky was blackish grey and the rain beat down on us. There was a continuous artillery barrage. When we had gone a few hundred yards and reached the corner of Invalidenstrasse and Lehrterstrasse, we halted. Here we had to surrender the rest of what had been given back to us— our watches, rings, and everything else in our pockets. The last shred of doubt about our fate vanished. I looked around: the thirty-five armed murderers walled us in. The SS men in front turned off toward the deserted Ulap—an old exhibition ground. Through our group went the unspoken cry: This is not the way to the Potsdamer station! It was a sinister, lonely place where only one thing could happen. Was this where Kurt had been taken when he was "discharged"?

"We're taking a short cut," shouted one of the SS men as we instinctively hesitated. The grotesque double meaning of the words occurred to me.

So this was the end. It would have been insane to try to escape. Although our situation was desperately clear, although everyone knew what the next minutes would bring, I think none of us could grasp the inevitable.

I thought what a grotesque mixture of brutal arbitrariness and bureaucracy our "release" was. First we got our property back and had to sign for it. Then they took it again and took us somewhere to murder us.

By now we were on the muddy ground of the colonnade on the exhibition ground, which was pitted with bomb holes and shell craters. The SS men stopped again. Half of our group was taken to another part of the lot.

From then on everything happened with gruesome rapidity. I was shoved forward, a hand grabbed my neck, I heard shots close by. Someone said, "It won't take long." Was that meant as consolation? I don't think I was wholly myself any more; I stared as if hypnotized at Haushofer who did not move. I tried hard to concentrate on the others, and I believe this was what helped me to stand waiting my turn. Certainly in those moments I felt neither fear nor desperation.

Someone near me cried out in fear of death and begged the SS leader for his life. I turned my head to look. The leader shouted loudly "Ready!" All the SS men repeated "Ready." I saw that a man had been mowed down by the whipping crack of a bullet. Something struck my neck and I was pulled back by the SS man and fell on the wet ground. Fully conscious, I heard shots, footsteps, whimpering, and crying. I lay motionless, without pain, only a warm stream of blood flowing down my face and neck.

I don't know how long I lay there or whether I lost consciousness. I doubt it, but my mind was not registering clearly. Then a hard boot pushed at my head. Someone said, "That pig is dead!" I kept my eyes closed and held my breath. There was some more whimpering, then two shots, and the whimpering stopped. I lay pressed against the wet earth, scarcely breathing for fear someone might be standing behind me. Then: "Let's get going. We have more work to do," and the sound of retreating steps. After that everything was still.

I began cautiously to turn over, always listening. There was no sound. Then I summoned all my strength to resolve, "Think of yourself! Go home! You can't help the others, they are dead. You must save yourself."

I tried to get up slowly and managed it with some effort. I had to keep wiping the blood out of my eyes. I touched my neck and my face carefully. Apparently the bullet had entered the neck very low—at the side, because of my twisting around—and had come out through my cheek, under the eye. It had passed through my turned-up coat collar and four thicknesses of a folded prison towel which I always wore like a scarf around my neck. I tried to stop the bleeding by tightening the towel and pressing my handkerchief on the cheek wound.

I started crawling on hands and knees, seeming to get nowhere. It's just as well to go slow, I thought, and stopped to catch my breath. The rain drenched me but it felt refreshing. When I had crept almost to the street I stood up and leaned panting against a log for a few minutes. My one thought was to go home. I reeled out onto the street, still feverishly aware that some danger might be lurking. Other execution squads might be bringing out fresh victims. A checkup might reveal only fifteen instead of sixteen bodies and they would look for me. The thought made me redouble my efforts to get out of the neighborhood.

I felt my way along house walls and past ruins, like a wounded, hunted animal, always listening for a step or a voice. I moved like a snail. Suddenly, around a corner, a military patrol stopped me. I pointed to my bloody face and they let me go on, only calling after me the address of the nearest first-aid station. But I did not want any help of that sort . . .

My shoes seemed to be nailing me to the ground. I took them off and walked in stocking feet. Very soon my socks were worn through. The debris on the street hurt the soles of my feet.

A man on a bicycle passed. When I called for help he replied "I'm busy" and rode on. I could barely drag myself along; the bleeding would not stop and kept making me weaker. The road seemed endless. From time to time I almost gave in to the temptation to drop down and sleep. But I could not let a military patrol pick me up. I had to save myself; I wanted to live.

Normally the walk took three quarters of an hour, but that night it seemed an infinity. After two hours, at 3.15 A.M., I staggered into the house in the Hagenauerstrasse and crept up the stairs. Kurt was at home! Neither he nor Hedwig recognized me when I fell into their arms. I must have looked awful—smeared with running and crusted blood, my face swollen out of shape, wet, barefoot, and filthy from lying on the ground. They washed me, gave me something to drink, made a temporary bandage, and put fresh socks and shoes on me. Although I badly needed rest, they agreed that for the time being it was too risky to keep me at home. And so Kurt took me at four o'clock to an acquaintance, Helle Schönemann.

But my condition was so bad that Kurt decided I needed immediate medical attention. Somehow he managed to get an ambulance which took me to the first-aid station in the morning. He claimed that he had found me unconscious in the street. I was taken to a hospital in the Christburgerstrasse, where I finally received medical treatment. Kurt said my name was Herbert Weiser, that that was all he knew about me; apparently I had been wounded by a shell fragment. I myself did not speak a word.

The doctor had ordered that I get hot soup, coffee, and be nursed back to health. I must have lain there as if dead, for the nurses gave me none of the prescribed food. One of the nurses said to another, "We can leave him alone, he can't live much longer." I was so infuriated that I rallied enough strength to jump out of bed and slap her in the face.

I stayed in the hospital for four days. Kurt came to tell me that more wounded were arriving—SS men who had been stationed in a near-by brewery. If the Russians found me there they might take me for one of these. Kurt put a Volkssturm arm band on me and helped me home. No one stopped us; the confusion was too great. We reached our apartment after dark and they put me to bed. I lay in a stupor, craving nothing but sleep.

On April 29 someone was sniping from one of the houses in our street. The SS searched every house. Kurt and Hedwig hid me behind the clothes press in a pile of bedding. I was still ill enough to suffer badly from lack of air and tried painfully to breathe through a hole. Fortunately they did not search long and I could return to bed.

Two days later, on May 1, the whole thing was over.

EPILOGUE TO CHAPTER II

The Other Front

A s a result of his wound, Herbert Kosney now suffers from headaches; his right ear is deaf, he tires very easily and occasionally feels dizzy. He owes his life to the fact that the bullet passed through his head beneath the brain.

In September of 1945 Kurt and he made a fresh start at earning their living by taking over a radio store and starting to repair radios.

PROLOGUE TO CHAPTER III

"You Are a Traitor..."

KNUD CHRISTIAN KNUDSEN was born in Berlin in 1916. Some of his ancestors had moved from Denmark to Germany, and his father, a professor of the history of drama, taught him Danish and occasionally took young Knud to Denmark.

An organization which desired to promote international understanding and peace selected Knud as an exchange student, and in 1932 he went to school in France. He was just seventeen years old when Hitler came to power. He had to serve a year in the spade-carrying Arbeitsdienst in order to be admitted to the university. After starting to study law he changed to history of art and in 1941 was awarded the doctor's degree. In connection with his studies he traveled extensively. He also took painting and drawing lessons, and some of his portraits were published in German and foreign newspapers.

Soon after the war began Knud was drafted and assigned to a Luftwaffe construction company. Four months later he was transferred to one of the Luftwaffe painters' units to draw portraits of soldiers. His duties took him to France, Greece, and Denmark. While in Denmark he got in touch with an anti-Nazi underground group, and although nothing came of it at the time, this contact influenced his growing abhorrence of the Nazi tyranny and the war.

III

"You Are a Traitor..."

KNUD CHRISTIAN KNUDSEN

THE GREAT barracks of the Adlershof airfield near Berlin reflected the glaring heat of the last days of August, 1942. Many Berliners had sought refuge from the heat on the shores of the Baltic Sea. I was in Luftwaffe uniform, standing at attention in a close, hot barrack room before a fat, bemedaled major who was studying the articles of war of the Wehrmacht very carefully. It was not just the heat and standing at attention which made me perspire so. I was being given a formal hearing on charges of sedition.

"How long have you been a lieutenant?" the harsh voice asked in an unmistakable Austrian dialect. I would never have thought an Austrian could speak so sharply.

"Five days, Herr Major."

"That will soon be over. We will make a report on your seditious activity against the Wehrmacht, on your defeatist statements and incitements to mutiny. I hereby place you under arrest until you are tried by court-martial. The witnesses will be heard beginning tomorrow. If you are fortunate you will get off with six years in the penitentiary, but if the charges are supported . . ." He drew his hand across his throat in a meaningful gesture.

Then he jumped up so suddenly that his medals clattered, and exclaimed, "Do you know what this means—destroying young people's faith in their superiors and in their Führer?"

"No, Herr Major. I belong to the group that was given a lieutenant's commission for the duration of the war. I am not even in the reserve. I am a portrait painter and was drafted to draw pilots and to paint generals."

"Even so you must know what it means to stab our brave troops

54

who are fighting in Stalingrad in the back. You are a traitor and will be tried as such." Argument was useless. Speaking of the senselessness of the war against Russia to this Nazi officer would only have made matters worse.

I was taken into custody. With difficulty I was able to get permission to telephone my parents so that my frightened mother, who did not know what had become of me, could bring me the necessary toilet articles. I was forbidden to tell her anything of my arrest. But when I kissed her she read in my eyes the answers to many of her questions. She gave me a book before she left. It was a Danish translation of a volume by Jane Nicholson which described the firm stand of the English in their most difficult hour. It was to give me much confidence during the hard times ahead.

I was interrogated every day; I was confronted with other soldiers and cross-examined. The charges were based on statements I had made on a return trip from the Caucasian front. I had been assigned there for six weeks as part of an artists' unit of the Luftwaffe which drew portraits of soldiers and officers. The results had been very meager, for I had no intention of supporting the war or acting as a propagandist for the domination of other peoples by corrupt and megalomaniac leaders.

I had been on most of the fronts as a painter, and my experiences had only increased my dislike of war. This was evident in my drawings, and I had had great difficulty in retaining my position in the painters' unit. At the beginning of the war I had determined to maintain my pacifist attitude and to kill no man, friend or enemy. I wished my life to have value for the progress of humanity rather than for its destruction. As early as the fall of 1940 I had foreseen that the war would be lost. In my quasi-civilian position I wanted to free as many young men as possible from the insane illusion that they were serving their Fatherland when they were merely preserving the lives of a few criminals.

After finishing my work in the Caucasus I was put in charge of a truck convoy of noncommissioned officers and soldiers going to Berlin. They were to be assigned to western Europe. During the ride I talked at length with a German who had been born and raised in Russia. I assumed that he was not blind to reality, and expressed myself freely to him, pointing out that a line as extended as the German front in Russia could not, in the long run, be held. He always agreed with me, and so I became more outspoken. As soon as we arrived in Berlin he reported me to the authorities.

Before reporting at Berlin-Adlershof I had made available to the soldiers in my unit a truck and enough gasoline so that they could take their baggage home and spend a few hours with their families after their long absence. This permission, granted on their word of honor, was a small concession to men who had made the dangerous trip through the Russian steppes and the Ukrainian guerrilla areas. This act of decency, which any humane person would have performed, was also held against me.

Sitting in my cell I thought about all this and recalled Hans, an eighteen-year-old corporal with whom I had also shared my ideas on the long trip back from the Caucasus. If he repeated only a fraction of what I had said to him, they would have a second witness and I might indeed be executed. He had been full of the clichés about the superiority of the Führer and the need for eastern Lebensraum, and to show him the real Germany which had found its true expression in the music of Beethoven and Bach, in the works of Goethe and Heine, was not easy. Using Denmark and Switzerland as examples, I had explained to him that a country does not have to be large to make great contributions to civilization. Some of our discussions had lasted till dawn—but had I changed his views?

Still another thought tortured me and kept me from sleeping. My father was close to Prussian Finance Minister Popitz, who was trying to bring some of the leading political figures of the Reich into opposition to the Nazis. I was afraid that the charge against me would draw attention to my whole family.

But my situation improved before long. Although Hans was interrogated several times, he did not betray me. The thought that I had perhaps converted him gave me considerable satisfaction. The assertions of the one informer were not supported by any of the other soldiers. Some of them contradicted themselves. When I was questioned I played the role of a dumb, harmless, unpolitical artist. A report on me had been prepared but not yet passed on to the court because of the uncertainty of the charges.

I was at the end of my strength after the many hours of cross-questioning. The mental struggle involved in keeping up an innocent appearance, the knowledge that a search of my Berlin apartment would uncover many forbidden books and my drawings against war and dictatorship kept me in constant fear. I developed a bad case of jaundice and was taken to a Berlin hospital. I was so sick that bedside interrogations were conducted but seldom. Hans visited me once, and my talk with him convinced me that I had given him faith in the triumph of humanitarian ideas and in a decent and democratic future.

In the first days of 1943 I was allowed to leave the hospital for a few hours. My apartment had not been searched; the Gestapo would have been more thorough than the army was proving.

I got off with a miraculously light sentence: eight days in prison—perhaps because the defeat at Stalingrad was shaking the faith of many people, including even some of the most fanatical Nazis. But I was removed from the painters' unit of the Luftwaffe and given a punitive assignment to a training company of the Wehrmacht. This so-called "training company," I found out, was to be used as cannon fodder in dangerous sectors of the front where the SS was no longer to be sacrificed. To give my life for the cause I was fighting against had no appeal for me; I must find some way of hiding, if necessary desert.

It had to be done quickly, for in a few days I would be transferred from Adlershof to the punitive company. I was given leave for one afternoon in order to visit my parents once more. I saw Hans again and wished him well: "Auf Wiedersehen till after the war. It would not be long, if only a few hundred thousand people shared our opinions."

Then I called a doctor friend who was stationed in an army reserve hospital in Berlin. An hour later I was with him. I could trust him, and told him frankly that I intended to simulate a recurrence of jaundice. He agreed at once to help me, but pointed out that I could not be placed in an army hospital unless I was assigned there "through channels." I promised him that I would appear to have the proper symptoms and would arrange to be assigned to the hospital through the dispensary of the Wehrmacht's city headquarters.

I went to the home of the sister of a well-known film director, an elderly lady for whom I had been able to do some small favors. Her son-in-law, who had become "unworthy of carrying arms" by marrying into a Jewish family, was employed in the Bayer factories as a pharmacist. He gave me a quantity of atabrine which, taken in large doses, turns the body, and especially the eyes, yellow as does jaundice. I went home feeling a bit easier but still uncertain of the success of my efforts. It would take several days for the symptoms to appear. I had to be declared sick in order to keep my headquarters in Adlershof from becoming suspicious. They were informed the next day that I was ill in bed and that an official army-approved doctor would be called. Apparently this aroused no suspicion, for the transport was not to start until a few days later.

The night of March 1, 1943, brought the first great air raid on Berlin. The earth trembled, houses collapsed, the sky was red and the air full of smoke. Whole blocks were in flames, while the people formed bucket brigades, hoping to put out the conflagration. Fire trucks raced through the night to the villas of the Nazi leaders and to the armament plants, while apartment houses blazed untended. I hurried to my parents' flat in Berlin-Steglitz, fighting my way through the scorching streets and passing screaming people whose last bits of property were lying about. I found my father tearing off his phosphorus-spotted clothes before hurrying to the roof, which was starting to burn. We managed to save our building. In the morning we sat together over a bottle of precious Rhine wine and discussed my desperate chances.

My brother arrived with an old friend, Hans Schmidt, who was an army doctor. "We will put you to bed immediately," he said. "I will give you an intravenous pyrifer injection, and tomorrow morning you won't recognize yourself." The next morning I had a very unpleasant fever. Dr. Schmidt advised me to go to the Zehlendorf army hospital, where he had spoken with a doctor friend. There I was assigned to a beautiful large bed, without waiting for permission from headquarters, as the fever made immediate admission allowable and the formalities of registration would be completed later.

A Dr. Ohm came to my bed every morning with a staff of assistants and nurses. He diagnosed jaundice. When I looked at myself in the mirror I had to agree with him. The atabrine had begun to work.

Although I had told no one in the hospital the facts of my case, I was aware of the sincere good will shown me. The doctors treating me seemed aware that I was not really sick. But one of the nurses was a different matter. She was fired by romantic ideas of battle and intoxicated by the heroic struggle for Fatherland and Führer. She was the sort who puts flowers on the caps of soldiers when they are ready to march out to defeat the enemy— all the more fervently since she herself had no boy friend. She took good care of the wounded in order to return them soon to their heroic task at the front; and she would immediately report as a malingerer anyone who was not anxious to go back.

This nurse gave me a blood test and told me I probably had never had jaundice; I should get out of the hospital promptly and go to the front where I belonged. If she denounced me I would be lost. According to the Wehrmacht's articles of war I could be considered a deserter; and this was a "second offense." Apparently she did denounce me to Professor Brenner, the head doctor of the ward, for that morning he entered the room followed by other doctors and the nurse. I lay motionless, my hands frozen to the cover. Professor Brenner looked at me a moment. Then he started a short lecture:

"My colleagues, we have a very interesting case here: a liver disturbance through excessive use of atabrine. The patient has been in Russia for some time, as I see from his files." He gave me an encouraging look.

"Yes, Herr Oberfeldarzt. I was in the malaria-infected areas of the Caucasus and near the mouth of the Don. I suppose I took an excessive amount of atabrine then and kept on, as . . ."

"Yes, you told me that one of your relatives returned from the tropics with malaria and so you were overly careful. My colleagues, that was an exaggerated type of precaution." He laughed and his listeners laughed with him.

"And here we see the result. Keep an eye on this case. Our pharmacological factories still have much to learn about the minor effects of atabrine. The patient will remain under my personal observation."

The professor turned to the next case. The nurse was astounded.

During the spring of 1943 I felt peace of mind again for the first time in years. The protection of Dr. Ohm and Professor Brenner had had a beneficial effect. When my old unit in Adlershof began to inquire as to my whereabouts, I realized how much the hospital administration had helped me. I had given my old FPN—Feldpostnummer, the German APO number—for the sick records, so that the Berlin army medical authorities were not aware of my belonging to a punitive company. It was surprising how helpless the bureaucratic machinery of the Wehrmacht became when one of its members was assigned to a hospital and therefore belonged to a different administrative machine. During the next eighteen months I continued to give various old and new FPN's. But I still consider it miraculous that the nature of my sickness was never investigated and that the confusion of FPN's allowed me to remain undiscovered.

My stay in the hospital could not last indefinitely. I received permission to go out afternoons. I used the opportunity to read up on internal diseases, especially liver and gall bladder ailments. Sometimes I visited friends, discussed my symptoms in great detail, and anticipated further development of my "disease."

Finally, in order to avoid unnecessary interest in me which even Professor Brenner could not prevent, a change of scenery became desirable, and I was sent to Karlsbad for a four weeks' cure. Although I had the assurance that Professor Brenner would take me back, I spent the beautiful spring days in Karlsbad in considerable anxiety. The Nazis had made every attempt to Germanize this area of Czechoslovakia, and even the doctors were thoroughgoing Nazis. Their goal was to make the resort famous for sending many soldiers back to the front.

I was given more blood tests. One, the Takata-Ara, would not reveal anything wrong unless I induced harmless infections in other parts of the body which could lead a doctor to diagnose inflammation of the gall bladder. Therefore before the weekly medical examination I exerted myself by running up and down the Hirschensprung, and then exposed myself to drafts in order to develop a bad cold. A mere cold or small infection on a finger was enough for the purpose. Even the ill-disposed physicians at Karlsbad had to assume a gall bladder ailment because of my earlier medical history.

I often had serious pangs of conscience that so many soldiers had to leave Karlsbad without being completely cured because of inadequate hospital space while I poured health-giving waters away and removed the poultices from my body to make my recovery appear as remote as possible. But I had no choice if I wanted to go on living.

After four weeks in Karlsbad I returned to Berlin for further medical treatment. Then a period of intellectual revival began for me, which was to be the basis for real resistance work later. Jochen Niemöller, the son of Pastor Niemöller, was in my hospital ward. He had been under close surveillance by the Nazis, and was now, like me, under the benevolent protection of Dr. Ohm. We saw much of each other on our free afternoons. "The prerequisite," I can still hear him saying, "for any successful resistance or for an active revolution is a real hatred of the Führer on the part of a majority of the people." We formed a discussion group of like-thinking people, which included Dr. Ohm and some charming and intelligent nurse's assistants who had already been imbued with a skeptical attitude toward the Nazi regime by their upbringing at home.

Sigi, an old friend of mine who was suffering from stomach ulcers, was put in the same ward purely by coincidence. He brought along an excellent little radio. Dr. Ohm managed to arrange things so that the ward was soon filled mostly with like minds, and we listened to the BBC. Each day we heard a political review at nine o'clock and at twelve the broadcast for women in Germany. Dr. Ohm and Jochen spread the news among the other wards. Even those soldiers who were not anti-Nazis were interested in hearing it and did not report us. Listening to the BBC was never without danger, for a network of Nazi agents and denouncers pervaded the German Army. The penalty could be death. But we were reasonably safe, for this Zehlendorf hospital was a veritable hotbed of conspiracy. It was no coincidence that Field Marshal von Witzleben, who was one of the leading conspirators in the July 20 attempt on Hitler's life, often visited Professor Brenner's internal disease ward. Officers, including many generals, were placed here in private rooms, often for a long time. Probably the conspiracy against Hitler was going on under our very noses.

Of course, incidents did happen. One day a lieutenant with an amputated leg was brought into our ward because the surgical wards were crowded with casualties from the eastern front. On his uniform coat, which was hung over his chair, one could see, among a number of other medals, the silver wound medal.

"Well, how are things on the eastern front?" I asked cautiously.

"Excellent." I looked at Sigi.

"But the troops are withdrawing toward the Doniets," I remarked, groping a bit further.

"Of course, but you have no idea how strong the fortified lines will be. They can't get beyond the Doniets."

Some weeks later I observed, "It seems the fortified lines at the Doniets weren't so strong; here we are withdrawing to the Dnieper."

"Of course, but you have no idea what sort of fortifications are built there. The Dnieper is much more formidable than the Doniets. The Atlantic Wall is nothing compared with the line built there."

Several weeks later, when the Russians had already passed the Dnieper, we asked him if his formidable fortifications were at the Dniester or the Bug. He turned out to be a bit uncertain, but he could not be shaken.

One day he murmured, "I want to get out as soon as possible."

"But not on one leg?" I queried. "Do you want to go to the front with an artificial limb?"

"That's it exactly. I'll take a tank course and command a Tiger. Think of the chance I have. I need three small wounds for the golden wound medal. If I'm lucky I'll get a piece of shrapnel in the artificial limb, and that counts the same as an amputation. Then I'll have the gold medal!"

As time passed air raids became more frequent and more destructive. We were hit like a bolt of lightning by Goebbels' order for everyone who could to leave Berlin. Indescribable confusion was the result, and I could no longer count on the protection of Professor Brenner. Before the patients were moved I procured a syringe and vials from my friend the pharmacist.

One morning the trucks were ready, loaded and overloaded with blankets, mattresses, and other necessary equipment. The patients had to ride on top of all this. We were taken to the Grunewald station, piled into long rows of cattle cars, and given straw to lie on. Only the severely wounded were brought in ambulances. I managed to keep Jochen Niemöller and a few other soldiers with me in a railroad car with some officers.

The only thing Professor Brenner and Dr. Ohm could do for us before we left was to give us sick records which made our diseases look rather serious. They also assigned us to keep an eye on a colonel who had recently suffered a stroke and had poor control of his thoughts or words. We were glad of this, thinking that his presence and rank might be useful to us later.

The trip was far from monotonous. Before we started a very excited and emotional elderly captain landed in our car. He muttered something about being there by mistake and kept calling to the passing nurses and doctors that he belonged in Berlin and should be sent back. He continued his protests even after the train was under way.

We had been told that we would be sent to a small village in Silesia. It turned out that this excitable captain, a former high-school teacher, was not at all abnormal. He did not want to end up in Silesia, closer to the approaching front. He had come to the Berlin-Zehlendorf dispensary for treatment of a slight case of diarrhea, just as we were being evacuated. During the confusion he was loaded on the train before the doctors had a chance to give him any medicine. So here he was, on his way to Silesia— so he thought.

"What will the Supreme Command say?" he kept repeating. He calmed down only when he discovered that he had his air-raid kit with him, including his toothbrush.

Next morning we found ourselves in the heart of Saxony. The

confusion had struck even the railroad, an unusual situation in 1943. So, instead of going to Breslau, we were set down at another hospital evacuation point at Meerane. The women and girls here were attractively dressed in the well-known Meerane Scotch plaids and wore unrationed hosiery from the hosiery mills in near-by Chemnitz.

The country doctor, who was also head of the army hospital, came to the station on his motorcycle. He was quite overcome by the sudden influx of so many sick and wounded, and for a while did nothing but draw on his pipe. He was anxious to transfer the higher officers as quickly as possible, in order to avoid difficulties. Sigi, Jochen, and I succeeded in convincing him that the three of us must stay with the colonel who needed us: he appeared to be severely wounded, his head being almost completely bandaged, though it was merely because of a boil on his neck.

We were assigned to a near-by mansion. When the excited captain heard that he suddenly lost interest in returning to Berlin and was quite content to join us. However, the colonel seemed to prefer staying in Meerane, or perhaps did not want the privileges accorded to his rank. He had some difficulty in speaking, but kept mumbling, "I—no mansion." I had learned in the meantime that the mansion belonged to a prince who was widely known as a philanthropist and a highly cultured person. His friends included university professors, noted musicians, and the publisher of Rainer Maria Rilke's poems. His intellectual background led me to believe he would be an opponent of Nazism, and I hoped to find his home a congenial refuge.

I took the first chance to explain to the country doctor that the colonel meant he possessed no mansion himself but was quite satisfied with the arrangement. That afternoon about thirty of us were driven in a converted hospital truck to an idyllic little town in the Mulde Valley. We were quartered in a wing of the prince's large Norman-style mansion, which had been converted into a hospital.

This area of the Erzgebirge seemed hardly to have been touched by the war; an officer as high ranking as a colonel was rarely seen in the country between Zwickau and Chemnitz, least of all in Meerane. But one could sense the conflict between the minority of right-thinking people and those who had acquired the odious Nazi spirit which now pervaded most of formerly Communist Saxony.

The prince's physician was the head of the army hospital. To our great joy we found him and the rest of the prince's circle to be genuine opponents of the Nazi regime. In the afternoons and evenings we could go about freely, and often joined the residents of the mansion. We also met frequently in the near-by home of the doctor, on the wooded slopes of the Mulde Valley, and I spent hours among the rare volumes in the prince's library.

There were men like the fanatical lieutenant with the artificial leg here too; the number of wounded quartered in Meerane increased steadily. These men could not help noticing that our group had been here an unusually long time, and sometimes a strong word from the doctor or some mediating action by the colonel was required to turn aside their suspicions.

"What a pity that the colonel wasn't promoted to general before he had his stroke," Sigi remarked; "then nobody would have noticed that he's not quite normal." But his condition soon improved enough to permit his discharge into civilian life, even though he could speak only in confused sentences.

The power of the prince's physician was not so great as that of Professor Brenner. The doctors here were under the strict supervision of the higher authorities whose duties were to declare a large number of patients fit for service as quickly as possible. Visiting inspectors came almost fortnightly. The more cannon fodder they discharged from the hospital, the more rapid would be their promotion.

Up to the summer of 1944 I had to resort about fifty times to the only available means of feigning illness, the intramuscular injection. Because such an injection required undisturbed preparation I rented a room in town, allegedly for family visits and in order to study quietly. I did not want to risk keeping a sterilizer, which could not easily be hidden, so I used pure alcohol to make sure that no infection developed at the point of injection. These injections quickly created disease-and-fever symptoms, so that I was always considered sick by the time I was examined.

The prince and his family sat for their portraits, and in the course of time I received several commissions to paint industrialists living in the vicinity. The prince, who became increasingly well disposed toward me, allowed me to use a little chalet of his for the storage of evacuated goods belonging to my relatives and friends, as well as the last valuable possessions of some Jewish families in Berlin. He also sold me a small plot of land, where I proceeded to build a house with the aid of two French prisoners-of-war. This place, in a heavily wooded area with a magnificent view toward Thuringia, was intended to serve as a refuge for my family and a storage place for my father's library. Here I worked with my two French colleagues, a printer from Laon and an engraver from Amiens, and two other confidants from the hospital. We felt secure here, away from all spying.

In spite of all precautions a few Nazis in the small town must have gotten wind of something. Perhaps the Nazi Kreisleiter had become suspicious at our relatively long stay, or the idle gossip of the townspeople may have planted the seed. One day a factory owner whose portrait I was drawing warned me that we were being watched and must be careful. A postal official had told him that our mail was brought to the Kreisleitung every night and opened surreptitiously, before we received it the next morning. Nothing incriminating could be found, for all our friends had learned to write in such a way that outsiders could never have suspected anything, and we had gotten used to reading between the lines. We continued to be careful, and the Nazi censorship never led to any action against us.

In the course of time the doctor thought it wise to transfer Jochen Niemöller to a replacement unit, where there was a friendly chaplain. Thus we lost one of our most valued companions.

I considered going to Denmark, the country of my ancestors, and fleeing to Sweden from there. In January, 1944, I got four days' home leave. I took an express train to Berlin, where I could arrange to get travel orders to Denmark from a captain in the Supreme Headquarters of the Wehrmacht. I did not tell my parents of my intention, as I wanted them to have a clear conscience if they were interrogated.

I got the travel papers for Copenhagen without difficulty and took the train. In Copenhagen I changed into civilian clothes and immediately looked up the friend who was to help me get to Sweden. He discouraged me, saying that the situation had changed, that officials who had been providing false papers had fled or been arrested. After we had discussed the problem for a long time he convinced me that I could do more in the final phase of the war by staying in Germany.

When I returned to the hospital after five days, claiming to have been late because of an air raid, I came back with peace of mind and an inner resolve that my life of inactive opposition should now become more active and useful.

The news of the Allied invasion electrified us and marked another step toward the end of the war.

Shortly after that a friend offered me a job on a soldiers' newspaper, *Front und Heimat,* in Berlin. The physician gave me a certificate of chronic and incurable gall bladder disease, so that I could continue to evade the punitive assignment if I was discovered. In the course of two years on the eastern front the punitive unit to which I had been assigned had been decimated. I cautiously got in touch with the replacement unit. They did not seem to know anything about my record and informed the hospital administration that they did not object to my Berlin assignment, but that I must first report to the headquarters near Bielefeld. It was in Bielefeld on July 20, 1944, that I heard the first rumors of the attempted assassination of Hitler. A wave of hope swept through the barracks, and some officers stated rather openly that they were only waiting for an order from Berlin to overpower the Nazi organizations of the area.

When I began work on the army newspaper, I immediately started putting out feelers to find other anti-Nazis. I soon discovered that in the subordinate positions on the paper the skeptics and anti-Nazis tar outnumbered the Nazis. Many convinced patriots had come to realize that they had been doing themselves and Germany a disservice by their blind fidelity.

In August I managed to get Sigi transferred to the newspaper, and that fall I succeeded in establishing a small resistance unit in the office. An engraver and artist whom we nicknamed Pitt joined us, as well as three of the editors. We met regularly and started making plans. Several times we managed to have galley proofs arrive late in the other towns where they were to be reprinted. Articles were often directed wrongly. The transport chaos was a convenient scapegoat when questions were asked about the strange disturbances in publication dates.

Pitt and I kept irregular working hours, as we were both assigned to drawing. We were often asked to work in the evening and late at night. We therefore had a relatively easy task, for in the evenings and on Sundays, when many offices were empty, much information could be gleaned from the desks. All of it was immediately passed on to our friends and intermediaries with foreign news services.

When the staff held conferences one of us would invariably manage to work in the next room. It was easy to hear because the old wall, blasted by a bomb, had been replaced by a thin temporary partition. In that way we learned that the Amsterdam editor of our soldier paper had retreated with his whole staff to avoid being ordered to take part in the defense of Dutch cities, and was to be court-martialed. Few people had access to this information, which we immediately passed on. Two days later the Soldatensender West, a British propaganda station purporting to be a German Army radio station, carried the news. Sitting at the radio at night listening to English news for Germany, our hearts beat faster when we heard information which could only have come from us.

We also made it our task to provide forged papers for persons who were in hiding from the Nazis, particularly for Jews who were living illegally and foreign workers who had escaped from labor camps. A certificate saying that a man was on the staff of the soldiers' paper, or a letter with the party letterhead, taken out of the cabinet of the editor-in-chief, could be of great importance to men living illegally. Soldiers who had deserted were supplied with travel certificates and travel orders. Travel orders also were used to help persons in hiding get travelers' ration coupons and thus gain legal access to food.

We often sat in the editorial offices late at night carefully preparing forged identifications. I had soon learned to imitate the signature of Oberbereichsleiter Liebscher, the Nazi director of the newspaper. We were aided in everything by the confusion and anxieties of the last year of the war. A person who might have reported us only a year before would hesitate to do so now.

One of our most difficult operations was the use of the official seal, which was kept in a safe in the inner office. Since we could not open the safe at night we had to use the seal during regular office hours. Three or four of us worked out a carefully rehearsed, detailed plan of operation. If anyone was called to the main office he would look to see where the seal was lying. Then when the office was empty he would go in and use it while someone else waited outside to delay the director of the paper if he should come back, and one or two more watched to warn of his return long before he reached the office.

Once we had an uncomfortably close call. Liebscher left the room and I quickly went to the cabinet to take out the identification cards. Suddenly he was back. I had to talk fast:

"Oh, are these the new identification cards?"

"How did you get those papers?"

"They were lying here on the table," I lied, and appeared very surprised.

"Is that so?" he wondered. "Well—I must have left them there. Don't mention this, they are supposed to be treated as secret material."

"Yes, I didn't get much sleep myself last night—what with the bombings!" I laughed and left quickly.

Beginning in February, 1945, we started playing another trick that was useful for its psychological effect. During air raids we would go through government offices and other public buildings and tear down the Hitler pictures. It was easy enough because all the rooms had to be kept open during raids. Pitt always regretted that he could not take the frames along. Once we succeeded in hauling a colossal picture of Hitler out of an office of the propaganda ministry and leaving it in the street. The crowds who came by afterward could not believe their eyes. We purposely did not destroy the pictures but only put holes in them. We could tell from the pleased remarks of passers-by that the stunt was effective.

In the winter of 1944 the badly damaged Wertheim department store was still selling framed glass-covered pictures of Hitler. Good frames were rare, and that alone made the pictures worth buying. Glass was almost impossible to get. Millions of Berliners remember the unpleasant sound of knocking the remnants of broken glass out of their window frames after an air raid. I had to stuff my windows with cardboard five or six times, as no glass was available to replace the thousands of panes broken by the bombs. So I went to buy a Hitler picture.

The little salesgirl looked at me for a moment.

"Two more Hitler pictures, please."

She smiled. I smiled back at her.

"Do you know how to do it?" she asked.

"Not exactly." I hesitated, to see how far she would go.

"You cut with a knife behind this groove and bend back the little tabs. Then you have 'the desired.' "

"And what does one do with 'the undesired'?" I laughed.

"Well," she said nonchalantly, "the best thing is to burn it."

"Or to hang it," I added. We both laughed.

For a long time after that I supplied the little salesgirl with anti-Nazi information, and found her a person whose political ideas were akin to mine.

Many of the printers and typesetters were ready to help us print a complete anti-Nazi newspaper, or at least some information sheets. In the engraving department we found a man who was willing to prepare one of those ridiculous pictures of Hitler on horseback in the armor of a medieval knight, staring defiantly at some invisible enemy. In this phase of the war such a picture was bound to create a ludicrous impression. We wanted to print it on leaflets containing information and suggestions for resistance measures to be taken against the Nazis.

We were too few to do anything on a large scale, but one of us had made contact with a Communist resistance group. The Communist leader, Werner, was extremely cautious and very doubtful about us at first; but we helped them with false papers and gradually won their confidence. They realized that our access to a printing plant and to certain information could be most helpful. Werner was Jewish and had been living in hiding under an as-

sumed name for two years, without food ration cards and under
the most primitive conditions. We gradually arrived at really
sound cooperation, for although the members of this group,
Kampfverband Freies Deutschland, Sektor Berlin, had different
political convictions, they all had the common aim of fighting
Nazism. Later I got an insight into the extent of Werner's activities: as early as 1941 he and a small resistance group had
mimeographed an open letter against the war and the Nazis
addressed to Field Marshal von Brauchitsch, and sent copies
anonymously to consulates and embassies, to the press and leading
government officials.

So it was that right in the office of an army paper we prepared
anti-Nazi leaflets. Members of the group would then make typed
copies. We took every reasonable precaution, worked with gloves
on and used many different typewriters so that the type could not
be easily identified, and destroyed all carbon papers. The leaflets
were divided among members of Werner's group, who distributed
them at night and during air raids, usually by simply inserting
them in mailboxes. A few were sent to the garrisons of the replacement centers near Berlin, where Werner pleaded for days
with a commanding officer to forego senseless resistance. He also
persuaded a number of soldiers to desert, and we later provided
some of them with identification cards.

The number of leaflets distributed was small, not over 150.
But Pitt, Sigi, and a few others managed to remove a mimeograph
machine from the press building and carry it to a cellar in
Leibnitzstrasse. Then we had enough leaflets to post on walls.

Another Berlin underground group had started the "No" campaign. Everywhere, on house walls, in the streets, in railway stations, one could see the word "Nein." We cooperated and took
every opportunity to write "Nein" wherever possible. The Nazi
propagandists immediately sent their block wardens and Hitler
Youth around to paint the word Kapitulieren? above the "Nein."

A crisis arrived when the editorial office was to be removed to
southern Germany. A rump editorial office remained, which
later was transferred to northwestern Germany. Sigi, Pitt, and I
were supposed to go along, but we simply refused to leave Berlin.
As alternative we should have joined the Volkssturm, which con-

sisted mostly of the sick and age groups previously considered unfit for military service. When we did not do that we were technically deserters.

We were determined to do everything possible to shorten the useless final struggle and persuade people to surrender their city blocks by raising white flags. In the confusion of moving we managed to remove large envelopes marked "Order of the Führer" which the newspaper used to expedite some materials to its branch offices. During the last weeks Werner found these envelopes most useful in his courier trips for the underground group. He put the leaflets in them. When he wanted to pass the ever-increasing numbers of tank barriers, he would ride up to the guards on his bicycle, hold up the envelope, and shout at them, "Can't you see, I'm a courier and must pass! The Führerbefehl must go through! Everything is at stake!"

Indeed, lives were at stake. The sight of the body of a young soldier hanged in the city, bearing the sign, "I failed to fight to the last for my Führer," restored our inner firmness and strengthened our devotion to our cause.

In the last weeks and days of the Battle of Berlin units of the SS and police swept through the streets and conducted quick, on-the-spot trials and executions of deserters. Only a few days before our part of the city was taken squads of fanatical Nazis in the Volkssturm, wearing red swastika armbands, searched every house for more men for the barricades.

Werner always encouraged us, allayed our fears, and was an example to us. We worked at an accelerated pace in April and turned out two series of leaflets a week, exhorting all to fight the Nazis and to stop the war. We were preparing a leaflet in my apartment when a Russian dive bomber flew over. A bomb hit the room directly above us and shook the house, but we escaped unscathed. A similar bomb went from attic almost to cellar in the house next door.

We considered the bombing a negligible danger compared with the situation we faced on April 21, 1945, a little more than a week before liberation. It was inevitable that sooner or later our leaflets would get to the Gestapo and be traced. I heard later that police near the Olivaer Platz had traced them to a young

man in a stylish grey hat with a broad brim who was seen going
to the Bayerische Strasse. We had always known Sigi's weakness
for being well dressed and wearing the latest clothes, but had not
thought he would wear his new grey hat in this smoke-filled and
dusty city.

On that April day Pitt and I were just coming from the Leibnitzstrasse to see Sigi. We paid little attention to the SS vehicle
standing in front of Bayerische Strasse No. 2. The SS often
parked their cars in the side streets when visiting offices on
near-by Fehrbelliner Platz. I had about fifty new leaflets, of
which Sigi was to get thirty. For some inexplicable reason I had
taken them out of my briefcase, folded them carefully, and
placed them in my inner coat pocket.

Pitt rang the doorbell. I noticed that the apartment door was
slightly ajar and we heard deep voices. Suddenly the door was
thrown wide and an SS man dragged us both in, shouting, "WE
HAVE BEEN WAITING FOR YOU!" Another SS man said,
"You are arrested. Resistance is useless. Don't try to escape." Indeed, there was no possibility of escape. The hall was full of SS,
military police, and Gestapo officials.

Sigi was flanked by two SS men. They reported to the Gestapo
official that they had searched the apartment without finding
anything.

I pulled myself together. As quietly as possible I expressed my
astonishment over what was going on. Without waiting to be
asked I pulled my identification papers—the ones I had forged
myself. When I pulled out my wallet, my hand trembled as it
touched the leaflets. The identification papers seemed to have
the desired effect. The SS were impressed by our job with an
army paper. Apparently they did not know that the paper was no
longer published in Berlin. Their uncertainty gave me added
courage. I told the official there must be a mistake, a really comic
mistake. We were doing important war work and had obviously
been denounced by some resistance group, a malicious trick of
vengeance. Of course this comrade—I pointed at Sigi—had to do
vital editorial work.

The Gestapo official wavered. I still feared a search of my person. A few more questions—and the sirens howled. The Nazis

grew restless. The Gestapo official rose. The search had revealed nothing, their consciences were at ease, and an air raid was coming on. They left quickly, but posted a guard in front of the apartment.

I went to the toilet and flushed the leaflets away. We breathed more easily. After a few minutes we looked outside. The guard had disappeared.

As the fighting came closer we joined the rest of the residents in the cellar of our apartment house. There was constant shelling, and the men left the cellar only to help when someone had been hit. We prepared our last leaflets, with instructions on how to behave in the final days, including hanging out white sheets as a sign of surrender. My brother, who was working in an armored-vehicle plant on the outskirts of Berlin, distributed leaflets there. The women in our apartment house, among them the theater executive Renate, also helped distribute them. By now all but two Nazi women in the house admitted that the jig was up, and before long they too acquiesced and sat listening to the BBC. We even encouraged them, making them help us raise the white flags. It was amusing to see their wishful thinking and watch their phantom Wenck army vanish into nothing. This "army," led by General Wenck, actually consisted of only a few divisions outside Berlin. Hitler placed his last hope in them, expecting them to break through the Russian cordon around the city and then, with the troops in Berlin, defeat the Red Army.

After two more days of fighting our part of town was turned over to the Russians. When the first one of them, a tank officer in a leather jacket, entered the courtyard of the apartment house, I walked up to him with a white handkerchief attached to a broomstick, rejoicing that the pistols and guns no longer held danger for me or for anyone. This was the longed-for day of liberation.

EPILOGUE TO CHAPTER III

"You Are a Traitor..."

KNUD CHRISTIAN KNUDSEN is now a publisher. He continues to paint and do sculpture and some of his work has received considerable recognition. A collection of his stories has been published,* as well as an attractive folder of pictures of his portraits and sculpture.†

His father, Professor Knudsen, was assigned to a Volkssturm unit during the war and was hospitalized for exposure which he suffered when he escaped from it.

Werner became head of the Berlin-Wilmersdorf Cultural Office and was instrumental in getting the Berlin Philharmonic Orchestra to give its first concert in the middle of May, 1945. It played music Germans had not heard for many years—Mendelssohn's *Midsummer Night's Dream* and Tchaikovsky's *Fourth Symphony*. Werner later became the editor of a theater magazine.

Sigi entered the technical department of Radio Berlin, and Pitt worked in the new Academy of Art. Jochen Niemöller was assigned to a unit at the front shortly before the end of the war and was killed. The misfortunes of war dispossessed the prince of his land; he moved to a furnished room near Hanover where he started to work as an interpreter.

* Berlin, Pontes Verlag, 1947.
† Berlin, Daco Verlag, 1948.

PROLOGUE TO CHAPTER IV

Shadow of a Star

VALERIE and Andrea Wolffenstein, the daughters of a Jewish architect, were baptized in childhood and raised as Protestants. Andrea became a pianist and music teacher, Valerie a painter. The death of their father in 1919 and the inflation forced Valerie to take up secretarial work. For some years she was secretary to the art custodian of the Weimar Republic, and later became film secretary. The rise of Hitler led to her discharge. After several years of unemployment she became secretary to an art historian and architect, until he emigrated to the United States. From 1937 to 1941 her work consisted in helping Jews who were emigrating with registration and the shipment of their goods. In June, 1941, she was assigned to the Jewish labor draft.

IV

Shadow of a Star

VALERIE WOLFFENSTEIN

IT WAS a bright June day in 1941. I was on my way for the first
time to the Zeiss-Ikon-Goerz factory to which I had been
assigned by the Labor Office of Berlin. At a street corner
near the factory buildings I saw a small group of emaciated,
careworn women who were walking in the same direction. One
of them asked me if I were one of "the new ones." They told me
that the Jewish women had to clean toilet rooms, twenty-eight of
them a day. One pointed to a fat, sloppy-looking woman and explained, "That's our forewoman. None of us ever saw her do a
stitch of work. All she does is make it hard for us. She is Polish,
and her husband is a garbage collector." Another added, "One
good thing about her is that she's so lazy she doesn't check on
us as much as the one before her. She was a slave driver! She
made the Jewish women get down on their knees and scrub the
urinal drains in the men's toilets."

And so I too started to clean toilets. I found it hard work for
my legs were weak and I had never been able to stand very long.
Most of the women had been working there a year and a half.
When they began they thought they could not keep it up long.
They looked completely run down. One could still see signs of
past beauty in the tired features of one woman. No one would
have guessed, looking at another, that she had once owned a big
real estate firm. I felt particularly sorry for a pretty twenty-year-
old girl who was engaged. She had started working with energy
and cheerfulness. Now, with the odor of the toilet constantly
about her, she began to loathe herself and had fallen into a
depression. I realized that I too would become despondent and
that my legs would not hold out unless I could transfer to another job. The oldest member of our group had been married

to a Gentile and therefore had some influence over our Polish forewoman who looked upon her as better than the rest of us. The old woman intervened on my behalf. As a result the forewoman sent me with my request to the foreman, who exploded but nevertheless assigned me to another job: peeling potatoes for the factory canteen.

Together with another Jewish woman I sat and worked next to the garbage cans, at the end of a semicircle of chattering women. After the filth and smell of the toilets I felt almost as free and happy as if under the open sky. But the next morning the other women refused to sit with us and threatened to report the keeper of the canteen to the Nazi party if he made them work with Jews. They called us a "criminal pack" and said we were responsible for "Aryans" like themselves having to work so hard.

So from then on the two of us had to peel our potatoes in a deep-lying, windowless little cellar room. We peeled six hundred pounds of potatoes a day—about three times as much as the other women had to do. Occasionally on sunny days the keeper of the canteen let us work outdoors, but behind a wall, hidden from the view of the others. During the first few weeks we got some hot soup at noon, but later that was stopped. Everything left over from the four thousand portions which were issued daily was thrown into the hog troughs. Every few hours someone from the canteen came to urge us on with nagging and threats. When I got home in the evenings I was hungry and exhausted. In the winter we suffered terribly in the cellar from the cold and from constantly handling the chilled and sometimes frozen potatoes.

My sister Andrea, who also worked in a factory, had similar experiences.

When there were air raids at night we Jews had to go to unheated parts of the air-raid shelter; the Gentiles lay down in warm shelters. Sometimes the all clear came so late that there was no use in going back to bed, for I had to rise at four every morning in order to be at the factory before six. In contrast to Munich and many other cities where Jews were not permitted to use public transportation at all, in Berlin we were permitted to use it if the distance was great, but we had to take the route indicated on our identification card and ride standing up. The blind and diabetic husband of one of my fellow workers had to walk four hours to reach the office of the Jewish community, where he had been summoned by the Gestapo. Many Gentile workers were indignant over this rule and gave free vent to their feelings. People occasionally gave Jews something, such as a cigarette or an apple. Once an old Jewish lady, identified by the yellow star, was standing in a crowded streetcar. A big Berliner saw her, got up and said in his earthy dialect, "Little starlet, come and sit down now." Only one person in the car started to abuse him. He answered quietly, "I can do what I damn please with my own buttocks."

One morning in December, 1941, as I was climbing the stairs to the station platform of the S-Bahn or rapid transit railway, very tired after two consecutive air raids, I turned my ankle, lost my balance, and fell fourteen steps. I hit my mouth against the concrete, knocking out several teeth, and was bleeding badly when I landed at the bottom of the stairs. Although crowds of people passed by as I sat on one of the steps, no one dared to help a woman marked with the yellow star. After a while I was able to get up and limp home. I could not turn to any Gentile doctor or nurse.

After I had been absent from work several weeks the factory office sent me to the doctor of the Krankenkasse, the public accident and sickness insurance system. He pronounced me well before I had recovered. Returning to work, I found I was to be punished for my long absence by being sent back to cleaning toilets. But the factory doctor secured me a transfer to a different place of work. I was sent to an armaments plant in the Frankfurter Allee, assigned to a group of a hundred Jewish women, and put to work at a drill. I stayed at this job throughout 1942.

The young foremen, intoxicated by their new powers, shouted and bullied while instructing us in the use of the machines. They did it, it seemed, less out of political conviction than in hope of raises and promotions. But a few tried to help us, regardless of the dangers to which they exposed themselves and their families. The forewoman of the manual work section practically considered us her protégées. She was a simple working woman whose husband was at the front. Nothing could intimidate her or deter her from kindness. Once, when she heard that a Gestapo inspection was being made in the building, she ran from one Jewish woman to the next and offered to hide all the things we might have which we were no longer allowed to eat, such as fruit, tomatoes, and sandwiches with meat. We would have been deported if any of these had been found on us.

When friends gave me an onion, Andrea hid it in the air-raid sandbox on the stairway of our apartment house. Good foodstuffs were not allotted to Jews, but sometimes a kind grocer sold or gave us something "forbidden." In the factory where Andrea was working some of the workers occasionally gave her meat stamps. But in our section of the factory, in contrast, foremen even walked by at lunch time to see if any of us had sausage on our bread.

The talk of Jewish women always ran to the obsessing questions, "When is the next transport? Who will have to go this time?" More and more women failed to return in the morning, or came to work in tears. One day they even deported the children left by the mothers in the Jewish kindergarten during their working shift. Sometimes women whispered hesitantly of escaping or obtaining forged papers, but the number of those who even contemplated that was woefully small. Many were so unmistakably Jewish in appearance that their looks would give them away. Others had only Jewish friends and did not know anyone who might hide them. And most of them were married. It was particularly difficult for the men to find a hiding place. They were always suspect if they were of military age and not in uniform, and were checked more closely than women. At one time the Gestapo resorted to the stratagem of deporting other occupants from an apartment in which they could not find the person they had listed for deportation. After that, all timid plans for escape were given up.

When the deportations first started, the persons received a letter notifying them what day they were to be ready. They had to make a list of all their property and take it to the office of the Jewish community. The Gestapo delegated the preliminary work to this office. Here one had to sign a declaration that, as a Jew, one was an enemy of the state—to which all one's property now belonged.

The suicides after deportation letters were so frequent that the Gestapo changed its tactics and picked up Jews without notice, usually at night. Often I lay awake waiting for the sound of the notorious covered truck and listening to the footsteps of all who came in. We were frightened whenever the bell rang. Andrea and I each lived in dread lest we come home in the evening and find the other gone.

If a Gentile coveted a Jewish apartment the residents had to leave it and move in with other Jews. When that happened to us, we rented a room in the house of Frau Rumpler, the widow of an airplane designer. Being too frail to work, she did not report to the Labor Office and had no job. She risked being deported all the sooner, as the performance of useful work afforded some temporary protection; but she counted on being safe because her husband had been well known and highly esteemed. One day in September, 1942, however, her notice came. About that time she received a letter from a former maid, then living in Vienna, inviting her to come to her to "submerge." Frau Rumpler immediately went to see Dr. Kaufmann, a Jewish lawyer who had been procuring false identification cards for many Jews. The fact that his wife was Gentile gave him some freedom of action. He had been converted, and belonged to Niemöller's Dahlem congregation, which had done much to help Jews. He supplied Frau Rumpler with a false identification card and a button of the National Socialist Frauenschaft. Camouflaged with these, she left for Vienna two days before she was to be deported.

As a result of her flight Andrea and I were in grave danger. Would the Gestapo come to get Frau Rumpler? Or would the Criminal Police come instead and arrest us as accomplices, torment us with interrogations, and turn us over to the Gestapo? We did not know at that time that the Berlin Criminal Police did not always cooperate with the Gestapo but carried on a passive resistance against them. I doubt that any of the "U-boats"—as those who went into hiding were sometimes called—would have been able to remain submerged without the connivance of the Criminal Police.

We were fortunate. The first Gestapo official who appeared in the apartment liked the large refrigerator and had it loaded into his bright blue car. Some days later the janitor's wife opened the apartment to two other Gestapo officials who sealed Frau Rumpler's rooms. Andrea was in her own room at the time, with a Gentile friend who had brought her vegetables and apples. She quickly hid them under a pillow. The Gestapo men were in a hurry and did not bother to pay her a visit.

We did not want to remain where we had to fear the Gestapo more than ever; but neither could we bring ourselves to move. However, it happened that the apartment looked desirable to a high-ranking officer who forced us out. A Jewish woman sublet us two little rooms on the top floor of a house near the Bellevue S-Bahn station. The rest of the house was occupied by a Gentile doctor. Our Gentile friends were not allowed to enter Jewish apartments, which were marked by a yellow star; but when they visited us here they might be considered patients of the doctor. They continued to bring us food, even flowers, and always took along some of our clothing or property to store for us.

For some days in December we heard our new landlady moving things about in her room. Then came complete silence. That evening we braced ourselves and entered her room, fearing to find that she had committed suicide. But the signs indicated that she had fled. We were again in danger. The janitor would certainly have to report the disappearance of the owner of an apartment.

By this time the Gestapo were deporting Jews from factories as well as homes. Working in a factory had ceased to be cause for deferment. Those of us who remained were replaced at the machines by deported Russians and transferred to manual work —a sure sign that we were soon to go.

Seeing that no serious efforts had been made to locate Frau Rumpler, we too started to think about submerging. Our Gentile friends rejoiced, and tried to help us procure forged papers, spending much money in their efforts. We felt that we must submerge only after getting identification papers, in order to bring less risk upon those who might give us refuge.

Getting the papers was, of course, a dangerous business. Dr. Kaufmann, who had furnished Frau Rumpler's, had been arrested by the Gestapo and executed. We had heard of cases in which Gestapo men themselves offered such papers; then, after the victims had received them and thought their road to freedom was open, they were arrested. Once a large number of Jews who were getting forged passports and exit permits to Sweden were arrested just as they were going aboard ship.

Our friends were unsuccessful in their many attempts to procure false papers. Then someone offered to get us identification cards of the Nazi Labor Front for 4,000 marks. That was a lot of money, but we paid it. One disadvantage of that type of card was that its stamp had to be renewed every three months, but as we constantly deluded ourselves into thinking that the Nazi regime would soon collapse, this did not seem to be a very serious matter.

On Saturday, January 9, 1943, friends came to see us, in great anxiety over our race against time. Our Labor Front cards were to be ready Monday. On Tuesday we wanted to submerge. But our friends talked us into leaving at once and taking refuge with them temporarily. We agreed to leave our apartment Monday evening. I would go to friends in Berlin-Neuwestend, and my sister to others in Berlin-Wilmersdorf.

We were packing, and all our things were lying about the room. Andrea was kneeling in front of the stove and burning our old identification papers which were marked with a large J, when someone knocked. It was the janitor. He came in, looked around, and said, "I'm checking up on what has to be done to the room." A pause. "I'll have to report to the Gestapo that the tenant of the apartment has disappeared, or I'll be punished myself." We asked him if he had to report right away—and he said no. We wondered what he had concluded from the disorder of our room and whether he would speak of it.

Toward eleven that evening we were ready. We wrote on a slip of paper, as we had been advised to do, that we were committing suicide, to give the Criminal Police the excuse not to search for us. We could not leave from the near-by S-Bahn station, for some railroad official might recognize us as daily passengers who in the past had always worn a Jewish star. Instead we walked to the next station with our rucksacks and bundles, which in all the excitement we had not tied up well so that they kept falling open as we walked. At the station we bade each other good-by.

Walking to the villa of my friends in Neuwestend, I felt as if I had lost a heavy burden simply by removing the Jewish star. For the first time in years I was outdoors at night, after the eight o'clock curfew for Jews. Even crossing a square planted with greenery or entering a park had been prohibited, and on my daily way to work I had had to detour around the Lietzenseepark. Now suddenly, as if by magic, I was out at night. The air was fresh, the moon cast long shadows on the clean snow. I felt a new awareness of beauty.

In the midst of the happiness over our successful escape and the warm reception of our friends, the misfortune which fell on our former neighbors weighed heavily on us. Flensburger Strasse, where we had lived, was "cleaned" of Jews: everyone was deported six days after our departure. A few weeks later Jews were rounded up in all the factories and loaded into trucks for deportation without any of their belongings. We heard that Andrea's name was at the top of her factory's list because she had been sick for several weeks that winter.

Then came the news that Harro and Libertas Schulze-Boysen had been executed on December 22, 1942. Libertas had been my friend since childhood. Her husband, an officer in the Luftwaffe headquarters, had been chief of an extensive resistance group which worked actively against the Nazis and even obtained military information that they broadcast to Russia on their own secret radio station. He was about to have himself transferred to Supreme Headquarters in order to assassinate Hitler, when the whole group was arrested. I remember walking along the street with Libertas when she told me of Harro's intention to assassinate Hitler. She was violently opposed. "Even if I have to stand guard in front of his room, it must not happen. For then people would consider Hitler a martyr." Almost all the members of Harro's group were executed. One of the few survivors is the distinguished playwright, Günther Weisenborn.

Very soon we got our first big disappointment. The Labor

Front cards on which we had counted so much never came. There was no way of finding the swindler who had taken the 4,000 marks.

After I had been some weeks in Neuwestend Petra Hagmann, a recent acquaintance who was half Japanese, asked me to share her small room in the basement of a house in suburban Dahlem. I gladly accepted. Her room was a good refuge, for the house had many exits, and the janitor and his wife hated the Nazis and approved of her taking me in. The maid of a family living in an apartment above us occupied a room adjoining ours. She was busy upstairs during the day, but when she was in her room at night we had to talk in whispers. We also had to be careful during the day, for a large window faced a neighboring horticultural establishment where a gardener was constantly working. In the past Andrea and I had had only ourselves to look out for, but now we had the responsibility to our benefactors of avoiding acts that might lead to police inquiry.

We avoided as much as possible going out on the street during the day. But protected by darkness, I occasionally walked to the church of the Niemöller congregation. The first time I entered it the whole congregation was reciting the 126th Psalm: "When Jehovah brought back those that returned to Zion, we were like unto them that dream." January 30 was the tenth anniversary of Hitler's coming to power. At the end of the service, where a prayer for the Führer was prescribed, Pastor Dehnstedt, Niemöller's successor, said, "Lord, do what seems impossible to us men, perform a miracle: turn the obdurate heart of our Führer." Since most of the services of the Confessional Church—the anti-Nazi Protestant denomination—were attended by Gestapo informers, he took a grave risk. He even read out the names of the pastors who had been thrown into prison or concentration camp. Members of this congregation did much to hide Jews and faced the many risks involved in helping them.

During the first months Andrea had a much harder time than I. At first she lived in a large apartment house with Anna and Christel Schulze, good friends of hers. They warned her to keep out of sight because many residents were good Nazis. But once she had a violent toothache and had to leave the apartment several times to go to a dentist. She was seen on the stairs then and feared the consequences. When the warden received strict instructions to keep records of all those permitted in the air-raid cellar, it got too risky to stay in the house any longer. After a particularly heavy raid Anna Schulze took Andrea to a Fritz Strassmann who occupied a small flat on the top floor of an apartment house. He himself was air-raid warden and that made things simpler. Although he hardly knew Andrea he immediately agreed to hide her.

Four months after we had submerged we finally got two identification cards: one of a Berlin housekeeper, Charlotte Maly, and an expired postal identification card of a Viennese language teacher, Editha Mailand. We never learned whether the Maly card was a gift or had been stolen or found. Editha Mailand had expressly given her card to one of our acquaintances for us. Andrea became Charlotte Maly and I Editha Mailand.

A young engraver who belonged to the Niemöller congregation and who often forged identification cards for Jews mounted our photographs on the cards in the place of the original owners' and completed the portion of the seal of the Third Reich which had covered the original photograph. He charged a small fee, and did it so well that a Criminal Police official to whom my sister showed it after the Allies had come agreed that only a very experienced eye could have detected the forgery. Knowing this earlier might have spared us years of anxiety.

Having no ration cards we had to live, wherever we were, mostly from the ration cards of our hosts. We heard of a driver for a wholesale grocery firm who delivered food to grocery stores and to the magnificent villas of the Nazi bigshots in Dahlem. He regularly filled paper bags with small quantities of the same things and brought the little packets to Jews in hiding.

Even though we rarely went out, we feared being recognized as long as we remained in Berlin. Friends who knew a Protestant clergyman in the province of Pomerania asked him if he would hide one of us. He was quite willing and we decided that Andrea should go, but just then he was called into the army medical service. He arranged however for her to live with the family of a pastor who had been imprisoned several months because he had permitted Poles to be present during his services. Andrea stayed with them for a year. Then she moved to be with another pastor's wife, whose husband was at the front, also serving in the army medical service. Andrea had better fortune with her shelter than I. In the two-and-a-quarter years we were submerged I had to move eighteen times. Each time I was tormented anew with fear of discovery on the trip and of unknown dangers in my new refuge. Often I did not know until just before my departure what new asylum had been found for me.

A close friend, Esther Seidel, living in southern Bavaria, knew a nun from the Order of the English Ladies who secured me a refuge with a farm family named Gasteiger not far from Munich. Esther of course could not write openly. As a signal for departure she sent a post card saying, "Farmer G.'s wife will take one of the two puppies, the plump one with the brown eyes"—an excellent description of me. In spite of being cautioned against taking the express train to Munich as I might be stopped for identification papers, I went by the night express and was not disturbed at all. But on the local train from Munich to Traunstein an official asked to see my papers. I tried to appear calm, though I thought he would hear the beating of my heart when I handed him my postal identification card. He simply glanced at it and returned it.

That May I reveled in the beauty of the mountains and the friendly way in which the Gasteigers had taken me into their home. They almost competed with each other in their kindness. But unfortunately they had a bombed-out woman from the Rhineland quartered in their house who was an ardent Nazi. She was suspicious because I kept to myself and ate alone in my room, and said to a neighbor that I might be a spy. During my second week with the Gasteigers their little girl got jaundice. We were afraid that I might contract it too. When I did develop a stomach disorder because I was not accustomed to the good food, someone in the house who was not informed about me wanted to send me to a hospital. Hence it seemed best to leave quickly and try to find another place.

I went to the next village, where I phoned Esther Seidel, using a fictitious name in case anyone was listening. She suggested that I come to Munich the next day.

Esther met me at the station. She had already found a shelter for me with the Ammanns, acquaintances who were living in Freimann, a suburb of Munich. I was to stay there five days until some other place was found. But on the first evening Herr Dr. Ammann—an engineer in the Bavarian Motor Works—told me he was happy that he could help save a human being from Hitler and asked me to stay with them for three weeks. In the course of my submerged life I was their guest three more times, each time for several months. Whenever I did not know where to go I went to them and they always received me as if I were a member of the family. And it was a big family: they had six children.

It was difficult here, as at several other places, not to arouse the suspicion of the maid. I had been explained to her as temporary domestic help; yet she was bound to notice that I never got mail directly but only through Frau Ammann. Also there was the question of ration cards. My friends in Berlin sent whatever stamps they could spare, but my hostess always had to add something. She often gave me food from her own supply, which I took to the kitchen and gave to the cook as my own. In another family I was a guest, so far as the nurse knew. Once, when I helped her, she shouted with enthusiasm, "What you're doing is Patriotic German Service which would please our Führer!"

One day Andrea suddenly appeared in Munich to visit me. She had traveled from Pomerania with a nurse who was coming on a week's visit. I was so frightened by this foolhardiness that I could hardly enjoy our days together. Also I felt oppressed by the extra load on my hosts. The trip from Pomerania had been uneventful. But when Andrea, starting back, was sitting in the waiting room of the Munich station, a man came up to the woman sitting next to her, identified himself as a Gestapo official, and asked to see her papers. At that time the "total labor levy" had been in force for about a year, and Andrea was still in the age group for compulsory work. She sat waiting for the moment when the official would turn to her. When he was through he walked over to another group to make another sample check.

The police were always looking for people. Sometimes raids were made near Munich where the Isar country with its dense growth of bushes offered protection to deserters or anyone who wanted to hide. Also, the police occasionally made checkups, suddenly blockading a street and stopping every person there. I usually stayed in the house, but was not safe even there. From time to time party members entered to commandeer rooms for bombed-out parties or to take the names and birth dates of all residents.

At first I had a hard time remembering to answer to my new name when anyone spoke to me. If I had ever been interrogated, I am sure that my presence of mind would have failed me and everything would have come out. At least I had practiced the signature "Editha Mailand" so long that it had a fair resemblance to the signature on the identification card.

As a result of the attempted assassination of Hitler on July 20, the Gestapo and police became more thorough in enforcing their regulations. Police registration had to be made without fail within twenty-four hours of arrival anywhere. The checkups on the trains were more frequent than ever, and more travel restrictions were put into effect. A longer trip could be made only by "stuttering": that is, taking a train part of the way, getting another ticket and taking the next train on, and so on.

After some time with the Ammanns I went to live with a family near Ulm. Then Esther Seidel invited me to come to her home near the village of Stephanskirchen, close by Rosenheim. She thought I would be safer there than in a town or a city. I was to come in September, after her thirteen-year-old boy who had known me in Berlin had gone away to boarding school. But on Saturday, August 27, I heard that more travel restrictions were to go into effect the following Monday. I made up my mind to leave at once, taking advantage of the fact that checkups were less likely in the crowded Sunday trains. I would stop for a few days en route with the Ammanns, or at least inform them where I would be. Andrea knew that when I moved she could always locate me through them.

But in Munich I could not reach the Ammanns because all telephone booths near the railroad station had been destroyed by air raids, so I decided to go straight on to Esther. While I stood in line to buy a ticket it was announced that no more tickets were available on that train. Everything seemed to be going wrong. Just then a man called out, "Who wants to buy one ticket on the next train to Rosenheim?" I bought it. I arrived at the Stephanskirchen station at 11 P.M., still an hour and a half's walk from the Seidels'. There was no place I could spend the night in Stephanskirchen, so I set out on foot. At first the moon was shining, but after a while it started to rain and got pitch dark. I could not find the meadow path leading to the Seidels' house or tell the difference between meadow and lake. I found a bench and resigned myself to spending the night outdoors.

The rain drenched me; it was a miserable night. But at dawn the sun rose upon the loveliness of the Bavarian mountains all about me. As I was drying my things I noticed in horror that my postal identification card was soaked and the forged stamp a blur, making the card practically useless.

Esther received me with open arms. I was introduced to the children as Editha Mailand, a house guest who would help out temporarily. To our surprise not even the oldest boy recognized me. It was fortunate, because his parents had decided not to send him to boarding school on account of the air raids.

The house was tiny. Its first floor consisted only of one room and a kitchen. But the Seidels made room for me and made me feel at home.

In the summer of 1944 Andrea was still living in Pomerania with another pastor's family. Her situation was not enviable, for her presence had to be hidden from an evacuated woman living in a room above, who was at home almost all the time because she was expecting a baby. Andrea had to stay in her room and in bed much of the time to avoid being heard.

As the Russian front came closer women were drafted to dig trenches. Anna Schulze who had hidden Andrea in Berlin phoned the pastor and advised Andrea to come back to Berlin and bring work clothes along. She had no difficulty getting a travel permit, as she stated that she was going to participate in the "total labor levy." Anna, it turned out, had a new identification card for her and a plan for registering her with the police and getting ration cards. A Herr Helmrich, who had been head of a food office in Poland during the German occupation, had helped many Jews escape and would be glad to give her a certificate releasing her from the jurisdiction of the area served by his office. With that she could go to some town near Poland, such as Frankfurt on the Oder, and claim to be a refugee from the part of Poland which the Russians had now conquered. She would have both legal status and an alibi for having lost her other papers. Andrea asked to talk to Herr Helmrich first and at least learn about the part of Poland she was supposed to come from, so that her ignorance would not betray her. Moreover, she was not eager to go east, closer to the front.

Frau Helmrich studied Andrea when she entered, and exclaimed, "Aren't you Andrea Wolffenstein?" Upon Andrea's surprised "Yes" Frau Helmrich embraced her joyfully: "I'm so glad that it's you my husband is helping. I've always wondered what had happened to you." They had been childhood playmates. Suddenly all problems seemed solved. Frau Helmrich had the courage to go to the police and register Andrea then and there as Charlotte Maly, a refugee from Poland. Thus she got a ration card and legal status immediately. It did not seem wise, though, for her to stay in Berlin. Someone might recognize her, and her resuming work, as she would have to, might lead to undesirable inquiries.

But where could she go? Someone she consulted recommended Württemberg where the Confessional Church had been particularly helpful to Jews. That appealed to her, since it would bring her closer to me. But there was a new restriction limiting travel to a hundred kilometers. How would she get a permit to go further?

Frau Helmrich was always ingenious in thinking of ways to outwit the Nazi bureaucracy. She wrote a letter signed by an imaginary woman doctor from Tübingen, expressing joy over Andrea's return from Poland and offering her a job as medical assistant. With this letter Andrea got the travel permit without question. She took the evening train to Stuttgart. An acquaintance who met her at the Stuttgart station advised her to stay there, in a larger city; but since Andrea believed me to be still near Ulm she went on. She phoned my old hosts, only to find out that I had left some time before.

The Ammanns in Munich had no idea where I was and thought me still at Ulm. Andrea tried to trace me from one host to the next. Her inquiries were made more difficult because the heavy July air raids had destroyed much of the telephone and transportation systems. Her imagination conjured up all sorts of possibilities: I might have been arrested; or had an accident, been taken to the hospital, discovered there, and turned over to the Gestapo.

Andrea had to register with the police. As the Munich police required one to fill out a detailed questionnaire, a friend offered to go in her stead, so that Andrea would only have to come and sign. Two Catholic women, who had helped me in the past and had often sent me food stamps, introduced her to an anti-Nazi woman official at the Labor Office. She gave Andrea a job which she could do at home: embroidering Luftwaffe officers' insignia. Thus she could avoid working with others who might ask too many questions. Each insignia took hours to complete and she continued embroidering to the last months of the war.

Meanwhile I was still with the Seidels. Herr Seidel worked at the Kolbermoor branch of the Bavarian Motor Works, the same firm that employed Dr. Ammann in Munich. At a meeting in Kolbermoor Dr. Ammann asked Herr Seidel if he knew anything of my whereabouts. "Of course," was the reply, "she is at our home." Joyfully Dr. Ammann wrote to his wife, "The battery arrived!" Andrea came out to see me and we celebrated a happy reunion. After that she came every few weeks, as often as her work permitted. In the presence of the children we could not risk being known as sisters, so we pretended to be merely friends. Each good-by seemed like an eternal farewell. The center of Munich where Andrea was living was at that time a nightly air-raid target, and at first she was in constant fear of the systematic investigations of the citizen registry office in Berlin; but their work became less effective as the chaos caused by the raids increased.

I stayed with the Seidels until the winter of 1944. A popular

walking path led by the house and as long as it was warm many
people bathed in the lake. Often villagers and people who had
been evacuated there from bombed cities came to ask favors or
seek advice from Herr Seidel. The front door led directly into
the kitchen and visitors sometimes saw me before I could retire.
I especially dreaded one man who was in charge of the évacués in
the village and the surrounding area. Less than a week after my
arrival this official appeared and asked how long I had been there
and how long I intended to stay. Fortunately the children were
not around to contradict my story. I boldly replied that I had
come for the week end and would leave the following day. Esther
entered just then. She went with the official to the porch. I heard
nothing of their long conversation but ". . . with a 'y' or an 'i'?"
So he was asking the spelling of Mailand and putting my name on
his list—the first step toward discovery! After fifteen more anxious minutes he left and Esther explained how harmless the
visit had been. The question had referred not to me but to the
landlord, whose name was Mayer. But the official had announced
that he would soon come back to ask Herr Seidel for some advice.
Several times I barely avoided meeting him. Three times he announced his visit for Sunday, with the result that I left the house
early Sunday morning and spent the whole day in the woods.
Every day too I had to watch out for the mailman who always
came into the kitchen. I tried to keep the door locked, but the
children went in and out, and occasionally when Esther was out
I had to sign for registered mail. Not the least unpleasant thing
was that the villagers always noticed and talked about newcomers
or visitors. Once there was a murder in the vicinity, and the
sheriff investigated everywhere with his dog. Of course the children noticed that Aunt Edith went upstairs whenever anyone
knocked. I felt depressed, too, because the Seidels were endangered by my presence. I cannot be grateful enough for their
generosity. They never let me feel how heavy a burden I was for
them during all that time.

That winter of 1944–45 a notice appeared in the newspapers
that the postal identification cards were no longer valid as identification papers except in the post office. My host tried to reassure
me; he would consult Dr. Ammann, and they would do what they

could for me. Dr. Ammann had a good friend, Herr Heckl, whom he had known in a Catholic youth organization. Herr Heckl traveled to Lindau on Lake Constance in my behalf to induce the Nazi party chief there, Ortsgruppenleiter Strauss, to provide me with false papers: identification card, registration with the police, and food ration cards. Herr Strauss, who was now acting mayor of Lindau, had been in the same army unit as Hitler. But he was different from most Nazi leaders and led a modest and righteous life. He promised to get the identification papers. I was to go to Lindau with Herr Heckl. A secretary in the Bavarian Motor Works offered to lend me her identification card for the trip. In Lindau I would pose as a bombed-out refugee from Freiburg who was suffering from amnesia, and say that I had lost all my identification papers. That would have been quite an ordeal for me, as I had no gift for putting on an act.

But it happened differently. I went to the Ammanns' to get ready for Lindau, and at the last moment a new travel prohibition made the trip impossible. I stayed on with the Ammanns. In February of 1945 a great number of refugees from Silesia arrived in Munich. That gave us another idea. Frau Ammann had to register with the police two Silesian relatives who had taken refuge with her. She boldly registered me as another refugee. The police were no longer able to inquire in Silesia because that was the front then. Thus I had a food ration card, though I was still without a proper identification card. I continued to stay in the house most of the time for fear both of discovery and of the daily raids. In April when the Allied troops were approaching we had some exciting days. The SS blew up bridges near our house, and a near-by SS barrack, defended fanatically by fifteen- and sixteen-year-old Hitler Youth, was bombarded.

Andrea lived next to a bridge which the SS tried to defend against the approaching Americans by erecting barricades. At night the people threw the barricades into the river. When orders came at the last moment that Munich was not to be defended, the commander of the SS troops saluted the people on the street for the last time with a Heil Hitler, and marched off.

EPILOGUE TO CHAPTER IV

Shadow of a Star

IN TIME Andrea returned to piano instruction and Valerie to painting portraits, landscapes, Bavarian costumes, and flowers. But after the currency reform in 1948 Valerie received no painting commissions because most people had no money for that. Both sisters have used every opportunity to fight hatred and prejudice.

Dr. Ammann was one of the scientists who were brought to the United States in the fall of 1945, and his family followed him in January, 1947.

PROLOGUE TO CHAPTER V

"Your Mother Has Twice Given You Life"

Erich Hopp was born in 1888 in Berlin and served at the front in World War I. He is a poet, author, journalist, and playwright. He was a free-lance writer until 1934 when, being a Jew, he could no longer continue in his profession. He began then to do all sorts of menial work, which was usually too strenuous for his small body. On a limited scale he was also able to continue his previous work for the Jewish community in Berlin. When many Jewish workers were put to forced labor, he escaped for a time by not reporting to the Labor Office.

V

"Your Mother Has Twice Given You Life"

ERICH HOPP

IN 1941 Berliners were encouraged to visit an exhibition called "Soviet Paradise," shown in barracks across from the Royal Palace, where they peered at dirty huts with broken-down furniture. One day one of these propaganda barracks was burnt down, in open protest against the Nazis. In retaliation 250 Jews were shot.

One evening in late May, 1942, shortly before the assassination of SS-leader Heydrich in Czechoslovakia, my wife Charlotte and I were sitting with our fourteen-year-old son Wolfgang in our apartment in the Friedenau section of Berlin. For months I had been doing heavy labor: loading coal, digging foundations—work to which my occupation as a writer had not accustomed me. I was very tired. About nine o'clock the doorbell rang—an unusual hour for visitors. I started to answer it, but Wolfgang stopped me. "Don't open it, don't," he whispered. The bell rang again. Then we heard a letter drop into the mail box.

We found a large envelope which contained the dreaded message: prepare to be evacuated. We were to be allowed to take a few things with us, including toilet articles, a blanket, and one change of clothes.

All night we weighed our chances for life. If we avoided deportation, how could we get along without a place to live, without food ration cards, always in danger of being reported by self-appointed denouncers? But deportation meant at best a precarious living and perhaps death. We did not consider the only alternative, suicide. We finally decided to submerge, and live illegally. Though we could not know it then, the decision was to mean survival to us.

We had two days of grace which we used to perform necessary errands. We kept up pretenses by taking the required list of property to the Gestapo office at the Jewish community center. Charlotte searched for a place for us to live. She took off her yellow Star of David so that she could hunt more easily and quickly. It was safe enough because she did not look Jewish at all.

I went to an old school friend who held a prominent position in Berlin University, and asked if he could hide us for a while, but he refused with regret. A ministry official who had often been our guest also turned me down: our Jewish corpses, he was afraid, might be found in his apartment after an air raid.

Charlotte returned with word of three possible hiding places, but none that could take us all. It was too risky for a whole family to stay together. We decided that Wolfgang and I would go temporarily to a children's home run by a relative in north Berlin. Charlotte chose one of the remaining addresses. The Gestapo came to arrest the people in the third place shortly afterward and Charlotte would have been arrested with them.

We left a letter in the apartment announcing our intention to commit suicide, and asked to be buried together when our bodies were found. We all signed it: everything must satisfy the sense of propriety of the bureaucratic authorities. We took only a few of our belongings along, in order to make the suicide more plausible.

Then we said good-by to our home, to my library of three thousand books, to Wolfgang's playthings. He started weeping when he realized what it meant. We went out quickly and closed the door forever behind us.

At the children's home on Schönhauser Allee we were met with disturbing news. "You can't stay here. It's too dangerous. The mother of one of the children has escaped from the Gestapo, and they will certainly search for her here." We were told to go to the Rückerstrasse at ten that evening and meet a man who would take us to a place where we could stay.

We went out on the street again. I was very conscious of having lost my Star of David and thought that everyone who passed must notice it.

We were at our rendezvous in front of the house in the Rücker-strasse at ten o'clock. The man appeared and took us into his apartment where we waited till midnight. Then a woman came with a huge dog. Little was said. She took us to the Mulackstrasse, one of the worst alleys in Berlin, inhabited largely by prostitutes and the underworld. It was off limits to military personnel. Tough characters hung around the bars. The police tolerated them because they could raid so much more conveniently: they found everyone together. We were received by Lorchen, the madam, who led us to a clean room with two beds. The tables had bright-colored lamps which Wolfgang thought pretty. Tired out, he quickly fell asleep, but I lay awake, reviewing the paradox: here we were safe—in a brothel! And safe for how long?

As soon as she could, Charlotte came and told us what she had heard from someone in our old apartment house. The Gestapo had appeared at six in the morning to fetch us. When no one answered the bell they broke into the apartment. Apparently they accepted the suicide story. In fact, a policeman spread the word that our bodies had been found in a lake in west Berlin and that we had been buried. It was a relief to know that we were officially dead.

We would really have been dead if we had not gone underground. Right after Heydrich's assassination we would have been at the collection point awaiting deportation. In reprisal for the assassination, three transports totaling three thousand men, women, and children were killed. We would have been among them.

The people in the house on the Mulackstrasse were very good to us. They brought candy for Wolfgang and cigarettes and detective stories for me, and even put a radio in our room. Lorchen baked a cake for Wolfgang, and he found his new environment of absorbing interest.

A house of this sort was a hazardous refuge. The occasion for leaving came only ten days after our arrival. On the floor below us were two French girls who had been put to forced labor in

Germany, had escaped, and now were leading a life of ease. These mischievous demoiselles stuck their tongues out at a Nazi woman living across the street and she threatened to get the police. We knew we must disappear again.

Charlotte came to see us. "How are my men?" she asked Lorchen. "How are they? They are gone." Charlotte's first thought was the Gestapo. But Lorchen told her we had gone back to the man in the Rückerstrasse who had taken us in before; and there she found us. He did not know where to hide us but he kept us that night.

Next day we rented a room in north Berlin. The landlady soon found out though that all was not right with us and told us to leave. Then we thought of Emil. Emil bought up used furniture, and had helped a number of Jewish families to settle their affairs before being deported. I had known him for some time and he was always very pleasant to us. We saw him and he gave us the address of a woman who dealt in old clothes and second-hand goods and who he was sure would have room. She lived in Wedding, a district of Berlin full of large close-set grey tenements which housed thousands of people. When we knocked on the door an old woman opened it and a pestilential odor issued from the room. Our first thought was to leave, but "illegals" cannot be choosy. We entered, and told her we were bombed-out people from Hamburg.

Charlotte was still at her original refuge. She spent every day, from morning till night, looking for food. Many people we knew gave her something, or named other people who would give. Wolfgang went by himself and ate unrationed soup in restaurants. For days I never dared to leave our room, partly because I look Jewish, partly because I did not have the necessary identification papers. As a man I was much more likely to be stopped than a woman, in whose military status the police were not interested. Hours on end I sat beside a shaky old table, meditating. Then suddenly a miracle took place in me. I no longer saw the ugly tenement room about me nor thought of our plight. I took paper and a pencil out of my suitcase and wrote what had grown in me out of these uprooted weeks: psalms of supplication in distress, psalms of human love, of confidence in God and faith in the victory of good.* I wrote day and night. My hand could hardly move fast enough. It was as if I were under some unexplained command and not I but some inner force were writing. In a few days I wrote twenty-eight psalms. That mood of inspiration never recurred in all my illegal life. I felt that I understood how the biblical composers of psalms who lived thousands of years before had suffered and hoped. They too had felt confident of eternal and divine justice.

We knew we could not stay very long in this place. Our hostess had rented a room to a post office electrician who had stolen quantities of electric cables from the post office and brought them to the house. Someone might come at any time to investigate. We lingered a little while until we could find a safer hideout. Then Wolfgang joined his mother; and the widow of a cousin, Selma Hopp, a Gentile, agreed to take me in. She was living in seclusion in Lichtenberg, an eastern suburb of Berlin, on the fifth floor of an apartment house. She told me she had been advised not to let me come as she might be watched by the Gestapo because her husband had been Jewish. But the old lady welcomed me and treated me with kindness. I lived in a room with dark green wallpaper and slept on a sofa so small that I had to curl up like a question mark.

I did not leave this apartment for twenty-one months. During heavy air raids the house would shake and quiver and sometimes rock. Plaster fell from the ceiling and pieces of glass flew about. Instead of talking I had to whisper; and when I walked I had to tiptoe. I could not cough out loud, or make a sound when Selma had company. The room was cold, and for exercise I walked its length, a distance of about four meters: 25 times to go 100 meters. For hours I had nothing to do, for I could not read all the time. So I stared at the dark green wallpaper and developed a phobia for green which I still possess today.

Charlotte and Wolfgang had to keep changing their hiding place. Most people were willing to risk taking them for only a week or two. Their presence for such a short time could always be

* Published as *O Mensch, verzage nicht* (Man, Despair Not) (Berlin, Pontes Verlag, 1947).

explained easily as visiting relatives or bombed-out people. Staying longer could raise doubts, and put too much of a burden on the hosts, who usually shared some food with their illegal guests.

Once some rabbits were stolen in the garden colony where they were living in an empty summer cottage; and someone suspected them. On New Year's Eve, 1942, they found a note on the table: "Flee at once! Grave danger!" Once again they were without shelter. Charlotte, who was herself at the point of desperation, comforted the chilled and crying boy. With her abundant energy she found a hiding place with a deaf-and-dumb person in the northwest part of the city, and later in the cottage of an old sideshow owner who fell in love with her. Sometimes when she and Wolfgang had no place to go Selma gave them shelter—but it was too risky for all three of us to be there long. The neighbors were always suspicious.

One day Charlotte did something unusual. Years before she had taken a course of lectures from Anna von Gierke, the well-known social reformer. Now she turned to Frau von Gierke for aid. I was skeptical, remembering my earlier experiences with people of note. But Frau von Gierke and her sister gave her addresses and made helpful suggestions. For a while Charlotte found refuge near Potsdam with the family of the art historian Dr. Beier. His wife was Jewish and so the risk was great for both parties. But they treated Charlotte like one of the family, and the children, Michael and Anita, anticipated her unexpressed wishes.

Frau Beier was later sent to concentration camp because having just returned from Crete, she did not know of the Nazi rule that all Jewish women must sign with the middle name "Sarah." She died, worn out, shortly after liberation.

While Charlotte was with the Beiers Wolfgang lived with a landscape architect who, in spite of being a member of the Nazi party, took him in. When it seemed unwise to stay longer with the Beiers, Charlotte moved in with a family who had accepted some of the Quaker doctrine and who generously shared their small apartment with her. Their children wanted to give their last bit of food to their guest; and above all they never talked about her in public.

All this time I stayed with Selma, meditating in the solitude of the dark green room. The dear old lady shared her food with me and helped to pass the time by talking with me, always in whispers so as not to arouse suspicion in the next apartments. We had a happy time when Charlotte and Wolfgang came to visit and all three of us could be together for a few hours. Bernd Tönnies, a friend who was a legal philosopher, came from time to time and gave us some of his cigarette and food ration stamps. It was a great pleasure to talk to him.

With all the time in the world, I could not write much. All I managed was a poetic dialogue, "On the Way," in which symbolic figures of Faith and Doubt discuss the problems of humanity.

One day as we were talking in Selma's room there was a knock on the door. Selma opened it and a policeman stood there. Selma stammered that she had company. He looked at me suspiciously. I felt I had to do something and forced myself to greet him with a friendly "Heil Hitler!" It turned out that he had come to check on places that could take in bombed-out people. The danger had passed, but my nerves were taut for a long while afterward. Besides, this raised a new difficulty. I could not possibly stay if bombed-out people should be assigned to Selma.

But when it became too hard to find a place for Wolfgang, he too came to stay with Selma. As he was getting no education I gave him some lessons in those months.

Wolfgang would often pick up cigarette butts on the street or take them from ash trays, and I rejoiced to get the tobacco. But once this quest almost turned out to be fatal. Wolfgang had found a smoker's ration stamp somewhere and went to a restaurant to buy some tobacco for me. When the proprietor looked at the stamp he was furious: it was from a previous ration period and was no longer valid. He thought that Wolfgang was trying to get away with something, and called a policeman from another part of the restaurant. The policeman wanted to take the boy with him to the station. Wolfgang saw camp gates closing behind him. Then suddenly one of the patrons said, "Let him go, I know that boy; he's Otto Schmidt from the Parkstrasse, I'll speak to his parents." And the policeman let him go.

In September, 1943, Charlotte again spent a week with the Beiers in Potsdam and then looked for another shelter. Just when she was at her wits' end where to go she was invited to a concert at the home of the two Wichert brothers in the Tiergarten district of Berlin. The brothers shared some of their food ration with her and told her that a Professor Karl Marguerre, an aeronautic engineer who lived in suburban Eichwalde, would keep her for a week in his home.

The professor met Charlotte at the station and installed her in the basement of his villa. When the week was over she tried to thank him and go, but the professor told her she could stay as long as she liked. At last she had a real home and could devote herself entirely to the task of getting food for her family.

The ration allotments in 1942 and the years following were just large enough for one person. It was impossible to expect anyone to share their ration card with three others. We approached the problem by preparing a list of people who might contribute something. It was made out in code, of course, so that the donors would not be endangered if we were arrested. For instance, a family by the name of Strauss was called "Blumentopf" —flower pot—and Edith or Bernhard would be abbreviated E or B.

Charlotte started visiting these people systematically. Gradually she developed a fairly regular weekly schedule. Each of these helpful and compassionate persons gave what he could; no matter how little it was—fifty grams of bread, five grams of fat, or a paper bag full of flour, some potatoes, or a bottle of thin soup— it helped. Any housewife can imagine the work it took to combine the many small bits into something adequate. We did not expect to live well—we only wanted to live.

Charlotte put her daily collections into a small briefcase and then came to us. This old briefcase gradually assumed a preternatural importance for me. When Charlotte arrived in the evening I approached the shabby container with almost devotional care, for its contents determined whether our lot for the next few days would be food or fasting. Occasionally it was impossible for Charlotte to come or we thought it unsafe. Then we called it a fast day. But we never lost hope, and even though our stomachs were empty our hearts were full of confidence.

And so, for three years, Charlotte hurried from house to house, from apartment to apartment, from one part of the city to another, asking for food to keep her family alive. She went without it herself for our sake and often would take only a plate of soup. She left no possibility untried, though it often cost her great embarrassment. Once in a small run-down lunch room a man spoke to her and promised to get her some vegetables or a quarter of a pound of margarine if she would meet him again.

Not all donors gave gladly, but some even thanked Charlotte for the opportunity to help. Others did it with the evident though unspoken thought, "Haven't we done enough for you already?"

A friend and former judge, Dr. Fritz Roland, was removed from office after 1933. In the course of the Jewish pogrom in November, 1938, he was arrested and taken to Sachsenhausen. His wife, a Jewess, informed her father-in-law, a Gentile from a distinguished old family, who was a member of the Order of Knights. He protested to Göring, informing him that his son was not a Jew. Soon afterward Dr. Roland was discharged. It turned out that he had passed himself off as a Jew in anger over his discharge from office, and had accepted all discrimination against Jews himself. After he was released from the camp he continued to collect funds for the Jewish community of Berlin. One day when Charlotte called on them Frau Roland said she had no bread this time. Dr. Roland, overhearing, cut off all the bread stamps still left for that month on his ration card and declared he preferred to go hungry himself than have us suffer.

Another time Charlotte was lucky enough to get the whole ration card of an engineer working on the V-1 weapon, who was going to Paris where he would get army rations.

Gradually the number of donations diminished and their sources changed. In the beginning many Jewish families still gave a bit, but eventually almost all were deported. Couples of mixed marriage often were most timorous. They did not know when their turn would come, feared they were being watched, and avoided anything which might add to their danger. Besides, they had too little themselves. Finally only the Gentile donors remained. Over the years there was an incessant fluctuation between getting enough to eat and real privation.

It is necessary to go back to the year 1919 to explain how we got meat and fat, important items for us, as most people did not have much of either for themselves. I had been commissioned by the Lord Mayor of Berlin to write and direct a play for a district anniversary celebration. The actors were amateurs and I selected a stout young man as just the type for a comic part. Twenty years later I was visiting in an apartment whose Jewish owners were having to move their furniture out quickly. Someone said that the only mover who could do it in time was Hockenholz, and he was called. When he saw me he stepped up and burst into a song from that play of twenty years ago. I recognized him, and after this Charlotte always found him a helpful donor of horse meat and horse fat. I doubt that we would have had the strength to survive without it.

Money was another essential item, if only to pay the small expenses of daily life or utilize donated food stamps. It could also buy a meal in a restaurant or soup or a cup of hot ersatz coffee. Some people wanted Charlotte to take a lot of money but she never took more than she needed for the moment. In contrast to others with similar fates who sometimes had to give their hosts large sums to hide them, no one ever asked a penny of us for anything. In order to earn their survival other illegals had to perform the lowliest and most difficult tasks. We were always treated with generosity and kindness.

When Wolfgang got to the age where boys were assigned to such posts as antiaircraft artillery assistant, he too was restricted to the house. Before that he camouflaged his origin by doing everything that everyone else seemed to do, even running around with a collection box for the Nazi Winter Aid. When I heard about this activity I put a stop to it.

I had nothing as identification except a military pass from the first World War. As a precaution I changed the religion on it from "mosaic" to "dissident." Wolfgang used every chance he had to obtain identification papers. He got a pass for the city transportation system under the name of W. Horn, a reader's card at the Lichtenberg Public Library, a postal savings book, and other things. Some illegals went to a police station after an air raid in order to get papers as bombed-out persons. That often worked, but sometimes they were arrested and deported.

Once Charlotte was visiting Herr Schmidt who knew a number of people working in the government. He was one of our most unselfish helpers, generous with both food and money, and never hesitated to receive her. She talked about the problem of identification with him, and he told her, smiling, that she would not need any; nothing could happen to her. But this did not reassure her, and so he promised to see what he could do. The next time she saw him he gave her a blank sheet of stationery from the Propaganda Ministry, signed by Goebbels. Charlotte typed onto it that she, Charlotte Horn, was employed in the press section of the Propaganda Ministry. It was not official as it lacked a photograph and seal. Charlotte suspected too that such ministerial documents might ordinarily carry some significant initials or code letters without which anything could be recognized as forged.

Toward the end of 1943 the air raids on Berlin grew more frequent. Wolfgang and I, who could not go to the shelter during raids, remained in the room on the fifth floor. We looked on as the bombs fell and fires started near by. Wolfgang's whole body shook; he clung to me and I tried to quiet him. "Come, boy, let's play 'friendly horse'!" I would say, thinking of the way a tired horse will rest its head on the neck of its teammate. He would come close, hide his head on my shoulder so that he did not see the fires, and feel more secure. Once, when a bomb fell next door, "friendly horse" did not help. I tried to reassure Wolfgang by telling him to follow the example of his (outwardly) calm father. "Yes, Vati, it's easy for you, you are a trained soldier," he said with a sigh.

Another time Wolfgang showed more presence of mind than I. Because the auxiliary firemen of each house had to inspect apartments when there was danger of fire, doors were supposed to be left unlocked. One night, when a near-by factory was burning, we heard someone coming down the hall. Now we would be discovered! What could two men be doing in the apartment during a heavy air raid when they should be in the cellar? Signaling the enemy perhaps? Goebbels had spread a great fear of spies among the German people.

We both sat as if paralyzed. Suddenly Wolfgang jumped up and locked the door. They tried to open it and complained that it was scandalous for doors to be locked during a raid like this. The danger was not over yet—the room had another entrance which could not be locked. But they turned away and we were safe.

In October we got the bad news from our friends, the Walters, that the Gestapo had come to them to inquire where we were. The good people had seemed surprised and claimed not to know anything about us, saying they thought we had been dead for a long time. They were repeatedly ordered to the Gestapo offices and questioned. So the Gestapo knew that we were hiding! We guessed who might have told them.

A young Jewish girl whose parents had owned a restaurant frequented by Jews had purchased her life from the Gestapo by becoming a spy. She would walk about with two Gestapo men and point out people she recognized. Many Jewish illegals were her victims. Unfortunately she knew us. Before she started her unhappy work she occasionally saw Charlotte and Wolfgang visiting the Walters and had once treated Wolfgang to a lunch with her food ration stamps.

On Frau Walter's birthday the Gestapo suddenly appeared again, hoping to find my wife and Wolfgang there. Fortunately they were wrong. But we had to face the fact that we "dead" had been officially resurrected. Charlotte was afraid to go out on the street, and Wolfgang received strict orders not to show himself. Every time the bell rang we were scared.

During the Christmas holidays Professor Marguerre went to visit his family in south Germany and Charlotte was left alone in the villa in Eichwalde. The Foreign Ministry had evacuated some offices to this suburban town. One night while these offices were being bombed with incendiaries Charlotte sat alone in the basement of the villa. Some incendiaries penetrated through the floor into the coal cellar, and she went in to put out the fire. Another bomb blew the cellar door closed and she was shut in with the smouldering fire. She found an old rusty water pipe on the wall but could not open the faucet. Almost frantic, she discovered an ax and split the pipe with it. The water poured onto the coal fire and the smoke threatened to suffocate her. Choking, and with singed hair, Charlotte forced the cellar door open and ran outside.

A neighbor in the yard was surprised to see a strange woman coming from the supposedly empty house. Charlotte explained that she was a friend of the family whom the professor had asked to guard the house in his absence—a plausible excuse. Called back by telegram, the professor praised the courageous action of "Carla Horn" to the townsfolk. As a result of this introduction she could show herself on the streets more openly, for she was recognized as the protector of the house. The professor also suggested that in the future she should not stay alone in the villa. But who could stay with her? Here fate intervened.

I shall never forget the night of January 3, 1944. After the air raid ended, about 3 A.M., Selma, Wolfgang, and I went to sleep. At half-past three someone knocked on the door: the house would have to be evacuated at once because a dud was lying in the yard. There was much excitement, doors were flung open, and everyone hurried to the air-raid shelter which was designated as a collection point. Selma took her little bag and left the apartment. Of course Wolfgang and I could not stay. In order not to be seen we waited till everyone had gone down and then we too sneaked down the stairs, each carrying a small bag. When we were almost at the bottom a police lieutenant in a steel helmet came in the front door. He looked in surprise at the two of us paralyzed on the stairs and shouted, "Hands up!" We dropped our bags and obeyed. The officer approached us cautiously. "Do you have any weapons?" "No." He apparently took us to be looters, of whom there were a number in these days of confusion and open doors. "What have you got in your bags?" We showed him some bread, a towel, and soap. Then the fateful order: "Your papers."

I pulled out my old military pass. It was of course in my real name, but Wolfgang's papers were issued in the name of Horn. The suspicion of the police officer grew. "Aren't you father and son?" he shouted. "Why do you have different names? Where are you from and where do you live?" So many questions and so few answers. I tried answering him in Berlin dialect. "Man, do you think we want to blow up with this place? Didn't you hear that the house was to be evacuated because of the danger of explosion? Don't hold us up any longer." And I said to Wolfgang, "Come, let's go." But the officer thought differently. He ordered us to come to the air-raid cellar with him. After that he'd see what to do with us, for we were obviously suspicious characters.

Again our struggle for life appeared lost. We slowly followed the policeman. To get to the air-raid cellar we had to cross the yard. There an excited crowd stormed the police lieutenant with questions—and in the confusion we escaped to the street by a side entrance. We ran through the burning streets, always thinking that we were being followed. Only toward dawn did we sit down to rest. At half-past six we phoned Professor Marguerre in Eichwalde and he told Charlotte to bring us both out.

We met Charlotte at a surburban station. She gave me a gift of cigarettes from the professor. Then she took me to have my hair cut and went to a restaurant with us.

After more than a year and a half in one room the world was new and strange to me. I tired easily, being unused to the fresh air, walking, or direct sunlight.

The professor greeted us warmly when we reached Eichwalde. The three of us rejoiced to be together again. We sat down to a good meal in a room with no trace of dark green wallpaper; and our kind and intelligent host visited with us. Wolfgang soon went to bed, but Charlotte and I sat up late, listening while the professor played Mozart, Schubert, and Beethoven on the piano. It was the beginning of a lasting friendship.

But the joy of being together could not last long. After the unexploded bomb in Selma's yard had been removed we decided that we had better go back there. To stay longer seemed too much of an imposition on Professor Marguerre. Although the police had not looked for us during the week we had been away, we entered the house with apprehension.

Later, bombed-out people were assigned to Selma's apartment and put in the room next to ours. We had to watch every move we made, could not clear our throats, and even had to stop whispering. The situation was becoming impossible, though Selma was as generous as ever. Then, after a few days, the refugees moved out again because they had found something better.

Occasionally Charlotte had us out at Eichwalde. We happened to be there in the early summer of 1944 when the apartment house Selma lived in was entirely destroyed in a raid. Fortunately Selma was safe in the air-raid shelter. After that the basement of Professor Marguerre's villa became our only refuge.

Finally the professor went to south Germany to stay with his family. Charlotte was left in charge of the whole house as his representative. She was not, of course, registered with the police, as the law required all residents to be, but passed herself off as a bombed-out person from the district of Neukölln in Berlin. The villa was rented to Herr Gerlach, who knew our true identity but was generous enough to permit us to continue living there. Charlotte prepared his meals and took care of the house.

The basement of the house was six feet below the level of the street and very damp. I usually spent the hours there sitting on a stool placed between a large wardrobe and a wash basin. When Herr Gerlach came home in the evenings it was safe for Wolfgang and me to come up out of our subterranean home and putter around in the kitchen.

Once when we were upstairs a post woman appeared out of nowhere and seemed much surprised to see two total strangers. She looked at us suspiciously. The postal officials had contact with every household and could report anything they considered peculiar. Again we had some uneasy weeks. Another time while Charlotte was out a chimney sweep made persistent attempts to get into the house. The two of us stayed in the cellar, making no sound. We could hear him walking around the villa, pounding on doors and windows and calling out angrily, "I'm sure there's someone at home, there's smoke coming from the chimney now, and there wasn't before. I'll get a locksmith and have the doors opened by force." Finally he went away, still grumbling.

One evening after dark there was loud knocking at the front door. Professor Marguerre had been back for a short visit and left, and we were again alone in the villa. We heard an excited group of people having a heated discussion. There was the sound of glass being broken. Then the noise subsided and they walked away. Later we found out what had happened. Professor Marguerre had forgotten to turn off a hall light, and it violated the black-out. The people were trying to figure out a way of putting out the light. As no one opened the door they broke a window-pane and used a long iron hook to tear the electric fixture off the ceiling. The upshot of this incident was that the professor got a fine and we were badly frightened.

One day Herr Gerlach told us that he could no longer risk having us in the villa. He had no desire to lose his head. His doctor had told him to be careful and the doctor should know for he was a cousin of Göring. Only Charlotte, who was now well known in the town, could stay. Charlotte almost collapsed that evening when she came home and heard about the ultimatum. Then for days she searched feverishly for a place for us. It was much harder than it had been, because many more houses had been destroyed and people had doubled up in the remaining quarters. Also, the tension in the population had risen and the pressure of the Nazi organizations increased every day. Street and house checks for deserters and suspects were more frequent, the younger boys were drafted for air-raid defense and the older men into the Volkssturm. Charlotte could find no place for us to live and had to ask if we might stay a little longer.

In the meantime Herr Gerlach had been called up for duty in the Volkssturm. Charlotte helped him obtain deferment on account of illness, by procuring atabrine and real coffee for him. By taking the atabrine and a great deal of coffee just before his medical examination he was able to simulate a weak heart. He was excused from service in the Volkssturm and permitted us to stay out of gratitude.

What the police, the Gestapo, and air raids could not do, disease almost did. While cutting horse meat which we got from Herr Hockenholz, I cut my finger. The meat was no longer fresh, and I immediately developed a serious infection. I ran a high fever, and pain tortured me day and night. I thought that my last day had come and instructed Wolfgang, if I died, to empty my pockets and then take my body into the woods. But after three months' illness I was again quite well.

The female Nazis were often the most fanatical and repulsive of the species. We heard after the war that one of these inquired at the police station if Carla Horn was actually registered with them. When they reported that she was not, she arranged a search of the house, which was to take place during the night. They did not make the search. A few mornings later, after an air raid, Charlotte was startled to see a policeman at the door. But he merely told her, "You should sweep up the glass on the sidewalk."

Once, late in the evening, someone knocked at the cellar window. This time it was no enemy but a friend: one of the Wichert brothers, who could not think of enough ways to help us. He had come out from the city with a rucksack full of potatoes. He never realized what a scare he had given us.

The war situation grew worse from day to day and restrictions of all sorts had to be laid down. We heard one day that the public transportation system could be used only by those with special passes. This was serious for us since it cut off our source of food: Charlotte could not go to Berlin to collect it. She used the last day of unrestricted transportation to gather as much food as possible. On the way back she ran across a Jewish woman lawyer, Anita Eisner, who was also living illegally. Through someone who had contacts with Army Headquarters she procured Charlotte a transportation pass and saved the situation.

The restrictions included increasingly sharp control of the S-Bahn in order to apprehend deserters, Allied agents, or other suspect persons. Once when Charlotte was riding in the S-Bahn three Gestapo men in civilian clothes entered and called out, "Identification with photo to be held ready. Show all papers! No one gets out until the check is over." Charlotte was terrified. She forced herself to seem calm and searched in her handbag. There was only a little red card from her doctor.

Some time before, she had had to go to a doctor. As the ones she knew had all been deported, she did not know whom to turn to. Then she ran across the name of a woman doctor which was the same as her own maiden name: Charlotte Wendriner. She looked up her namesake and the doctor gave her, as she did to all of her patients, a little red card with her alias on it: Carla Horn, the name she had adopted when we submerged.

The Gestapo men looked over the papers of a woman sitting near Charlotte. Nothing she produced satisfied them. Passes from an office where she was working were rejected as inadequate. She was questioned intensely and arrested. Now the wolves turned to new prey—the terrified Charlotte. She tensed herself not to lose her nerve now or to betray any confusion, and took out the red medical card.

There is a tale of a tyrant who ordered all mothers to sacrifice their newborn children. One woman hid her baby under her apron. The tyrant asked what she was hiding and she answered "Flowers." And when she showed her "flowers" at his command, the tyrant saw red roses.

The Gestapo must have seen red roses too. "Thank you, gnädige Frau," they said, and passed on.

During another checkup in a suburban train Charlotte sat opposite a man who could not or would not answer questions. Quickly Charlotte suggested that he might be a foreign worker, and offered herself as interpreter. She talked to him in all the languages she knew. The Gestapo official nodded to her in thanks and walked off with the arrested man without asking for Charlotte's pass.

April, 1945. The front was coming closer. We could see red, green, and white flares, and hear the noise of the artillery apparently only a few miles away: the Battle of Berlin had begun. We rarely got newspaper reports, but heard all the more rumors: the Russians had broken through and were marching on Eichwalde; the SS had dug in at near-by factories, and all flat roofs like that of our villa were to receive machine-gun emplacements; the neighboring town was already destroyed.

One day in late April Charlotte went to Berlin and gave some clothes to bombed-out friends there. She came back with the terrible news that the S-Bahn was going to stop running. Most people had at least put some food away, but we had so little that we could not save anything. We had some hard bread which we rationed strictly. At noon we drank a little bitter ersatz coffee.

We knew though that the end was coming. The windows were constantly rattling from concussions, the bombardment kept coming closer, and often at the sound of explosions near by we threw ourselves on the concrete floor.

The night of April 24 we went to bed confident that the approaching Russian Army would be no menace to us. Around midnight we heard heavy tanks roll by, but after a short council of war we decided there was nothing we need do.

In the grey of the morning Wolfgang and I cautiously looked out into the street; a soldier in a brown uniform was walking by. Wolfgang thought it was a Nazi Storm Trooper but I remembered the brown uniforms of the Russians from the first World War. Then Wolfgang sighted a strange vehicle: small horses drawing a two-wheeled cart on which two Russian officers with bright gold epaulets were sitting. There was no doubt about it: Eichwalde was in the hands of the Red Army. At last, after three long years of constant danger and deprivation, the hour of liberation had come.

I am not ashamed to admit that I wept a great deal that day; and I took my beloved Charlotte in my arms. When I embraced my boy, who was now seventeen years old, I said, "Wolfgang, promise me never to forget what your mother has done for you. She has twice given you life. You must thank her a thousandfold. I will do it with my last breath."

People were walking along the street with white arm bands, to signify that the town had capitulated. Soon white sheets were hanging from all houses. Exultant, Wolfgang climbed to the attic to hang a signal of peace on the flagpole which for twelve years had carried the damned swastika flag. Charlotte would not let me show myself on the street yet, for we still feared a counter-attack or a break-through of the surrounded SS troops toward Eichwalde. But five days later, on the first of May, 1945, I was able to end my three years of cloistered life.

I was not very steady on my feet; Wolfgang and Charlotte took me between them and we walked to the town hall to receive official papers and food cards, so that we submerged ones could live again. A door on the second floor had a sign, "Committee of

Free Germany." About twenty men were sitting in a small room —the new masters of the situation. When we entered they stopped their talk and rose, surmising that they were witnessing a rare scene. I was white, and years of hiding and hunger were evident on our faces. We tried to tell what had happened in three years. First we stammered and then we could not talk fast enough. A murmur went through the group. Could this happen in a town like Eichwalde with a predominantly Nazi population? A miracle in their midst!

A man came up. "I'll take care of the formalities for the family." And he did. When Wolfgang got the food cards he proudly called out to me, "Vati, now you are again head of the household."

EPILOGUE TO CHAPTER V

"Your Mother Has Twice Given You Life"

AFTER the liberation Herr Hopp wrote plays and assisted in their production in Eichwalde. Then the Hopps left the Russian Zone and lived very primitively in a DP camp in Berlin, where he edited the camp newspaper. His psalms were published at that time.

The suicide note the family left behind when they went underground was so effective that when a friend from Shanghai was searching for Herr Hopp after the war, the Hebrew Immigrant Aid Society received a police report that he had killed himself.

The Hopps were evacuated to another camp in Kassel in the summer of 1948 and in the spring of 1949 they emigrated to Israel.

Professor Marguerre is working in France.

Selma, who is now seventy-three years old, is living in Strausberg near Berlin.

VI

In Our Hope

MORITZ MANDELKERN

I was born in Grodek, in Poland. In 1918, when the war was over, I came to Berlin. I am a tailor, and even though I have to walk with two canes because I have been paralyzed since childhood, still I can do my job well. I married my good Henriette in 1922. We were very happy when our boy Siegfried was born.

Our trouble started in 1938: they didn't want to renew my working permit. But they finally did let me continue my trade because I was tailoring for Jews.

A persecution of the Jews in Germany broke out in November, 1938. They wanted to deport me. But I was in the synagogue when they came to the apartment to pick me up. That was my salvation. God held his protecting hand over me. Someone warned me not to go home that evening, so I stayed overnight with friends.

Then all was quiet again, but we feared more trouble and new measures against us. What could we do? We could only wait and pray.

The war started with the invasion of Poland in the first days of September, 1939. On September 13, the day before Rosh Hashana, the Jewish New Year, they came for me in the morning at half past five. I got sick from the excitement and had to go to the toilet. They posted a guard in front of the open door with a loaded gun. I thought, "What am I in their eyes? A criminal?" Did they think I was dangerous, with my two canes?

At the police station there was a kind man. He had pity and said, "This man is unfit for arrest." So I was discharged, and our Rosh Hashana was a very happy one, and we thanked God for his intervention.

Our luck did not last long, for only six days later all foreign

Jews between fifteen and sixty had to report at the police stations. Apparently they feared us as enemies.

Two policemen came to get our boy and took him away like a criminal. He was fifteen years old, and such a fine boy. They put handcuffs on him, and he simply held out his hands. I hobbled alongside as they took him away, and my wife supported me, for I was always tripping. My eyes were only on Siegfried and not on the street under my feet. I wanted to encourage the boy, but what could I say? My glasses were wet with tears and I could not speak.

He went with them like a lamb. I sometimes think today that we did everything wrong then. But might was against us and who could help us? We were like prisoners from the beginning. We could do nothing any more, only beg and obey and look on quietly at what they did with us.

I begged them to let Siegfried go. A doctor in uniform shouted, "Shut your big mouth, you dirty Jew! You can be glad that we let you go home!" And they kicked me downstairs.

My poor wife cried and raged and was like mad when they took our boy away. We had to leave our son in their hands. From then on our hearts knew only sorrow and the thought of our Siegfried. My wife kept saying, "Can't a mother do something for her own child?" And she sat staring at nothing and would not eat.

The boy was taken to a collection camp on the Kaiserdamm. My wife and I saw him twice. After ten days they were all taken away. We did not know where our prayers should seek him.

Then came a note from Sachsenhausen—so now we had to make ourselves realize that our son was in a concentration camp. We said to ourselves, "Why?" For the boy's only guilt was that he was a Jew. But in Germany this was a crime.

Day and night we wondered what we could do to save him. My wife saw lots of people and got advice. It was always the same: it was no use trying anything. But they told her at the police station that if our Polish relatives would offer to receive Siegfried, he could be freed from the camp. We finally managed to have friends smuggle a letter and money to Poland, and the request was made.

My wife was hopeful and we started to breathe easier. Half a year passed by, waiting and waiting. Then the answer came, "The request has been refused." A mere letter, and I read it again and again, and don't want to believe it, and say, "You read it." And my wife reads it and goes white and says nothing, and the letter falls on the floor.

Then we become quiet and think: God is punishing us. Strange how one can go on living. But we did not give up hope, though we did not dare talk about it. Only sometimes I noticed my wife looking at me as if she wanted to say something; but she turned her head away and went on pulling threads and was quiet. And I too was quiet, but both of us knew what we were thinking.

A day came which started like all the others: I was tailoring, and my wife was working in the kitchen. She often did the ironing for me because it was hard for me to stand. We heard three knocks at the door, the way our boy had always knocked. I dropped everything, but then I said to myself, "Moritz, you are a fool!" And again the knocking, three times, the sound of knuckles on wood.

Then I shouted out and went into the hall, where I collided with my wife—she was quicker than I, for I had forgotten my canes and had to lean against the wall. She threw the door open, and—I don't remember any more, I must have fallen. But it was a good awakening: my boy held me in his arms, and he had his good tender laugh again as in the days when he was small. He kept saying, "Are you glad?"

It was August 30, 1940, may the day be blessed forever! To see that one day was enough, and everything that came afterward we were able to bear, thinking of that one day.

We had experienced a miracle and I believe that our prayers did help. Our request had brought it to pass. Our boy had to report to the Gestapo, and they sent him to the police who released him.

My wife held the boy, and she looked as she had seventeen years before, when we stood at the altar. Her face was shining and her fear of the Gestapo and the police was forgotten.

Siegfried was told he would have to go to Tarnow in Poland; he could stay at home until the order came.

And now we enjoyed every hour we had with our beloved son.

But sometimes it was strange: when he saw a soldier, on the way to the synagogue, he would jump to attention. That always hurt me. He was so different—he might have been away five years instead of nine months, his ideas and views were so old. Often when he talked the two of us just looked at him and wondered that this was our child.

All the time we tried to find a way of getting him across the border illegally. He might have got to Yugoslavia; but then he said, "What if they catch me? No—I was in concentration camp once—" When he said that he did not look at us.

Often he was silent—not at all like a boy of sixteen. He never spoke about his time in Sachsenhausen, and we were afraid to ask him. Maybe we were cowards in not wanting to know.

We could keep him a little less than two months: on October 25 he had to go to Tarnow. We had to say good-by again and it was hard. But this time we could help to support him, and we heard from him from time to time. He found work with the Jewish Council in Tarnow and was not badly off.

But early in 1942 Tarnow also had pogroms. The German Army had occupied it and things got worse. Siegfried was unhappy and we worried about him. We secretly sent him a message and money so that he could flee. He wrote that he had got Polish and "Aryan" papers identifying him as a Volksdeutscher—a Pole of German origin. We heard that he had gone to Lemberg, but we wondered if that meant safety or the beginning of new danger.

Then for a while we heard nothing. Whenever the doorbell rang we trembled, always expecting news. My wife went around as if she were sleepwalking. When I spoke to her she gave me strange answers, for she was always thinking of Siegfried, trying to imagine where he was and what was happening to him.

Our uncertainty did not last much longer. On November 8 a card came, written in the Gestapo prison in Lemberg. We didn't know how it was smuggled out. Only a few lines, illegible and blotted. But we could make out that the boy had been betrayed by acquaintances and that he had little chance of getting out.

That was the last sign.

From then on everything was different. I kept on going to the synagogue and tailored, and we waited for news. But in our souls we both knew, and were just acting for each other as if nothing could have happened to him.

We would both gladly have sacrificed our lives for our child. He was so young. Again and again I asked myself, why this horror? I lay awake nights and wondered why these misfortunes had to come over the world. But my mind never understood, no matter how much I meditated.

An old customer of mine, a Gentile who had lost three sons in the war, sometimes came to visit us in the evening when it was dark. He never complained, only talked about the time when his boys were small and how they played in the yard and made so much noise. I wondered how Henriette could sit there listening for hours, but she understood him and asked him to go on. He could not speak about the boys at home. His wife could not bear even to hear the names of her sons.

In December, 1942, many of our neighbors were deported to Poland. We saw the trucks pick them up, and Henriette asked, "Will you go with them? I'd rather jump out of the window! Those are the beasts who—" I thought as she did.

One morning my wife returned from delivering a coat which I had fixed. She was breathless and her face was white as chalk. I knew what it must be.

The truck had stopped next door and six men in uniform were there talking with the porter. Then two Jewish orderlies came slowly into the house. This was part of the ordeal, that Jews were forced to pick up their own brothers and to watch as they climbed into the executioner's cart. I had read about the French Revolution. Whenever I saw this truck I thought: will they take us, too, to the guillotine? We did not know anything about gassing yet, but we suspected that death was waiting for us.

There was no time to hide. We did not say anything but simply sat in our apartment hall and waited. The door was locked and we hoped it would look as if we weren't at home.

It seemed an eternity, though probably it was not half an hour, for next door there were only two Jewish families left, and in our house no one but us. My wife held my hand and sometimes she pressed her fingers against my lips for me to be quiet. I was afraid even to breathe. We cowered motionless in the cold hall-way, waiting, waiting. Heavy steps came up the stairs and our doorbell rang. Then everything was quiet. We did not move. The bell rang again, much harder, and someone knocked angrily and called, "Open up! Departure for Palestine! Palestine Express for Herr Mandelkern!"

I wanted to scream, but my wife held me and laid her poor frightened face against mine so that I would be quiet.

I don't know how long it was, but at last we heard them leave. I had a feeling that someone was hiding behind the apartment door waiting to pounce on us when we came out.

Toward evening we heard the gentle knock of Frau Schwarze. She and her nine-year-old boy had been good to us, though her husband, who was a Nazi block warden, paid no attention to us. Frau Schwarze sometimes brought us apples and a piece of white bread on Friday evenings.

When we realized that it was her signal, five knocks in quick succession, we opened the door. Our looks must have scared her, for she quickly drew us back into the room, said she was going to get us something and that we need not be afraid any more.

We were numb from fear and excitement. Frau Schwarze came back bringing rolls and a glass of wine. She heated water and made us drink tea. We thanked her without saying a word. My wife kept crying, and when I dried her tears she said, "I don't know why I'm crying."

We knew that we could not spend the night in the apartment, for next morning the orderlies would certainly be sent back for us and would break down the door if we did not open it. Good Frau Schwarze said she could hide one of us in a tiny chamber in her apartment, but we must think about it, because the room was unheated and had only a small garret window and there would be just a candle for light. It would be best to stay in bed on account of the cold. Would one of us dare to live up there?

I shook my head and just looked at my wife. But her courage rose. She said she would give me some warm feather bedding, and she would go to the country herself, to some farmer, and do tailoring.

"I don't want to," I said. Why go on when Siegfried was no longer there? "I don't want to live any more. A cripple can't do it. I would only be a burden to you, and it wouldn't work."

But the two women did not listen to me. They started to pack our things and they let me sit there, for I wasn't good for anything.

By eleven that night I was lying up there in bed in the attic room and trying to think it all over. I trembled wondering if Henriette would get away. She was to stay overnight with acquaintances and next morning she would have to take the yellow Star of David off and go by train to a village in the country, for from now on we would have to get along without food ration cards.

It was the beginning of a terrible time. We were always worried about each other. I caught a bad cold and kept coughing, but I could not do it out loud because so many people came to see block warden Schwarze. I had to crawl under the covers and my body shook.

Friday evenings little Bruno Schwarze brought me a piece of white bread and jam. I lit the candle, and he sat with me for an hour, warmly dressed so that he wouldn't freeze.

I lived in the little chamber for eighteen months. Worst of all was the terrible winter cold. If I could only have walked around to get warm—but I had to stay still so that no one would get suspicious. Even when my wife came and we knew that the coast was clear I hardly dared to speak out. Once the bread fell on the floor; another time I bumped into the door in the dark. I listened breathless, terrified that the block warden would scold his good wife for hiding me. But he was good too, for he often gave me cigarettes from the ration he got because he worked in a cigar factory.

I thought of many things during those months and said many prayers. In my loneliness I talked to my dear boy and he would answer me—imaginary conversations to pass the time.

My wife found refuge in the country with a cousin who had married a Gentile. Because of her marriage and the fact that she had children she was "privileged" and was not deported.

They were happy to have Henriette and claimed that she was an "Aryan" relative. She tailored for the farmers' wives and they paid with food. That was our salvation.

It was May, 1944. The air raids had gotten worse and I had to stay up there alone when everyone else went to the cellar. Then everything was dark and the house seemed dead and as if forsaken by God. Sometimes I shivered so with fright that I could hardly pray. Up there everything sounded threatening and I was always thinking: now the house will start to burn.

But on May 19 I wasn't so afraid. I was getting used to having death come down from the clouds to destroy the innocent as well as the guilty, the children and the weak as well as the strong. And that day something happened that I cannot explain. I can only believe that God's angels carried me out. For how could I— a cripple—have saved myself?

I sat up there as usual during the alarms, with my two canes beside me, a small pocketbook with my papers and a little money in it, and some bread. The sirens stopped blowing. Everyone had gone to the cellar. I gave myself the treat of going down from my little chamber into the Schwarze's living room; and I thought how wonderful it was to be in a room with real windows, with a picture on the wall, and a bookcase, and a rug on the floor. I sat there with my hands folded, thinking of my wife, for she always thought of me during air raids.

Suddenly there was a clap like thunder and the whole house shook. I could hear the crackle of burning wood and smell smoke.

I did not know what to do. The fire wardens must not find me here when they came up to investigate. It would be worse yet if Herr Schwarze were to inspect his apartment with some neighbors . . . I hobbled back to the attic and sat down on the bed there, shaking with excitement.

Smoke began to come up the stairs and I heard loud shouts from the yard. My wife had said to me each time she left, "Remember, the second key hangs to the left behind the door!" What key? I did not know what it was for. I stumbled into the hall and looked at the door.

Now I could see the fire. I touched the iron fittings of the door. They were hot and burnt my hand. I cried out in pain. And then suddenly I had the key in my hand and opened the door, went out on the stairs—and that is the last I remember.

I can hardly believe that I got down those four flights of stairs, through smoke and fire, without anyone stopping me or recognizing me. Can the fear of death have given me such strength?

When I came to, I was lying in the first-aid shelter. They told me they had poured water over me and then carried me there. Slowly I started to think again. And then came the realization that the danger was not past. Something warned me, "Careful, careful!" A first-aid man cared for me and bandaged my hands and was very friendly. And I kept trying to get it clear in my mind what was the most important thing to do now.

My coat—I had left it up there, with all my papers. But what good would the Jewish identification cards have done me? Suddenly I knew: I had to lie, for the truth would be death. Maybe my hour had not yet come, and I rubbed my head to be able to think clearly and to give the right answers.

Then I spoke carefully and slowly, and acted my part. It hurt my heart to think that God had saved me only for this. I told them that my name was Schwarz and that I was a cripple from the last war. The first-aid man didn't ask any more questions. That afternoon I was discharged.

For the first time in eighteen months I crossed the street with the sky above me and saw the stars outdoors instead of from the garret window.

The house had burned down. I didn't dare ask where the Schwarze family had gone. I stumbled along as fast as I could. I had a little money in my pocket and took the subway to another part of town. Then I sat down on a bench. What should I do now? There was only one answer: go to my wife. She was in the village of Schönebeck near Berlin. So I went to the station and bought a ticket. Walking came hard after the long months in the attic room.

When I finally was seated in the train I felt as if I were dreaming. It had been a long time since my last trip on a train. No one looked at me with suspicion or contempt. Of course I did not wear the yellow star and looked no different from the others who sat there tired and tormented, talking of their lot.

A woman next to me knew Schönebeck, so I cautiously asked her where farmer Hübner lived. It was dark when I got off the train and I had to look for a long time for the farm. They were already in bed when I got there. My good wife was so excited when she heard everything. Our relatives had pity on me and said I could stay for a few days and rest. I felt as if I had been reborn. Everything looked new to me: the animals, the fields, and the people. My wife was with me all the time and looked at me as if I had risen from the dead.

But the relatives were afraid to keep me for good. We went back to Berlin and found a place for me to stay with a family of mixed marriage in the Brunnenstrasse. We told them a tale about my having to come from Thuringia for treatment. I even went to the public air-raid shelter. Though it was already overcrowded people who thought I had been wounded in the war often made room for me. This good fortune lasted only ten days; then the landlord got frightened and said, "Find yourself some other place."

I was desperate. What was the use of going on living? I had become too much of a burden for my wife. The Hitler regime might last a long time yet, and I was terribly tired of fighting for my life. Why should I? There was no hope or joy.

I sat down and wrote a long letter to Henriette, explaining everything to her and begging her to forgive me this last cowardice. I wrote her that I knew it was bad of me to leave her now but that it was best for both of us. But when I had sent the letter off I was paralyzed. Instead of doing something as I had announced, I stayed in bed and thought I might die if I just stopped eating.

I acted like a child, without good sense. And suddenly my wife was standing by my bed and crying and scolding me all at the same time. She was so brave and courageous, better than I with all my faith.

From that moment on we did not separate any more. Henriette begged our relatives in Schönebeck to take me. So I had a room with them and tailored harder than ever before. I almost never went out, but when I did it did not matter much, for everything was in such confusion. People from the city were flooding the villages, and no one paid much attention to anyone else.

On April 25, 1945, the Russians came.

I can speak Russian, so I could talk to an officer. Nothing happened to the whole street, and no cattle were taken.

For a while I was interpreter in the village, but as soon as we could we went back to Berlin. We had to hunt for a place to live and were finally allotted two rooms.

My good wife is at my side and does the ironing and the errands. We go on living, only getting a bit older and weaker than before.

And our boy? Should one believe that God will perform another miracle for us? He has done it before.

Man should not live without hope. So we continue in our hope.

EPILOGUE TO CHAPTER VI

In Our Hope

IN ADDITION to their tailoring the Mandelkerns have devoted much of their time since the war to the service of the remaining Jewish community in Berlin. They searched for their protectors, the Schwarzes. Finding Frau Schwarze ill, Herr Mandelkern took her to the Jewish hospital, where she died three weeks later. Not long after that Herr Schwarze died of a heart attack. Their boy Bruno is in an orphan asylum in the Russian Zone. The Mandelkerns send him food packages and are trying their best to substitute for his parents.

Every Sabbath they take out Siegfried's last post card, now worn from handling. They wanted to emigrate to Australia to join Herr Mandelkern's brother, but did not get the necessary entry permit. They were happy when in 1949 they found refuge in Israel.

PROLOGUE TO CHAPTER VII

Tea Party

LAGI COUNTESS BALLESTREM-SOLF is the daughter of Dr. Wilhelm Solf, who died in 1936 after a distinguished career in the German Foreign Office. He had been successively Governor of Samoa, State Secretary in the Colonial Office, the first Foreign Minister of the Weimar Republic, and from 1921 to 1928 Ambassador to Japan. He was among the most progressive officials of the German Empire, and he and his family were never taken in by the specious appeals of National Socialism. Dr. Solf tried to bring about a change in the Nazis' treatment of their political opponents and of Jews, interceding with Goebbels and attempting to see Hitler. He saved a number of persecuted professors by getting them appointments in Japan; and after his death his family continued to help victims of the Nazis.

The anti-Nazis who met at their house became known as the Solf circle. Among them were Albrecht von Bernstorff, diplomat and banker who had been a Rhodes scholar, and Dr. Otto Kiep, who had been Consul General in New York and had become known during his diplomatic service—especially after 1933—for his anti-Nazi views.

Rudolf Pechel, who was imprisoned in the Ravensbrück concentration camp at the same time as Frau Solf and her daughter, Countess Ballestrem-Solf, speaks in his book on German resistance of "the courageous attitude of Countess Ballestrem, her sturdy opposition to the Gestapo—she did not conceal her hatred of the system—and her comradely readiness to help all fellow prisoners." *

* *Deutscher Widerstand* (Erlenbach-Zürich, Eugen Rentsch Verlag, 1947).

VII

Tea Party

LAGI COUNTESS BALLESTREM-SOLF

IN 1938 I returned to Berlin from Shanghai, where I had been living for six years. Shortly after my arrival I was called to a Gestapo office and questioned about my political attitude, because they had had reports of my "political agitation" in Shanghai. The "agitation" consisted in expressing my opinions freely, continuing to associate with Jewish friends, and helping refugees who were beginning to come to the Far East. The Gestapo accused me of never having appeared at the "German Corner," the Shanghai rendezvous of the German colony, and of trying to prejudice foreign diplomats and statesmen, all old friends of my father, against the Nazi regime. They released me after questioning.

Early in the war they summoned me again. I phoned my mother, who lived near me, and told her that if I did not come back within six hours she should take steps to help me. This time I was charged with being a "Jew slave." The Gestapo had received information that our family was helping persecuted Jews and that I was in the habit of going to the Jewish section of the air-raid cellar in our apartment house. I pointed out that the Jewish couple who owned the house were friends of mine. I was again dismissed. I suppose my mother and I were treated gently at first because of our close connection with foreign diplomats. The Gestapo did not want to create a scandal or alienate foreigners if they could help it.

No compromise with the Nazis was possible. To avoid even giving the obligatory Heil Hitler salute I often carried a shopping bag loaded with laundry or vegetables in each hand.

The many people who met at my mother's house were of one mind in their opposition to the Nazis. Her home became a sort of political oasis where our friends and other like-minded people could speak freely, vent their disgust and despair, receive information, and take counsel. We listened eagerly to foreign radio stations. Foreign diplomats visited us, and we made them realize that the reports they heard about concentration camps were not mere horror stories, as the Nazis would have it, but a small portion of the bitter truth. But although we considered ourselves cofighters for freedom and humanity, we were not heard abroad.

In the fall of 1940 I married Count Hubert Ballestrem, an opponent of National Socialism since his student days. He belonged to a group headed by Carl von Jordans who had been fighting the Nazis even before they came to power. Other members of this group had included von Bose, who was murdered in connection with the Nazi purge of June 30, 1934, and Wilhelm von Ketteler, murdered at the time of the Anschluss which he had tried desperately to prevent. Another member, Fritz Guenther von Tschirschky-Boegendorf, escaped abroad after the 1934 purge.

As the persecution of Jews intensified, I made it my special task to aid them. In 1939 I had been able to help Dr. Ferdinand Mainzer, author and gynecologist, by taking his jewelry out of the country and escorting his family to England. My mother and I did our best to get emigration affidavits for Jews and she visited innumerable embassies and consulates in quest of visas.

After the first few years of the war the deportation of Jews increased and the "stars" were rarely seen on the street. It became increasingly important to save Jewish families by getting them out of the country illegally or by hiding them. We sheltered some in our house and helped others to find hiding places. I would go, fearful of being caught, to the star-marked Jewish apartments that "Aryans" were forbidden to visit and get a list of things wanted—sometimes a newspaper, sometimes vegetables or things which were still unrationed. Our butcher's wife, with a wink, would weigh me up a larger piece of meat than the ration called for. Our janitor, when I saw him again after the war, said to me smiling, "I knew all the time who lived with you, but they would never have found out from me."

One day we learned of a chance to smuggle some of our protégés into Switzerland. Rumors constantly circulated among the "submerged" about possibilities of escape—some real, some dubious. This channel was a small farm close to the border in Baden, from which a few field paths led to Switzerland. This was a reasonably safe way of leaving Germany. The farmers who helped in such an undertaking usually did it out of sympathy and only occasionally from a desire to make money. They put the refugees up for the night, and just before dawn guided them to the path. A picture post card from Switzerland was indication that the fugitives had got through.

We wanted a couple who had been submerged for months to take this opportunity. The woman was hiding with us, her husband with friends. Shortly before they were to leave the Gestapo caught them in a restaurant. The next day a Gentile cousin of theirs came to us in dismay to say that the Gestapo had asked where they were keeping their belongings, so that they could be fetched, and they had given our address. I packed their things, anticipating arrest myself, but nothing happened. My mother then reserved this sure route to Switzerland for another couple she was helping. They too were arrested, interrogated, and probably tortured. They gave information about the route and said the tip came from Frau Solf.

As the war went on, we saw ourselves losing out in our struggle against the Nazis. Close friends of ours were arrested in 1942. After that my husband and I expected the Gestapo momentarily, and thought they would at least search the house. In June, 1943, our old friend Privy Councillor Richard Kuenzer was arrested, and our own expectation of arrest increased. No one who has not lived through it can fully understand the feeling of being cornered that haunted us day and night. We could trust no one except those whom we knew well. We could not use the telephone freely—it might be tapped. We were never sure we were not being watched.

A friend warned us in August, 1943, that he had heard from a confidant of the Gestapo that we were under surveillance. We became still more careful on the telephone. We saw fewer people, partly because the increased bombing made it more difficult to get around.

In September my mother attended a birthday tea given by Fräulein von Thadden, who had distinguished herself in Red Cross and social welfare work and had been headmistress of a girl's school. I could not go; I was in the hospital with a rupture I had contracted while helping to extinguish fires.

The guests were all friends except for one newcomer, a Dr. Reckzeh. He had introduced himself to Fräulein von Thadden the day before and given her a letter from Maria Segantini, daughter of the Swiss painter. The letter, written in good faith, introduced Dr. Reckzeh as "of like mind." Although the conversation at the tea was more guarded than usual because of his presence, everyone in that circle was so accustomed to speak freely with the others that an outsider could easily pick up anti-Nazi statements. Dr. Reckzeh offered to take letters to Switzerland. My mother gave him three for the Danish Minister to Switzerland. They were harmless, concerned only with personal matters, and quite unimportant; they were not even closed.

Soon afterward we were all warned by Count Moltke, one of the members of the Hitler opposition, that Reckzeh was a Gestapo agent.

Dr. Reckzeh tried rather clumsily to induce my mother to put him in touch with the German emigrant circles in Switzerland. She of course refused. Even without the warning, we were too careful with messages abroad to entrust them to any but the closest friends.

When September and October passed without arrest we began to breathe more easily. But we had little reason to.

November saw the first really heavy air raid on Berlin. I was bombed out and moved to my mother's house. Soon afterward that too was demolished. We both escaped miraculously from the burning house, but we lost everything. My mother left Berlin for her sister's home in Partenkirchen in Bavaria. I had to have an operation and could not follow her until January 10, 1944.

The morning of January 12 seven Gestapo officials appeared at my aunt's house in Partenkirchen and searched it for hours. Then they took all of us—my mother, my aunt, our housekeeper, and me—to headquarters in Munich. Mother was interrogated at once. The rest of us were locked in a windowless tower room, with two women to guard us. We stayed there two days. The third day we were told that my mother was to be sent to the Gestapo prison in Berlin. Actually she was put in a cell of the Gestapo building at Sachsenhausen.

We were held incommunicado. My brother and my husband were on the Russian front and could do nothing for us. A Gestapo official remained in the house in Partenkirchen to collect incoming mail, answer the telephone and tell anyone who called, "The ladies are away." Though the Gestapo were often fiendishly clever in their methods, they could be exceedingly stupid. The whole neighborhood was aroused when the seven of them arrived in two cars to arrest us. By evening all Partenkirchen had heard that the Gestapo had taken us away. The silly statement that we had gone away, when everyone knew that we had just arrived, bombed out and sick, aroused suspicion in even the most simple-minded. I smuggled two messages out of the Munich prison to tell friends what had happened, but they had received news of our arrest long before. Time and circumstance had developed people's skill in passing on important information, and our arrest closely concerned them.

I tried in every way to effect the release of my ailing aunt and our old housekeeper, but got no answer to my pleas.

One day I was questioned about a list of names in code. Years before I had worked out this code for use in correspondence from Shanghai, so that I could write more freely about German, Chinese, and Japanese diplomats and statesmen and refer to the propaganda office, the Gestapo, or the SS. The code list contained the names of friends the Nazis had recently arrested—Otto Kiep, Richard Kuenzer, and Arthur Zarden. This made it appear more incriminating than it actually was, for it was ten years old. From then on I too was treated like a criminal.

After six weeks in prison an official told me that the situation looked bad for me and that there had been many more arrests of "high personalities from the best families."

During the two months in Munich I saw the Gestapo methods in action without being exposed to them myself. Others arrested in connection with the tea party were severely interrogated, mistreated, and tortured. Every day I saw men return from interrogation with obvious signs of beatings; sometimes they were covered with blood. A young man in the cell next to mine had been so brutally used that he was afraid he might reveal the names of friends in the next interrogation. That night he strangled himself. We saw women of the Jehovah's Witnesses with blue, swollen faces and hands; hundreds of them passed through our small prison each day on their way from one concentration camp to another. One heard many languages and saw men, women and children, some of them still stunned by their fate, others hardened by years of imprisonment and torment. Pregnant girls who had associated with prisoners of war worked in the prison. Their babies were taken from them soon after birth and they themselves were usually sent to Ravensbrück.

One morning an official came into our cell and told my aunt and the housekeeper, "You are discharged, and—" looking at me with spite, "we'll send you to Berlin." I was secretly happy, hoping that I might soon be somewhere near my mother.

On March 15 I was taken to Berlin by train, seated among other travelers. Two Gestapo officials in plain clothes guarded me, one a man, the other a Fräulein Gründorfer who looked exactly like Himmler and turned out to be his niece. Not knowing who sat with them, the passengers around us talked almost exclusively about air raids, and occasionally execrated the Nazis.

We reached Berlin just after a night raid. Then I learned that we were going to Fürstenberg in Mecklenburg; our destination was Ravensbrück. As we were changing trains in the crowded station my male guard suddenly gave me my ticket, suitcase, and pocketbook, and said, "In case we get into different cars, don't forget that you get out at Drögen."

This was a grotesque situation. I had money, my identification card, my baggage. The crowd was so large and dense that it would be easy to lose the guard and escape. Was it a trap, or was he sure I would not go? For two hours while we waited for the train I weighed the pros and cons. But I knew the Gestapo too well to think lightly of what they might do to my mother if I escaped. So I stayed and took the train.

We were picked up in a police car at Drögen and driven to the huge camp. That raw, gloomy evening I saw for the first time the dreary barracks and the columns of inmates in their striped uniforms. The car stopped in front of a narrow low building, the Ravensbrück prison. It had been built as a disciplinary barracks for camp inmates and was still used for that purpose. Part of it, though, had been made available to the Gestapo. One of their Berlin offices had been hit by bombs and they had no room for us there. They also wanted us to be safe from air raids so that they would not lose valuable information by any premature decease.

I was locked in a bare cell on the north side of the prison. I could see the large open space of the camp square and hear the shrieking siren and the roll calls and camp activities. It took considerable effort to draw myself up the wall to the ledge where I could look out through the small, barred window, listening all the while for sounds from the corridor so I would not be caught.

The first day I was taken to the prison yard for a quarter hour's walk. The newcomer in a prison tries to grasp the general lay-out as quickly as possible. I wandered along the yard till I could see the whole southern wall of the cell building. Suddenly I heard my name called from a near-by cell. I looked up as unostentatiously as possible, knowing I was being watched from the other side of the yard. Mother's sad face was pressed against a barred window. I had to control myself in order not to show the shock I felt, for she looked emaciated. But it meant much to see her at last and to know that we were both in the same building. In time it was possible to see her occasionally and to exchange a few words. As I got to know the prison better we managed at times to send written messages and letters. The other inmates helped a great deal in that. Many of us had known each other, and the spirit of comradeship among the political prisoners, who were of all classes and nationalities, was both help and solace.

After about two weeks I was moved to a cell on the south side of the block, from which I could see the prison yard. I soon realized that our whole circle of friends was in the prison. One slender man with a deathly pale face looked especially familiar, but I could not identify him. He was doing his daily fifteen minutes' walk alone. That meant either punishment or that he was condemned to death. Only after long observation and after he had seen and nodded to me did I recognize him. It was Nikolaus

Christoph von Halem, one of my husband's best friends, who had once been big, strong, and humorous. With von Mumm, he had composed "Führer Speeches" and verses which bitingly satirized Hitler and the Nazis. Now he looked weak and spiritless. I could see by his detached, other-worldly expression that he had finished with life. Like Mumm, he had been under arrest since 1942 and still had a long road of suffering before him.

I missed Dr. Arthur Zarden, a State Secretary in the Finance Ministry. When I inquired about him someone whispered that he had jumped out of a window of the Main Security Office of the SS shortly after his arrest. I was deeply affected by this news. He had been a dear friend, a man of cosmopolitan outlook and great intelligence.

Every day was like the next, until one afternoon at four o'clock I was taken out of my cell. I was kept waiting until ten that evening and then interrogated till 4 A.M.

"What is your attitude toward National Socialism?" was the first question. I said I was opposed to it. In none of my interrogations did I ever compromise; I always emphasized my complete and total rejection of Nazism. I was told later that this was enough to convict me. There was actually no conclusive proof that any of us had committed high treason, but the Nazis had been watching our circle for years and viewed us all with hatred and deep mistrust. They wanted to destroy us and all we stood for, and tried to find some legal basis on which to do it. They knew a lot, but we occasionally managed to make them uncertain.

I was questioned several other times in the course of the next few weeks, while my mother and other friends of ours were being interrogated in their turn. The technique used on me was always the same: the Gestapo made wild threats and from time to time attempted to get information by various promises. One of the inquisitors, Kriminalrat Leo Lange, sometimes stormed so that I thought he would hit me. Lange later gained notoriety for his interrogations about the Twentieth of July.

Once we were all examined by SS doctors to determine whether we could take torture. My mother and I escaped torture, but the men did not. Privy Councillor Kuenzer, who was in his seventies, and Count Bernstorff were tortured until, half unconscious, they admitted charges pressed against them by Lange and his cohorts. It was to no avail that they denied everything in writing after they recovered.

My mother was subjected to third-degree interrogations to which a weaker person would have succumbed. Lange gave her sleeping draughts, then roused her for inquisitions which usually lasted six to fifteen hours. He tried to frighten her with the death sentence. He threatened to arrest her youngest son; told her she would have to cart rocks; that he would put me in a dark cell. Mother was depressed and quite broken physically. It took much self-control not to reveal anything harmful to others, not to show fear, and not to lose her temper. When nothing else worked she was put for weeks on a starvation diet of decaying turnips.

I saw her from the window and was dismayed at her pitiable condition. She whispered to me about the starvation diet. I nearly went mad from grief and anger. I refused to eat—I could not have eaten anyhow. During the sleepless night which followed I remembered that a fellow prisoner had told me in Munich: "They don't like it at all if one goes on a hunger strike." I decided to try, and carried it out for several days, although a well-meaning official urged me to stop lest it lead to grave consequences. But I succeeded in one thing—my mother got part of my food.

One day Lange appeared in my cell, and we had a clash. He shouted at me. Unstrung by grief over my mother, anger and hunger, I shouted back. Lange raved that my mother would die unless I would incriminate Count Bernstorff, Privy Councillor Kuenzer, or others. There was only one answer I could give to that: "Herr Lange, you have it in your power to execute my mother."

About the middle of June most of our friends were sent away from Ravensbrück. We heard that the trial against "Thadden and five others"—the guests at the tea party: my mother, Fanny von Kurowsky, Irmgard Zarden, Dr. Kiep, and Legation Counsel Scherpenberg—was to take place before the People's Court on July 1. Notorious Judge Freisler would preside. I was not included because I had not been at the party.

The People's Court was a special creation of the Nazis which did not apply mere legal rules but followed the Nazi precept that what served them and their state was right. Its red-robed judge was imbued with a fanatic desire to destroy those who stood in the path of Nazism and was known for passing death sentences on the flimsiest basis.

The charges included high treason, sedition, favoring the enemy, and defeatism. The trial lasted from eight in the morning till eleven at night. The prosecution charged that Frau Solf had given Dr. Reckzeh instructions for peace negotiations. When questioned about this she declared that if she had wanted to do so she would have found a better messenger than a stranger like Dr. Reckzeh.

Freisler asked, "You called our treatment of the Jews 'inhuman'?"

"Yes."

"What was your husband's political ideology?"

"He was a humanitarian: he tried to be a good Christian, he served his country and helped his fellow men."

"Then he was a liberal?" Freisler taunted.

"Yes, he was."

Later Freisler asked, "What about the Quakers?"

"I believe they are the most unselfish and Christian people."

"How can you, as an internationally educated person, say that? Don't you know that they are pacifists and play their politics under the cloak of Christianity?"

"I do not think so. Charity stands above all things and pacifism is, in my eyes, no crime. Love and faith in each other should be our goal. That is what we have to learn again, and the churches fighting with us are going to help us."

Dr. Zarden's daughter Irmgard is said to have been one of the few persons who managed to make Freisler lose his poise. The judge was anxious to picture Dr. Reckzeh, who appeared as a witness for the prosecution, as an upright citizen who just happened to hear seditious statements and dutifully reported them to the Gestapo. He shouted at Irmgard in the stand:

"But you are also guilty because you listened to these treasonable statements without reporting them!"

Irmgard answered calmly, "Herr President, when I found out

that Dr. Reckzeh was a Gestapo stooge, I no longer considered a report necessary."

Freisler gaped at her a moment, cleared his throat, and said, "Well, h'm, h'm, yes."

Shortly before the summing up by the defense Freisler announced that Frau Solf would be withdrawn from the case "for further investigation." Fräulein von Thadden was sentenced to death and was decapitated with an ax. Dr. Kiep was hanged. Scherpenberg got two years in prison. Irmgard Zarden and Fanny von Kurowsky were acquitted. My mother was brought back to Ravensbrück.

Everybody was amazed at her withdrawal. Some were of the opinion that the neutral diplomats, headed by the Swedish Minister, had persuaded General Oshima, the Japanese Ambassador, to talk to Hitler. Her lawyer, Dr. Dix, thought that the tea party was not regarded as adequate ground for a death sentence; they wanted to try her with the Solf circle and make a new and bigger haul. The reprieve meant more uncertainty, more interrogations, more misery.

The failure of the Twentieth of July was a sad shock to us. Our first reaction was one of fright, for we knew that it would have a bad effect on our trial. A few days after the attempt the Gestapo made short visits to the cells to test our reaction and note our morale. One official asked what I thought would have happened if the assassination had succeeded. "A great deal," I said. "Above all, you would be in this cell and I would not."

Night and day we heard prisoners being taken away for interrogation. All rules were enforced more strictly. It was hardly possible to communicate any longer. Occasionally I got a glimpse of some of those who had been arrested after the Twentieth: Hjalmar Schacht; Count Peter Yorck; Erwin Planck, son of the famous physicist; Finance Minister Johannes Popitz; Ulrich von Hassell, former Ambassador to Italy; General Halder, former Chief of Staff; and countless others. Some women had been arrested in *Sippenhaft*—family arrest—because of the participation of other members of their family. I saw the wife and daughter of General Hoeppner, and the mother-in-law of Stauffenberg, the officer who had placed the bomb.

One of the few men still at large was Goerdeler, the former Mayor of Leipzig who was to have become Chancellor of Germany after the coup. A reward of one million marks was offered for him. A letter from him which had been found on my mother's desk took on new significance for the Gestapo when Goerdeler's role became known. Mother was questioned about it and about her connections with other members of the conspiracy. She was cross-examined about her friendship with and assistance to a priest, Dr. Metzger, who had tried to get a letter to the Archbishop of Canterbury via the Archbishop of Upsala, Sweden. The examination lasted all night and stopped only at 7 A.M. when Mother fainted.

In mid-August Count Bernstorff, Werner von Alvensleben, and I were suddenly put on a hunger ration. One guard had tears in his eyes when he brought me the "dog dish" of stinking soup. He was the only decent Gestapo official I had come to know. He had got into the service out of sheer stupidity and could not withdraw from it. One night when he was on duty he took me to my mother's cell. It might easily have cost him his head. After a week our hunger ration was stopped. In spite of my protest against his taking such a chance, the guard had persuaded the camp doctor to restore us to a normal ration.

The comradeship and sympathy of the other prisoners during that hunger week were very moving—not only of my own friends such as Princess Ruspoli and Puppi Sarré, who always tried to raise our spirits, but also of girls from the camp who had been imprisoned for offenses such as refusal to work. They gave me bread and other bits of food that one can easily pass on in a prison.

One day I was put into a damp cell in the basement where I stayed for two weeks without books, companionship, or exercise. I was told presently that my mother had been sent away. Nothing more. I worried about her more than ever.

After the Twentieth of July a new and grim mood prevailed in Ravensbrück and all conditions grew worse. Up to that time we had had older German SS men who were still human. Now they were replaced by younger and more "reliable" men who worked in shifts of six. We called them the "rats." They were mostly Rumanians and Hungarians, with a few Russians. They looked through the cell judases every twenty minutes. Leo Lange came to inspect each Sunday and to shout at all of us. In the cell below me was Finance Minister Popitz. I could hear Lange shout at him, "Well, Minister, you old pig . . ."

There were nightly checkups now. Senseless outrages were perpetrated, all apparently planned to make us lose our nerve. We were waked in the middle of the night and asked name, age, sex, religion, amount of savings, and other pointless questions. Once they roused me at 2 A.M. to ask to which units of the Nazi party I belonged. They switched the bright electric lights alternately on and off during the night. Another irritating technique was to have guards run through the corridors at all times of day and night, stamping, shouting commands, stopping at various cells, and marching away again. But we held on, and each one helped the others to bear up. During our free time I could occasionally whisper with Rudolf Pechel, whose unbroken fighting spirit gave us all courage. Count Moltke had secret means of contact with the outside. All of us saw with dread the prison filling with our friends who had been free up to that time.

Count Bernstorff had the cell next to mine, and we knocked at the wall, trying to encourage each other. Sometimes I pulled myself up to the cellar window and saw above me, on the ground, the women of the concentration camp standing for hours on end, a common camp punishment. The measure of daily misery and atrocity in the camp was beyond human understanding. Behind one wall of the prison building lay the crematory. It was smoking constantly, and as the year 1944 progressed the smoke got thicker and heavier. Near by was the execution square. During the warm evenings and nights of August and September I heard many shots from there.

Toward the end of August I was suddenly taken upstairs out of the basement cell. Weber, a Gestapo official who looked like a murderer, told me that Princess Ruspoli, the widow of an Italian diplomat, and I were to reorganize the jewelry deposit of the camp. The previous supervisors had been camp inmates who had helped themselves. Each morning Elisabeth Ruspoli and I were conducted to a larger cell where we had to sort paper bags containing jewelry and cards—more than 77,000 bags in all. Each new arrival at the camp had to give up all valuables and even personal trinkets of purely sentimental value. They were put in a bag, and the contents indicated on a card signed by the inmate. Some of the bags held priceless jewels, others a little brass cross or a ring signed for with three wavering X's. Many of the things had belonged to Greeks, gypsies, Ukrainians, or Poles. It was a depressing job, for as we worked we imagined the lives of the women who had owned them.

One day Weber appeared with six suitcases. With some embarrassment he asked us to take care of them "on the side." We were to separate the valuable from the worthless stuff and give the best to him. Three of the suitcases held a mass of jewelry, some of it beautiful, some crude, probably belonging to inmates who had been murdered. The contents of the suitcases were supposed to have been transferred to the Reichsbank and credited to the SS. Weber did not feel that necessary.

During September the prison was quieter and less crowded. Our work made the time pass more quickly, and Elisabeth Ruspoli was the best comrade I could have asked. Finally I had news of my mother. She was in the Cottbus penitentiary for three and a half months. On December 1 she was sent to the Moabit Remand prison in Berlin to await a second trial before the People's Court.

All we wanted now was to gain time, for the fronts were moving closer and liberation might come soon. But on October 18 this period of relative calm, with its false sense of security, came to a sudden end. An official appeared and shouted at me, "Get ready, you leave in twenty minutes." I was filled again with uncertainty and fear. Quickly I said good-by to Elisabeth Ruspoli, to Puppi Sarré, and a few others, and climbed into a prison van holding seven men, including Count Bernstorff. For two hours we rode without being able to see anything. When we reached Berlin Bernstorff was deposited at the prison in the Lehrterstrasse and I was taken to the women's prison in Moabit.

A few days later I received the indictment drawn up against "Solf and five others." The five were our friends—Privy Councillor Kuenzer, Count Bernstorff, the historian Dr. Hagen, Father Erxleben—all leading members of the Solf circle—and I.

Although my mother was in the same prison we were not permitted to see each other. Once the acting head of the jail and one of the women officials made it possible for her to visit me secretly in my cell. But most of the women jailors at Moabit were worse than the SS men in Munich and Ravensbrück.

During all my imprisonment I was allowed to see a visitor from outside but once. That was in December of 1944, when my husband came back from Russia on leave. Perhaps it was the worst moment of all that time. For fifteen minutes we sat facing each other, separated by a large table. Beside us stood a female official who constantly looked at her watch. Both of us were too stunned to say anything sensible, for we had to assume that we were seeing each other for the last time.

As time went on we suffered hunger increasingly. There were air raids day and night and we sat them out in our cells alone, not being allowed to go to the cellar. We had plenty of time to dread the trial, which was repeatedly postponed because the People's Court had more cases than it could handle.

The cells were unheated, with temperatures often far below freezing. Hygienic conditions were wretched, the women officials unscrupulous. Hunger tortured us. Hunger affects people differently: some grow gaunt, others swell like misshapen balloons. Mother became a living skeleton; I looked like a blown-up rubber doll.

The chief comfort during these bitter months was the visits of the prison chaplain, Poelchau, who cared courageously for the political prisoners and brought advice, consolation, and help of all kinds. He made it possible for Mother and me to communicate, carrying the letters himself. He smuggled food to us on every visit, and had a cheering word for everyone.

The attorney for many of the political prisoners who were being held on the most serious charges was Dr. Behling. His visits helped to stall off despair. He and the woman doctor, who could smuggle in an occasional piece of bread, were Mother's great consolation.

Our trial was scheduled for December 13, then postponed to January 18, 1945, and again to February 8. One of the worst air raids ever to hit Berlin struck on February 3. The huge old prison building with its thick stone walls shook to its foundations. We sat in our cells—I darning a bottomless pile of military socks —while the bombs fell all around and the air was filled with the noise of modern aerial warfare. It seemed to make little difference then whether we were killed that day or sentenced to execution five days later by Freisler.

Next morning fellow prisoners whispered, "Freisler is dead!" I could hardly believe it. It meant life for us—time gained, and the elimination of our most dangerous enemy. Freisler's eagerness to slaughter others had led to his own death. He had delayed going to the air-raid cellar and was killed by a bomb which hit the court building. Many records were burnt in the raid, among them our own. Our trial was again postponed to April 27.

From newly arriving prisoners we heard something of what was going on in the outside world. We knew that the war could not last much longer but that there was still danger of being killed, at the end, by the SS.

The sense of dissolution of those last months became increasingly strong in early April when artillery could be heard. Every day criminals and lesser political prisoners were discharged. Some of the women guards were doubly watchful: others no longer came to the prison, fearing that liberation might mean punishment on the spot, or even death. A fever seized all the prisoners; even the most apathetic developed a wild desire to live. On the daily exercise walks I saw signs of new life. The little trees in the prison yard turned green; birds were singing, and the chill lessened in the cells. All these seemed promises of early freedom.

The judicial machinery had become disorganized and most of the judges had fled from Berlin by April 20. On April 23, four days before the date for our trial, a woman official who seemed completely hysterical appeared in my cell and shouted, "Get ready for discharge."

In the office I found my mother; the widow of a former mayor of Berlin, Dr. Elsas; and her daughter. We were all bewildered and not sure what was happening to us, but we found ourselves indeed discharged and walking out of the prison.

We soon learned to whom we owed our freedom. A friend of both families, Dr. Ernst Ludwig Heuss, had persuaded an official to make out discharge certificates for us four. The main office when they heard of it wanted us back. And when Dr. Heuss and others tried to do the same thing for other prisoners, it was already too late. That night and the next two nights the Rollkommandos of the SS did their beastly work in the prisons of the Lehrterstrasse and Prinz Albrechtstrasse. The men were called out of their cells and taken in groups to bombed-out ruins where they were shot in the neck. Among those murdered were two of our dearest friends, Richard Kuenzer and Albrecht Bernstorff.

EPILOGUE TO CHAPTER VII

Tea Party

MOST of the people mentioned in this story are dead. Seventy-six friends and close acquaintances of the Solfs were killed, many of them during those last few days. The body of Richard Kuenzer was found in a mass grave after four weeks' search; Count Bernstorff's was never recovered.

Frau Solf now lives in England. Lagi Countess Ballestrem-Solf and her husband are in Berlin, and their fate is much the same as that of other Germans. Like many Berliners who see human values still ignored and a better world as far off as ever, they ask if the struggle was worth it. Countess Ballestrem-Solf wrote recently: "I do not want to think of the past because it has lost its meaning. The world has learned nothing from it—neither slaughterers nor victims nor onlookers. Our time is like a dance of death whose uncanny rhythm is understood by few. Everyone whirls confusedly without seeing the abyss."

VIII

Rags, Picklocks, and Pliers

ROLF JOSEPH

During the 1930's our family, consisting of my parents, my younger brother Alfred, and me, lived in Wedding, the workers' district of Berlin. From Hitler's *Mein Kampf* and the many other anti-Jewish utterances and acts of the Nazis, we could imagine what might happen to us, but we always hoped that other countries would prevent the worst. Emigration was out of the question because our father had been "60 per cent" physically disabled in the first World War and our mother was ailing.

In 1938 I had been a carpenter's apprentice for three years. Suddenly I was thrown out of the trade by a government ruling that the carpenter's guild could no longer hire Jews. I reported to the Labor Office and was at once assigned to work in the acetate spinning mills of the IG Farben factory in Berlin-Lichtenberg. The machines gave off an intense heat of about 200° F. The temperature in the room had to be kept constant around 110° F. No windows could be opened. We worked almost naked and perspiration ran down our bodies in streams. Moreover, the Jewish workers had to put up with tormenting by foremen and supervisors. Director Huber was a decent sort and when he heard of persecution of Jews he at least took the persecutor to task. Later I was assigned to work as carpenter for a company building barracks in Köpenick near Berlin. The company was thoroughly corrupt; most of the foremen or supervisors were interested only in lining their pockets. I was not surprised when the firm collapsed in 1941.

The Labor Office next assigned me to a factory in Berlin-Pankow which made kitchen furniture. I was still living in Wedding and had to walk almost four miles to the factory, but since the distance was not over that minimum I was not allowed to ride. Sometimes, when I was too tired, I simply took off the Jewish star and rode anyway. I kept thinking, "Now someone will recognize you!" but nothing ever happened.

About the time I went to work in Berlin-Pankow the deportation of Jews began. My brother Alfred and I talked over what we would do when our turn came. We decided that we would not go under any circumstances. At that time we were living on the third floor of a house next to a cemetery. We made a rope ladder and planned to climb down into the cemetery if the Gestapo came to take us away. A neighbor offered us a refuge in near-by Oranienburg.

But we did not have a chance to use our rope ladder. When I came home from work on June 6, 1942, the dreaded furniture van was standing in front of our house. I felt alternately hot and cold. My parents were always at home at this time. A neighbor waved to me to go away but I could not go. I ran up the stairs and listened at the apartment door. I heard my mother cry and a strange man shouting at her. I thought up all sorts of fantastic, impossible ways of saving my parents. But instead of doing anything I just stood there staring at the door. I imagined what was happening on the other side: Father, who could hardly move, and Mother, frail and trembling, thinking of her boys. I heard steps in the hall and in a panic rushed down the stairs. I ran through the streets till I was out of breath. Finally I stopped to rest in a doorway and sobbed and moaned. I tried to think of some way to aid my parents, but I felt utterly helpless. Mother was probably glad that I did not come in, but I still cannot forget that I saved myself and that my parents were taken away.

I found my brother at the house of an acquaintance, and together we went to some friends in Oranienburg who had promised us shelter. But they became frightened and claimed that they could not hide us because Gestapo men were living near by. We left, without having a place to go to. Now we were real outcasts. For the next three years our life was flight and hunger and fear. Things were made a little easier by the fact that we had some money. Mother was able to give a neighbor two thousand marks for us, and the neighbor handed it on to us. Yet even with the money I don't think we would have had the courage to go on living if we had known then that this existence would last three long years. But we were young and were kept going by our deep hatred of the Nazis and, I suppose, by a sense of adventure.

For the first four months we had no shelter. Fortunately it was summer, and we simply loafed around. Hundreds of illegals, as we called ourselves, were living like us: we would ride in the S-Bahn or U-Bahn till late at night, always in fear of being stopped to show our identification cards with the large "J" on them. We spent nights in parks and woods, and when the weather was very bad, in railway station washrooms. Once I overslept in a washroom. I was awakened in the morning by cleaning women who rattled at the door. They apparently thought that a drunk had locked himself in and before I was awake they had brought a railway official. I played up drunk, opened the door, and meandered out. No one stopped me.

Our friend Arthur Fordanski joined us soon after we went into hiding, and the three of us stuck together from then on. We finally found a refuge. Acquaintances of Mother's suggested that we see "Mieze," an eccentric woman in her late forties who made her living by delivering newspapers. She stored all those she did not sell. Her real name was Marie Burde. We found her in a basement in the Tegelerstrasse where she lived. Her readiness to help us was unlimited. She shared her food card with the three of us, always dividing everything into four equal parts. Fortunately she was a vegetarian. She even refused to sleep in a bed because the feathers had something "animal-like" about them, and slept instead on stacked-up newspapers. She got along with the money she earned and the proceeds from selling her meat stamps and tobacco ration card. She carefully stored her clothes, underwear, and books for the time when she would be in an old folks' home and have time to dress well and read in comfort. Mieze also collected empty bottles, rags, rusty nails, and assorted debris in the basement room. It was so full of the stuff there was hardly any space left. Yet all four of us slept there on the stacked-up papers. The place teemed with vermin, and one could hardly breathe. But in spite of her peculiarities Mieze was clever and very generous.

So as not to be seen by the people in the house we climbed out of the window into the street early in the morning and stayed away till late in the evening. When it rained we spent the hours in Mieze's cellar behind the piles of rags.

We were always expecting to be stopped to show our cards. The mother of a friend of mine, Paul Wagner, who had died, gave me his old card without the telltale "J" on it. From then on I felt much easier when I was on the street. We stayed away from places like railroad stations. Somehow we always managed to get something to eat. We would go to cheap inns and order *Stamm*— often just a thin soupy dish for which no food stamps were required. We were always hungry. We scrounged food from acquaintances and bought it whenever we could; but without ration cards we had mostly to get it "other" ways, at high prices.

One day near the Berlin-Wedding station I was stopped by men in civilian clothes who identified themselves as military police. They examined my identification card, looked at a list, questioned me, and arrested me—as a deserter. They had a Paul Wagner on their list of deserters and were convinced that I was he. They cocked their pistols and took me to the nearest police station. I had a choice between two bad alternatives—knowing that if they considered me a deserter I would be shot. So I revealed my true identity, and with it had to admit that I had been living illegally because I was Jewish. They put me in a police wagon, took me to the Alexanderplatz prison, and locked me in a large cellar with hundreds of foreigners. Since we got almost nothing to eat there was active bartering between the hungry prisoners and the trusties who moved around and could lay their hands on additional food. One prisoner gave a gold watch for a loaf of bread.

Two days after my arrest I was taken to the prison in the Dirksenstrasse for interrogation. There I shared a double cell with a Jewish girl, separated only by iron bars. The poor girl lost her nerve and I had to look on, powerless to stop her, while she slashed her wrist with a razor blade. They carried her body out, covered with blood. I had to try to forget this, as I needed every bit of concentration to face the interrogation.

The Gestapo insisted on knowing where I had been living. I

assured them that I had no shelter. Everyone refused to believe it. Time and again they demanded the names of the people who were sheltering me, but I refused to give them. Then they took me into the cellar, tied my hands and feet, strapped me on a wooden box, and gave me twenty-five lashes with a horsewhip on my naked buttocks. I had to count each stroke aloud.

That was the first time I had experienced Nazi methods on my own body. The physical pain was bad, but worse still was the fact that these criminals had the power to humiliate me in this way. It strengthened my determination not to let them break my spirit.

After the whipping I was taken to dungeon cell No. 1 in the Hamburgerstrasse, where Jews were collected prior to deportation. This was a cell in the basement, for the difficult cases. It was less than four feet high and there were no windows. I was alone at first, but later five men were put in with me. They had tried to escape from a deportation transport.

We lived in the most primitive conditions and had to sleep on the floor at first; later we got mattresses. We had a bucket for toilet.

The six of us got along well together and developed friendships which lasted beyond the time spent together in the cell.

We started making plans for escape. There was an open storeroom across the passageway from our cell, with stairs leading to a door with a simple steel lock. This door opened to the outside. But we had little chance of escaping as long as we remained in this windowless locked cell.

After four weeks I was put in cell No. 6 where there were twelve other prisoners. The other five had to remain in the locked cell. Like most cells, No. 6 was not locked, and opened into the basement corridor. When no SS man was around, the prisoners would meet in the corridor and talk. I visited with my five friends and spoke with them through the iron bars. It was a great consolation to us. When the Gestapo guard approached, the Jewish orderlies would whistle and everyone would rush back to his cell.

The six of us started working seriously on our plans for escape. Plumbers came often to work on the toilet pipes which ran from the upper floors to the cellar. That gave me a chance to "borrow" tools. A Jewish orderly smuggled a loaf of bread to us containing a picklock and a screwdriver. There was one other thing to think of. We could not be sure none of the orderlies would squeal to protect himself from being blamed. A Jewish nurse volunteered to get some sleeping powder and put it into the orderlies' coffee. She was kept in custody because she had struck an SS man, but she was very pretty and was made a trusty because SS leader Duberke had taken a liking to her. She succeeded in getting the sleeping powder. There was still one obstacle—Duberke's dog. He slept in the cellar, and we hoped he wouldn't bark.

The night of our escape came. The nurse put the sleeping powder in the orderlies' coffee. Everything was going smoothly—except that this night the dog chose, of all places, to lie in front of cell No. 1.

But everything went according to plan. The orderlies were sleeping; the dog did not move. I managed to open the cell door with the picklock. We opened the door of the storeroom by simply taking off the lock. We cut the telephone wires and dashed out. But no one had thought of the fact that the outside of the prison would be lit up brightly and that guards would be standing there. When the first one of us came out on the street a guard shouted, "They are breaking out!"

I was the last one out. A guard jumped on me at the door and we both rolled down the stairs. All my comrades were caught quickly too. Next evening we were again together in cell No. 1. Each of us got twenty-five lashes and SS leader Duberke ordered us to be handcuffed on the transport. We were worse off than ever.

After eight weeks the transport was ready and we were handcuffed together in a chain. I was the last on the chain and had one hand free. We climbed into a large furniture van where we discovered a tool kit under the roof. I took out a pair of cutting pliers and put them in one of my boots.

At the Putlitzstrasse station forty-eight of us were piled into a railroad car which was fitted with iron bars and could only be opened from the outside. There was a lot of confusion and noise, women were distraught and children crying. Two locomotives hauled the train eastward.

But we six veterans of cell No. 1 had a glint of hope. I took the cutting pliers out of my boot, and as the train rolled along we started to work on my handcuffs. It was a tedious job, but after hours of effort all handcuffs were cut and we were free. By this time it had grown dark, and we were a few hours and perhaps eighty kilometers away from Berlin. The train was moving along at the steady pace of a freight train. Now was the time for us to escape.

The orderlies in our car were scared to let us go—for fear they might be blamed. We had to intimidate them first. Then we knocked some of the boards out of the end of the car so that we could step out on the buffer and jump.

We all knew that it was a matter of life or death, and we got up courage to jump. Only six of us dared to. The others in the car were afraid in spite of knowing what lay ahead of them at their destination.

I was the first. I stepped out on the buffer and jumped far out. The others followed me in quick succession. We had hardly hit the ground when police and SS guards in some of the cars lit up the whole area with red flares and shot at us. But they hit none of us, and fortunately the train kept moving.

I had landed on hands and knees on the railway embankment and suffered only some bad scratches and bruises. One of the men had broken his leg, another his arm.

We knew we must get out of the area quickly. We lay low for a short while, then crawled a ways, lay still again, and crept farther till we reached the nearest forest and took time out to rest. We knew that the most difficult part of our trek was still ahead and decided to head for Berlin in three parties of two each. Our friend with the broken leg walked as well as he could, supported by another.

During the day we hid in woods or barns, and traveled on foot at night, without food. We did not dare talk to anyone, even to ask for bread. We got as far as the Spreewald, a picturesque area southeast of Berlin which is crossed by many streams and canals. The streams made the going all the harder. The police searched the area for us and combed it with dogs. They finally caught all of us. We learned that twenty men from the Wehrmacht and police had been searching for us.

We were kept in the police prison of Lübben for two days. Then they chained us up again, and put us in a separate compartment of a train going to Berlin. At the Schlesischer station SS leader Duberke was waiting for us with his staff. The reception we got can be imagined. At Gestapo headquarters in the Burgstrasse we received twenty-five lashes; in the prison in the Hamburgerstrasse we were beaten again. I was struck in the face with a whip. Suddenly body and mind revolted and I developed a high fever. The fever gave me an idea. I knew that the SS were afraid of contagious diseases, so I scratched myself up badly and said I had scarlet fever. The doctor actually diagnosed scarlet fever and I was sent, lashed to the stretcher, to the police prison hospital in the Iranische Strasse. I kept on acting as if I were seriously sick.

After two weeks the Jewish nurse in the prison told me that I was going to be sent to the SS barracks in Lichterfelde and shot. I made up my mind to try to escape once more. With death sure, I had nothing to lose.

Another prison patient in the ward, Erich Goldbach, and I talked the nurse into getting us trousers. We had no shoes and our shirts bore the stamp "Jewish Police Prison," which we could not get rid of. We put the shirts on inside out so that the lettering was not legible.

It was more difficult to manage the barred windows. With a tourniquet made of a wet towel and a piece of wood I widened the space between two bars so that we could just squeeze through. Our cell was on the third floor and below us was the asphalt court.

It was a leap into uncertainty but it might lead to freedom. Erich jumped first. I saw two guards run to the main entrance of the prison. They started their motorcycles and rode off. Erich couldn't have gotten far. I looked down. The courtyard was empty. My heart was pounding. I had a terrible moment of indecision. Were they watching the yard more closely now or was their attention diverted? I could not know. A tremendous will to live poured into me, with the knowledge that I had life to gain. It looked very far to the ground, but I jumped.

I hit the ground with a terrible thud and a shooting pain went through my spine. I felt as if I were paralyzed, but fear kept me moving. I climbed over the wall, let myself down into the street, and managed to jump on a passing streetcar.

I acted almost unconsciously and intuitively. I stood in front near the motorman. No one paid any attention to my strange attire—I was in stocking feet—maybe they thought I was bombed out. I covered my chest by crossing my arms, to make sure none of the prison imprint on the turned side of the shirt could be read. It was summer and wearing only shirt and trousers was not uncommon.

The streetcar was crowded and the conductor who collected the fare paid no attention to me. I got off at Tegelerstrasse.

My brother, his friend Arthur Fordanski, and Mieze had long ago given me up for lost, and our joy was indescribable. My body hurt terribly. I lay down right away. We did not dare to get a doctor. But I could not walk any more, and had probably hurt my spine and cracked some ribs. For three months I lay on the stacked newspapers. Alfred looked after me, massaged me, and rubbed me with ointment. It was not an easy time, for we had to live in incredible filth, without fresh air or enough food.

When I was able to go out for the first time I set out to try to find some food, because I had depended on the others for so long. I had heard that I might be able to get something in Heiligensee, a suburb northwest of Berlin.

On the way there I ran across Jakob Post, with whom I had once worked as carpenter. I had always thought him a decent sort of person. He knew that I was among the persecuted and asked how I was getting along. I described my escape from the prison hospital. He promised to get me food and invited me to come the next day to his apartment.

I went and he welcomed me warmly, but I thought it strange that he immediately asked me to wait, and left. I thought at first that he was getting the food—because I did not want to think differently. But it seemed peculiar when he did not return for some time. I was just thinking of leaving when he came back with two officers of the Criminal Police.

This time there seemed no way out, and I was too weak physically and mentally to offer resistance. I had no hope left.

They asked no questions, for Jakob Post had told them all they needed to know. I had to walk between them to the police station.

We had gone a short way when I stopped. Hardly realizing what I was doing, I said quietly:

"You can do what you like with me. You can shoot me right here. But I am not going with you. I'd rather die right on this spot—right now. I've had enough."

They cocked their revolvers. I did not move and just looked at them.

Everything seemed so unreal I was not even afraid. I only knew one thing: I wanted to get it over with.

Infinite time passed, perhaps really less than a minute. One officer said in a low voice to his companion, "Shall we let him run?"

"I don't care—" the other answered, "but he can't see that fellow up there where we just got him. That might make trouble for us. As long as the war is on, he can't do that."

I just nodded. If I had been able to speak I would have shouted for joy.

I turned around and walked slowly away through the streets as if in a trance. When I got "home" to Mieze's cellar I fell on my newspaper bed exhausted.

It was the end of 1943 and we still had many months of war and bombing ahead of us. Mieze continued to be generous in her help, but her peculiar notions were sometimes difficult to bear. She would not let the place be cleaned, and the vermin did not bother her in the least. At our request she did buy additional vegetables at times but she would not spend any money for soap. She collected human excrement in a bucket and from time to time took it out to her little plot of land in suburban Schoenow north of Berlin. She did not use it as fertilizer, though, but dumped it on a pile. "I want the soil to rest," she always said. The grass was up to our heads, for the soil had been "resting" for nearly twenty years.

Yes, Mieze was a character. Once she found a Turkish paper in the ruins and promptly bought a grammar so that she could study Turkish—later.

We owe Mieze much, and I don't want to make fun of her peculiarities. She continued to shelter us, although a neighbor woman got suspicious and wanted to report us. But we could keep that woman quiet by giving her bread. From then on we always talked in low voices in order not to attract attention, and when Mieze had company we hid behind the piles of rags and newspapers and no one noticed us. But the lice were a terrible nuisance.

We managed somehow to live on the little food we had. By selling her meat stamps Mieze could buy more of other things; and a Gentile relative often brought us food.

That is how we pulled through until the day in November, 1943, when Mieze's cellar was bombed out. We borrowed a hand-cart, put what was left of Mieze's property on it, and walked out to her place in Schoenow. On the way, in Buchholz, a Nazi official stopped us and asked for our identification papers. We told him that we were bombed out. He felt sorry for us. As it was very cold he invited us to spend the night in his barrack. We accepted with mixed feelings.

As soon as we reached Mieze's place we started to build a cottage. We picked up boards where we could find them, and even got a large iron stove from the ruins of Berlin. We managed to build a really beautiful cottage. Then we helped the neighbors. We were soon well liked because young men were scarce. We told the Nazi neighbors that we were working on the night shift, and I gave out that I was a draftsman from the Heinkel aircraft plant in Oranienburg. I left for work "officially" every evening at ten o'clock.

I prepared my own identification card. Arthur's girl friend, Lotte, who was partly Jewish and was working in a factory, "borrowed" a rubber stamp from the office of the factory. I used it to fix up another paper showing that I was of mixed Jewish parentage and that I was working in the factory. I had to show that card three times but never had any difficulty.

We even built an air-raid shelter out in Schoenow. Once, when incendiaries hit there, we helped to extinguish the fires. We lived in the midst of Nazis without being suspected. They were tired of the war, although outwardly they appeared quite confident. We did everything possible to help the underground, especially by distributing leaflets which we got from Ukrainian workers.

On November 27, 1944, my brother Alfred was arrested while distributing these leaflets. He will tell his own story.

ALFRED JOSEPH

ARTHUR FORDANSKI and I were together all the years we
lived illegally. We had known each other since childhood
and had always been inseparable friends. Both of us were
born in 1921. He was the only one of his family who was
determined to submerge, and the only one who survived. He and
his brothers and sister-in-law lived with their parents. A Jewish
orderly who rented a furnished room from them always told
them when deportations were planned.

In February, 1942, they were notified to be at home on a certain day, allegedly so that their property could be inventoried.
No one believed this, and the orderly confirmed their suspicions,
telling them that the Nazis wanted strong young men for railroad work in Poland and they would all be deported. Arthur
left at once, but the rest of his family did not dare to. They were
so intimidated that they observed all regulations.

A few days later Arthur risked visiting the apartment at night
and found it sealed. His family had been taken away. He learned
later that his parents had met ours in Theresienstadt, the Jewish
ghetto town in Czechoslovakia, but neither his parents nor ours
ever returned. We suppose they were all gassed. Arthur's brother
and sister-in-law were taken to Monowitz, one of the branches of
the Auschwitz death camp. One brother is said to have been
alive in Buchenwald till 1945. After that all trace of him was lost.

From that February day when he left home Arthur and I lived
a vagabond existence. Our headquarters was Mieze's cellar. She
was always going to let us into the cellar in the evening, but unfortunately she had no sense of time. Often we made a definite
agreement to be in front of the house at eight o'clock, glad to be
getting into a warm place after being out all day in the cold. But
good Mieze was visiting friends and did not return until twelve
or one o'clock at night, and was surprised that we were not there
waiting for her.

During the first three weeks of our illegal life, until he was
arrested, my brother Rolf lived with us in the cellar. It was much

163

harder for him to adjust to this new life as he was more sensitive and more disheartened than we. He found Mieze's unreliability harassing, especially when we had to find another place to spend the night because she did not show up. And he worried about endangering and burdening Mieze and anyone who helped us through our illegal life. But what else could we do?

Sometimes our legs would carry us no farther and we could barely wait till evening. Inadequate food and the constant hunt for food and shelter had greatly weakened us, but we would not let that get us down. Occasionally we even enjoyed our life, and acted a part which we thought would camouflage us as harmless foreigners. We wore berets and sometimes talked a strange mixture of syllables when we were eating in a restaurant. Once someone at the next table said, "What are they, Dutch?"

In the spring of 1943 Arthur and I found an empty apartment near the Alexanderplatz. The former inhabitants, a Jewish shoemaker and his family, had been evacuated. Although the apartment was sealed, the other residents of the house had broken in and were taking the belongings out piecemeal. It was a dilapidated, noisy house with the front door always unlocked. We were more tired than careful and often slept there. While we were lying in bed people would sneak in and take some chairs or the shoemaker's tools. None of them reported the strange men in the beds; as they were thieves themselves they probably thought we were the same sort. One night we thought we heard heavy boot steps. Police! We had no way out and hid in the clothes closet. The men turned out to be quite harmless and were just getting another piece of furniture. We stayed in the house about four weeks and then looked for another hide-out.

On the line to Oranienburg there were some old railway cars that were used by construction crews. We slept in these several times. But one night a group of railway policemen appeared with dogs. Arthur could hardly get me awake, but we managed to slip out the other side and get away before the dogs got wind of us.

Sometimes we tried to fool ourselves into believing that our life was just a sort of game, but we knew very well how bitter it is to live a hunted existence.

One night was a nightmare. I had been riding around in the subway because it was a cold winter night and I was too restless to wait in some inn. I don't remember why I did not go to the cellar; perhaps Mieze was not there to open up. I fought my way through a snow storm. Near Pankstrasse I just couldn't go on. Suddenly I saw an inviting round shack. I went in to warm up but apparently fell asleep standing, even though I was very cold.

When I woke I heard steps going back and forth with military regularity. I knew at once that I was in a sentry box. I did not dare go out. Then I decided I had to get out before daylight. As I darted out I ran straight into the sentry, but he was so surprised that he simply looked at me and did nothing. I ran around the corner and hid in the ruins of a house. I waited, expecting to hear shots, but nothing happened.

We were lucky when there was an air-raid alarm at night: that gave us a good place to stay. We rushed to a public air-raid shelter, threw ourselves on the cots and slept well and comfortably. Once someone felt sorry for us: "Poor fellows, they have to work all day and can't even get a good rest at night."

In the daytime we often went to the trenches in the Exerzierplatz—"Drill Square"—and stretched out there. During an alarm people clambered in and were surprised to find us there before them.

Later we stayed with Arthur's girl friend Lotte who lived with her parents in the Zehdenickerstrasse. They came under the Nazi laws for "privileged" marriages, because one partner was Jewish and the other Gentile. They had to be careful, however, because the Gestapo applied the rulings in their own arbitrary fashion. We were allowed to sleep in the attic, but we never came till nightfall so that the neighbors would not get suspicious.

It was a double blow for us when Mieze's house was bombed out on November 22, 1943, and our other refuge, the house in the Zehdenickerstrasse, the next day. I at once went out to Mieze's hut in Schoenow. Arthur didn't get there until the next morning because he stayed behind to help put out fires.

Gradually we got quite reckless. We wanted to do our share against Hitler and the Nazis. Whenever we could we would paint inscriptions against Hitler on the walls of ruins or in toilets or

post leaflets dropped by air. After these activities we were never
sure whether it was best to run or walk away as if unconcerned.
Usually we walked quietly away. Rolf had gone through so much
that he could not help turning around to see if someone was
following us.

Mieze was ordered to wash steps and halls in a house in the
Brüsselerstrasse. We knew she was not likely to keep another
house clean when she would not even clean her own place. The
occupants of the house complained, and to prevent Mieze's getting into trouble her brother Ernst and I often cleaned the house
together or alternately. People frequently spied on each other,
and they must have wondered why two apparently healthy young
men were washing the steps. One day when Ernst was there alone
police came to see his papers. He did not have any reason to hide
them: he was "Aryan" and deferred from military service because
he was ailing. So they left again, unsatisfied.

It was a matter of honor to listen to the British radio. One day
the radio suggested that we throw broken glass on the main highways. We threw glass on the road to Bernau, which ran near us.
Nothing happened to us. But misfortune overtook me when I
felt quite secure.

It happened like this. On November 27, 1944, I went to an
inn in the Bernauerstrasse where I often met Ukrainian laborers
who printed leaflets in the camp they lived in. They always gave
me a supply for distribution. They had captions like "REFUSE
TO WORK!" "YOU ARE HELPING PROLONG THE
WAR!" "DO MORE SABOTAGE!" "KILL THE NAZIS!"

Suddenly Gestapo officials appeared and arrested two Ukrainians with whom I was talking. I could not escape. One of the
Gestapo men took my papers out of my pocket and when he saw
the large "J" put handcuffs on me too. They took us to the Dirksenstrasse prison. We were interrogated at once. "Your name?"

"Alfred Joseph," I answered, and was slapped in the face.

"Have you already forgotten your damnable name?"

Then I knew what they wanted—the middle name Jews had
been ordered to adopt: "Alfred *Israel* Joseph." I thought of my
brother—and that now my turn had come. They wanted me to

state exactly where I had been living since June, 1942, for according to their files I had been evacuated on June 6. They did not believe my answer that I had been roving about, and got angry at my reply. The woman taking notes was sent out of the room, and they started to beat me. Then they asked me again and beat me again. I saw that I had to invent something, so I told them that I had stayed with a friend at a certain address. The house had long ago been bombed out and my friend killed. The story did not do me any good for they called the police station of the precinct and when they found out that I lied they beat me again.

Afterward I was taken to the Alexanderplatz prison. They continued to beat me, and lack of food weakened me. I knew that I had started on the long road of torment which Rolf had told us about. The awful thing was to have it happen such a short time before the end. We were expecting the collapse of the Nazis in a matter of days.

I knew Rolf would look for me in vain, just as I had looked for him. I wondered what I could do to escape. It did not look very hopeful. The Gestapo became more cruel as the war drew to an end. I was taken to the cellar prison in the Schulstrasse, where the mistreatment continued. After a week I was sent to the concentration camp at Sachsenhausen. The worst part came after six weeks: the labor transport to Ravensbrück. The place was so overcrowded that three of us had to share a wooden cot. We were given thin blankets. It was miserably cold. One evening a blanket was missing. When it could not be found for all the searching, the other blankets were taken away and the windows were lifted off their hinges so that we lay there shaking in the bitter cold all night. In the morning, half frozen, we had to face the evil of a new day. That was just one of the many tortures that were planned for us. Many perished, and it is a wonder so many survived.

Half a year later, in the spring of 1945, many of us were shipped back to Sachsenhausen. No one knew why. We were afraid of these transports, for there was always the chance that they might be taking us to our death. One day it was rumored that we would be sent to Bergen-Belsen. We had heard terrible things of this place. Living became a race against death by hunger, disease, or liquidation. Would the war end or would we die first?

The trip to Bergen-Belsen was interrupted at Oranienburg by a heavy air-raid. We stopped to repair railroad tracks. It was hellish forced work at a killing pace, and we were at the end of our strength. I weighed less than ninety pounds. We finally got to Bergen-Belsen.

Shortly after our arrival, toward the middle of April, 1945, we suddenly heard that the Russians were coming. We were half insane from excitement for we had reason at last to hope. The camp was broken up and the excitement of the Nazis was plain. Orders were issued and retracted. Rumors and alarms were passed around. No one knew what to expect. Some of the inmates were almost out of their minds at the thought of being killed at the last moment before liberation—for in those days the bestial qualities of the SS showed themselves in one last terrible outburst. Unfed, most of us almost too weak to walk, we were marched out of the camp, guarded by five hundred armed SS men.

There were about thirty thousand marching men. We slept in the woods that night. If anyone could not move on, he was killed without pity. A large group was taken into a valley and liquidated. I managed not to be included, suspecting their intentions. I slipped away from that group. Then the misery march moved on to Schwerin. Many of the SS men now tried to move west, not wanting to fall into the hands of the Russians.

Near Criwitz I escaped. A farmer took me into his house and hid me till the danger was over. I got enough to eat and recovered quickly, so that I could tramp to Berlin later. I found Rolf and Arthur with our good Mieze. Hitler was dead. We, the doomed, had survived him.

EPILOGUE TO CHAPTER VIII

Rags, Picklocks, and Pliers

ROLF, now twenty-eight years old, is prevented from working by a heart and lung ailment. Alfred is working for a butcher and Mieze is again gathering rags. Both Rolf and Alfred help her now to make her life easier. Alfred's friend Arthur owns a ladies' tailoring shop.

Rolf's five prison mates were executed in the SS barracks in Berlin-Lichterfelde. His fellow inmate in the prison hospital, Erich Goldbach, was caught after his escape, taken to Auschwitz, and threw himself against the high-voltage wires to avoid being gassed. The "friend" who had the two policemen arrest Rolf returned to his native country, Holland.

PROLOGUE TO CHAPTER IX

The Church Conspiratorial

EUGEN GERSTENMAIER is a Protestant clergyman and theologian. He was born in 1906 in Kirchheim/Teck in Württemberg. After eight years in business he attended the university and studied theology, literature, and philosophy, first in Tübingen and later in the old Hanse city of Rostock.

Allen Dulles speaks in *Germany's Underground* of Gerstenmaier's conviction that "a spiritual opposition to Nazism was not enough, and that Nazism had to be rooted out if Christianity was to survive in Germany." * Dr Gerstenmaier tells here what happened when he acted on his convictions.

* New York, The Macmillan Company, 1947.

IX

The Church Conspiratorial

EUGEN GERSTENMAIER

O N MAY 1, 1934, a festive procession moved through the streets of Rostock, the old Hanseatic port and university city on the Baltic Sea. It was intended as a demonstration of the new unity of the people under National Socialism, a symbol of successfully accomplished Gleichschaltung—the reduction of all the diverse groups in the German state to a Nazi common denominator. Baker and butcher, officials and workers, all marched under the swastika flags—the butchers in their blue-and-white striped working clothes, the railroad and postal officials in their uniforms, the Labor Front in blue holiday suits, and the university professors in their medieval gowns. Everyone kept step: it seemed that Gleichschaltung had been successful. But an attentive observer could note embarrassment and resentment in the faces of some of the workers and a certain discomfort among the academic group, who looked like bad actors. The procession had, of course, been carefully staged, and so had the shouts of Heil to the Führer. Numerous Storm Troopers and SS men were prepared to maintain order with nightsticks and revolvers, and emergency squads of police were ready for the slightest incident.

Goebbels had a diabolical ability to create mass hypnosis, to lead people astray and confuse their emotions, but even he never succeeded in persuading all the Germans to join the Nazis. After 1933 Hitler's following was never composed of volunteers alone. Neither Goebbels nor Himmler nor all the "special plenipotentiaries of the Führer" were able to complete the Gleichschaltung of the people. They had initial successes in the church struggle, as the resistance of the church came to be known; a Reich bishop was appointed by Hitler to head the Evangelical Church; a new

Concordat with the Holy See was assured. But before long even the Nazi press could not conceal the fact that the Gleichschaltung of the church had failed. God's truth could not be subordinated to the commands of Hitler. The church was henceforth labeled "the enemy of the people."

The National Socialists always underestimated the strength of a deep-rooted religious tradition sustained by a living sense of spiritual values. And the church had the support of the intellectuals because they recognized the cultural significance of its fight for existence. A wave of open resistance followed the publication of the so-called Aryan paragraph, designed to exclude worshipers and ministers of "non-Aryan" descent. These protests led to a demand that the Reich bishop resign.

At that time, in 1934, I was a student of theology at the University of Rostock and spokesman for those who supported the church against the Nazis. When the SA, the SS, the Hitler Youth, and other party units organized a mass rally to support the church program of the Führer, the majority of the students took our side and refused to attend. There were serious conflicts within the student body, and weeks of unrest in the university. When the spokesman of the Nazi group, a fanatic SS man, resorted to slander to discredit the church party, he was publicly repudiated by the student body, who prohibited his attending classes. But within twenty-four hours of his expulsion a warrant for my arrest was issued by order of the Nazi-appointed governor of Mecklenburg, on the grounds that I had committed an act of "incitement to armed revolt."

While in prison I meditated on the circumstances. It was true that my friends and I had taken actions which could hardly please the Nazis, but up to that time I had scarcely dreamt of an armed uprising. So far the church had been merely like a breakwater, which had tried to hold back the Nazi waves. Its freedom in the totalitarian state could be maintained only partially and with difficulty. Freedom of the individual had vanished, and with it justice and human dignity. Many considered it a hopeless task to fight to recover them; the church scarcely had the means to do so. Some salvation must be found—it was like a divine command. But what were to be the ways and means?

I was soon released from prison by an amnesty of President Hindenburg. In response to an invitation of the Theological Faculty of the University of Rostock, I began the procedure for admission to the faculty. I passed and completed the professional examination, but for a long time the Ministry delayed issuing the diploma. When I finally received it and had given the prescribed trial lectures at the University of Berlin, the "Representative of the Führer," the highest official of the party, declared me politically unacceptable. I was not permitted to lecture at a university.

I then entered the chancellery of the German Evangelical Church as a professional assistant, and for the next few years I was in the external affairs office of the church. Helping to prepare for the Oxford and Edinburgh church conferences in 1937 gave me an opportunity to become familiar with the ecumenical movement and its problems, as well as with foreign churches of various denominations. I also became acquainted with international political and economic questions, and met men of many countries who have remained my friends to this day. But two years of preparatory work was doomed to failure. When the German delegation wanted to leave the country, we were refused passports, and men from the Gestapo and from Rosenberg's office went to Oxford in our place.

The decisions of the Oxford World Conference enraged the Nazis so much that they demanded that the German Evangelical Church resign from the ecumenical movement and from the World Council of Churches which had just been formed. Bishop Heckel, head of the external affairs office, refused to accede to this demand, in spite of recurrent attacks. This enabled me to maintain the connections of the Protestant Church of Germany with other churches of the World Council. It also gave the German resistance a chance to remain in relatively close contact with other countries. Hans Schönfeld, who was one of our group, was director of the research section of the World Council of Churches in Geneva. Through his position he was able to perform services for the victims of National Socialism which would have been considered treasonable in Germany.

The work in the church became more difficult after 1937. It was more and more necessary to counteract Nazi propaganda and the Gleichschaltung policy to which the orthodox national churches of southeastern Europe were subjected. Of course these churches instinctively kept their distance from National Socialism, but we were interested in bringing them as much as possible into the struggle against its ideology and political influence. Our attempt was made the more difficult because Nazi propaganda in the southeastern region at times appeared friendly to the churches and was consequently more effective than in western Europe.

Looking for men who might be able to help in this work by virtue of their position, I became acquainted with a group of young officials of the Foreign Ministry. Outstanding among these was a young legation counsellor, Hans von Haeften, the son of a Prussian general. Hans was a devout Christian and an unswerving opponent of the Nazi regime, but he was so competent in his job that he was entrusted with important work. He rendered great service in the creation of a German opposition. We were joined later by Adam von Trott zu Solz, former Rhodes scholar who combined a superb education with a social conscience and a knowledge of the world. In the course of time I met young men from the group around Ernst Weizsäcker, Undersecretary of the Foreign Ministry, such as Georg Federer, Gottfried von Nostitz, and Albrecht von Kessel who was for some time at the Vatican. The loyal cooperation of these men both before and during the war made it possible to carry out the tasks of the church and to keep up political resistance through the international connections of the church.

In late July and early August of 1939 I attended a gathering of a small circle of English, American, and Scandinavian churchmen in the mansion of William Temple, the Archbishop of York. Men like Reinhold Niebuhr from the United States and Anders Nygren from Sweden, now president of the Lutheran World Federation, were present. Those at this meeting, like others I saw abroad, recognized the danger of war, but I noted with dismay how the Third Reich was underestimated. I remember meeting a senior officer of the British Navy who told me confidently:

"Shortly after a declaration of war by England, Hitler will be removed by a mass revolution and peace and order will come on earth."

When I was abroad or talked with foreigners, I was sometimes brought to the point of desperation by their failure to appreciate the true meaning of the totalitarian state and their naïve underestimate of how a ruthless police system and incessant propaganda can control the masses in a modern industrial state. Admittedly, a correct evaluation of the totalitarian state was at that time more difficult than today; but the moral condemnation of peoples forced into a totalitarian system appeared to me unsuitable and unnecessary, long before the days of the Communist putsch in Czechoslovakia in 1948. In the face of a vast and thorough police apparatus endowed with unlimited resources, it is remarkable that there was in Germany any systematic growth of an opposition.

The German resistance movement was formed over a period of time from widely scattered and often independent groups of varying political and social origins. A few individuals here or there would band together to plan some move against Hitler. For instance Count Fritz von der Schulenburg whom I had long known once asked Count Peter Yorck and me to join a group of volunteers who were someday to take Hitler's field headquarters. As a result of ever-increasing pressure these loose associations gradually developed some unity and cohesion. But I doubt that any person was ever in a position to survey the whole structure fully. It is in the nature of such movements that they cannot be fully known.

In the years before the war I had met some men whose plans were aimed at a coup d'état against the Nazis, alone or with other groups. We put our hope in the army, the generals. Anyone who was realistic had to rest his hopes in the military to carry out a coup. It would have been fantastic to expect a rising of the unarmed masses or such a peaceful "victory of the free spirit" as some dreamers hoped for. Totalitarian governments cannot be overthrown except by force of arms, and the military were indispensable because they were the only ones outside the Nazi ranks who possessed arms.

The beginning of the war brought closer the need and the possibility of a coup. The opposition groups were joining hands and becoming more active. Colonel General Beck was considered the head of the army resistance group, and the courageous Goerdeler, former Lord Mayor of Leipzig, was the chief exhorter and proselytizer.

When the war started I was in the Rumanian province of Transylvania, which has a high percentage of Germans, to speak at a conference of churchmen being held near Hermannstadt in order to strengthen the resistance of the German churches to National Socialism. I rode back to Berlin past mobilized Rumanian divisions that were anxious to fight Germany rather than stand at her side. In Berlin there was not a trace of enthusiasm. At most, people appeared resigned; some wept, others cursed under their breath. The city was already blacked out.

I talked with Josef Wirmer in Berlin, a lawyer and confidant of Goerdeler's who was slated to be Minister of Justice in Goerdeler's cabinet. When I asked him about the plans of the generals he told me that the final chapter had begun and that action was to be taken.

I was soon called to see Ambassador Fritz von Twardowski, head of the Cultural Department of the Foreign Ministry, who in clerical circles was considered a reliable representative of the church. Because he had been seriously wounded in line of duty— he had narrowly escaped death by assassination while in Moscow as embassy counselor—he enjoyed a certain amount of freedom in the Foreign Ministry; and he made use of his privileged position to offer my friends and me opportunities to perform illegal tasks.

Our first assignment was a secret mission to Norway to initiate intervention for peace. Hans Schönfeld and I sailed to Oslo, where we talked with Bishop Berggrav, a respected and gifted church leader. He understood our reasoning that the war must be brought to an end before it turned into a world conflagration, in order to prevent still worse disaster for the blood-soaked and partly destroyed countries of Europe. He agreed to take on the thankless task of intermediary, though we could promise him only the support of that relatively weak portion of the German

Foreign Office which was gathered around Twardowski and might possibly include Weizsäcker.

Hitler's arrogant speech at the end of the Polish campaign bade fair to destroy our last hope for tolerance and compromise. But Bishop Berggrav, endowed with the courage of one who strives to prevent endless misery, went to work energetically in London and Berlin. The result of his efforts in London was not encouraging; in Berlin it was virtually a personal humiliation.

For a while I lived with officers of the Supreme Command of the Wehrmacht and cooperated with anti-Nazis in the Foreign Office. I got to know many others of similar opinions, such as Johannes Popitz, the Prussian Finance Minister, an intelligent statesman who was constantly pressing for the overthrow of the Nazis; the superbly educated Ulrich von Hassel, diplomat of the old school and former ambassador to Italy; and Jakob Kaiser, trade union leader, and his friend Habermann. All were serious, determined men who worked ardently for the coup.

Hans von Haeften and von Trott zu Solz introduced me to young Count Helmuth von Moltke. On previous occasions, when he had been helpful in bringing escaping Jews to safety, I had admired his purposeful energy. Now I found his evaluation of the political situation and the views of the circle of young men around him to be closely akin to my own ideas. Thereafter my own work and my participation in the resistance were carried out more and more in the "Kreisau circle," so named for the former estate of Field Marshal von Moltke, which now belonged to the young Count and served as our gathering place.

At a meeting which I had arranged between Moltke and the elderly Bishop Wurm of Württemberg I first met Count Peter Yorck von Wartenburg. Afterward, when Moltke's apartment and mine were bombed out on the same night, we both lived in Yorck's house in Berlin. Moltke's planning and initiative were invaluable to the Kreisau circle, as was Peter Yorck's strength as a moderator. Our unity was welded through hard years of difficult struggle, of meticulous planning and deliberation. We lived together, faced common risks, imprisonment, and trial together, until death finally parted us.

Carefully selected young representatives of various callings and opposition groups were brought together in the Kreisau circle. There were trade union leaders like Carlo Mierendorff and Theo Haubach. Adolf Reichwein, brilliant teacher and writer and one of the younger Social Democrats, was a member from the outset; and Julius Leber, another leading Social Democrat, joined us later. Adam von Trott zu Solz and Hans von Haeften were the group's specialists in foreign policy; Paulus van Husen and Theodor Steltzer were of special value to us younger men because of their experience in internal politics. The Jesuit, Father Delp, and van Husen were the Catholic representatives, and I was the Protestant one. A group of trusted authorities from various strata of society and economic life was available to give expert guidance. It included Eduard Wätjen, one of the founders of the circle; von Trotha, a cousin of Moltke; and his friend Horst von Einsiedeln. We were to owe deep thanks in later days to Harold Pölchau, prison chaplain and one of the Protestant members of the circle, for his consolation and help.

From the beginning two factors endangered the success of the coup d'état. One was the vacillation of the generals in whose hands its execution lay. They had good reason to expect that the civilians involved would see to the establishment of agreements with foreign governments as a necessary prerequisite to the coup. The failure to conclude such agreements was a second important factor in the failure.

Numerous attempts were made to get some sort of assurance from other countries that they would recognize and cooperate with a new government after the overthrow of the Nazis. Many of the secret contacts of various groups of the opposition did not, of course, become known till after the war, for it is in the nature of conspiracy that the number of persons "in the know" should be as small as possible. The account of such negotiations given here is by no means complete.

Goerdeler was abroad in 1938 and 1939 and talked with Sumner Welles, Churchill, Vansittart, and Daladier about the plans of anti-Nazis. After the war started he informed the King of the Belgians of the objectives of the opposition and asked whether he would act as an intermediary with Paris and London concerning a peace after a coup. The 1940 offensive stopped whatever might have come of that attempt.

In the first days of September, 1938, Theodor Kordt, the German chargé d'affaires, urged Lord Halifax, British Foreign Minister, to flatly reject Hitler's demands.

Fabian von Schlabrendorff went to England just before the war to inform Churchill of the impending attack on Poland and tell him of the anti-Nazi conspiracy in Germany. Rather early in the war Churchill was also given our detailed evaluation of the political situation in Germany, an account of expected developments, and a sketch of the existing elements of resistance and their political attitudes. I have since learned that he marked this statement "very encouraging" and filed it away!

In August of 1939 von Trott zu Solz talked with Chamberlain and Halifax, and later came to the United States where he met the British Ambassador, Lord Lothian, at the Mayflower Hotel in Washington. While in the United States Trott was shadowed by both the Gestapo and the FBI. He came to be one of the main intermediaries between the German opposition and foreign officials, making numerous trips during the war to Sweden and Switzerland, where he was in contact with the American OSS.

Hassell, former Ambassador to Italy, had several talks in Switzerland with intermediaries of the English Foreign Secretary. He concluded that they did not have much faith in getting peace by overthrow of the Hitler regime.

In May, 1942, Dietrich Bonhoeffer, one of the outstanding young Evangelical theologians, and Hans Schönfeld had interviews in Sweden with Dr. Bell, the Bishop of Chichester. They gave him the names of the leaders of the opposition, and Dr. Bell agreed to act as an intermediary. He spoke to Anthony Eden, inquiring if the British Government would be willing to negotiate with a new German government which should overthrow Hitler. The answer finally came back via Switzerland—in substance a flat "No."

Moltke was in Turkey several times and kept Allied representatives there informed of the hopes and plans of anti-Nazi Germans.

I used every opportunity to talk with foreign clergymen who

had the ear of their governments. When I visited Sweden in 1943 I spoke with an official of the British Foreign Office.

The policy of unconditional surrender proclaimed at Casablanca in January of 1943 seemed to doom our last hope of getting assurances abroad meeting the prerequisite set by the generals. It was not even possible to secure a promise of armistice in case the coup d'état should lead to a clash with the Waffen-SS. The German generals have often been blamed for their hesitation and their fatal indecision, but one should not condemn them without considering the other side of the question. I still believe that the generals could be expected to and had to commit high treason: in other words, to overthrow the Nazi government. But to ask them to betray the country itself to the enemy in time of war was to expect them to commit a dishonorable act according to their standards. This could not be expected of them.

The internal difficulties were no less formidable. It took years to reconcile our consciences to the necessity of assassination. The feeling of solidarity among the younger men from the military and civilian groups of German resistance, whose vision was directed more toward the future than toward the past, proved a more powerful and penetrating guide in shaping plans than the efforts of the older generation.

As a result of deep disappointment over the failure of the military, Carlo Mierendorff from the end of 1942 on constantly urged action by the civilian group. In this connection he brought into the circle Julius Leber, one of the strongest representatives of the former trade unions. Then death entered our group for the first time in the late fall of 1943 when Mierendorff was killed during a British air raid on Leipzig. In little more than a year most of the rest of the circle would be dead. After Mierendorff's death Leber, Reichwein, and Haubach worked on, planning the participation in the coup of units of the prohibited trade unions. They cooperated with Leuschner—former trade union leader and close associate of Goerdeler—who was slated to be vicechancellor in the post-Hitler cabinet.

Hitler reaped victory after victory, without altering our belief that Germany would be defeated and largely destroyed if he remained at the wheel. But the prospects of a coup grew dim and the preparations increasingly difficult. Time passed, with countless arrests and growing hopelessness.

One day Moltke stated in the Kreisau circle that we could obviously no longer count on a coup d'état, but should continue to develop practical political principles and work out forms of organization in anticipation of the complete defeat and temporary occupation of Germany. Our efforts thenceforth were directed toward policy planning. We saw no promise in a revival of the constitutional and political conditions which had permitted National Socialism to come to power. The mere reconstitution of the Weimar Republic did not appear adequate to ensure democracy in Germany. We considered a federative structure for the Reich, as a basis for participation in a European union to which we aspired. We put great emphasis on the creation of a new German social and economic order transcending the old party doctrines, for we were constantly aware of the tremendous potential strain on the German economy, which would be largely in ruins if the war were lost. And we wanted all German and European reconstruction to be founded on Christianity, for this corresponded to our personal experience in our life-and-death struggle for justice and human freedom.

It has been stated that the Kreisau circle, and especially Moltke, abandoned the idea of active resistance at the start and rejected a coup d'état. This is completely erroneous. For years Moltke worked with his friends toward the one goal of overthrowing National Socialism—whether by a coup or by engineering a military collapse. But Moltke did not belong to the military, and he always said that the execution of a coup had to be a military matter. That accomplished, our task was to be the promotion of a far-sighted, truly democratic self-regeneration. The two farewell letters that Moltke wrote in the Tegel prison shortly after he had been sentenced to death can in no way be taken as evidence of the rejection of a coup d'état by the Kreisau circle. They were not intended to represent our plans accurately, but were part of the defense we had jointly prepared during our trials for high treason and betrayal of the country. The idea underlying both of Moltke's letters was to demonstrate the nihilism and brutal corruption of National Socialism.

Although neither Moltke nor I was convicted of high treason, it must not be deduced that we did not in fact participate in it. We both acted with full knowledge and intent to prepare, at least, for high treason; Moltke could not, of course, have done more, for on July 20 he had been imprisoned for months. Every German who really wanted to achieve peace on earth, freedom for his Fatherland, and respect for the rights of man, had no alternative but to strive for Hitler's overthrow, even by force—and that meant high treason.

In the latter part of 1943 Count Fritz von der Schulenburg established a close link between the Kreisau circle and Count Claus von Stauffenberg, a cousin of Peter Yorck. He was a young, able, and intelligent staff officer who had risen quickly to the rank of colonel in the General Staff. He had been badly wounded, wore a black bandage over an empty eye socket, and had only one arm and but three fingers on his remaining hand. Stauffenberg gave an impression of reticence and good sense rather than of aggressiveness or military bluster. His formulations were unusually thoughtful for a soldier, his statements well considered and calm. I had opportunity to learn of his readiness to help when he assisted me in saving a group of clergymen from seizure by the SS and the Military Selection Commission. Stauffenberg succeeded in convincing Generals Beck and Olbricht and others that they must stake everything on one throw.

In January of 1944 Helmuth von Moltke was suddenly arrested. The reasons were peripheral. There was no immediate danger. A few months later one of my closest friends and colleagues, Wilhelm Bachmann, secretary of the Evangelical Welfare Association for internees and prisoners of war in Germany, was arrested for surreptitious aid he had been giving them. Expecting my own arrest momentarily, I disappeared to a remote mountain village in the province of Carinthia in Austria. But as X-Day was postponed over and over again, I started back to Berlin. En route I visited in Stuttgart with my old bishop, Dr. Wurm, to make final preparations for his assumption of all ecclesiastical tasks in anticipation of a successful coup.

Having reached Berlin at 3 A.M. on July 20 my wife and I went to Peter Yorck's small house in Berlin-Lichterfelde. A note in cipher awaited me there saying that Reichwein and Leber had been arrested. Peter Yorck came home a few hours later. "This is X-Day," he told us, and gave me the password of the conspiracy. A warrant for my arrest had already been issued. We were sure that the house was being watched.

We tried to get a little sleep. Then Yorck went to the War Ministry in the Bendlerstrasse.

The plan of the coup d'état, as I later came to know it in detail, called for the assassination of Hitler, Himmler, and, if possible Göring. Then detachments of the Reserve (or Home) Army were to march on Berlin and occupy it, to furnish military strength against the SS. Meanwhile, the Berlin Guard Battalion was to surround government buildings and protect the War Ministry. Similar plans had been made for the Reserve Army through all of Germany. The code word was "Walküre," the signal of army headquarters to all its subordinate commands that a state of emergency existed. Commanding officers would then open their top secret Walküre envelopes and carry out the instructions which had been prepared for, say, the collapse of the front or an Allied parachute attack in force. But they would also find something more that would startle them.

To the original Walküre code, which was merely the signal for an emergency program, the conspirators in the Reserve Army had added further sealed orders including provisions for the establishment of martial law, the cessation of all political activity, and occupation of all public buildings. They also included the location of the Gestapo's secret headquarters, data on the reliability of various district army officers, and a list of the potential hiding places of the top Nazis, as well as the names of civilians who were to advise the military commander of each district.

Further orders were to be given to the military forces abroad, who were to arrest SS officials under their command. Once the orders had been issued, General Beck was to announce on the Deutschlandsender that Hitler was dead, that he himself was now Chief of State and Witzleben Commander of the Armed Forces, and that there would be a three-day state of emergency during which Nazi resistance would be liquidated and a cabinet formed. The new cabinet would start armistice negotiations immediately.

Stauffenberg had volunteered to place the bomb, and was therefore assigned to a position in the Reserve Army where, as Chief of Staff, he would have access to the briefing at Hitler's headquarters at Rastenburg in East Prussia. The assassination was twice postponed because Himmler was not present. The first time the code word had already been issued in order to reduce the three-hour time lapse between the order and its execution. It was not easy to explain away this false alarm.

Finally it was decided to carry out the assassination on July 20 even though Hitler might be alone. Carrying the briefcase containing the bomb, Stauffenberg entered the barrack in Rastenburg which was used for the briefing at about 12.30 P.M. He placed the briefcase on the floor.

Shortly after the briefing had started Stauffenberg's adjutant, Lt. Werner von Haeften, brother of Hans von Haeften, called him out on the pretext that he was wanted on the telephone. Before leaving Stauffenberg pushed the pin of the bomb in the briefcase. Then he hurried to his car. One hundred seconds later, before they had reached the car, they heard a loud explosion. A few moments later they were on their way to the airfield. They flew to Berlin-Adlershof.

In the meantime the chief conspirators, including General Beck, were assembled at the War Ministry in the office of General Olbricht, deputy commander of the Reserve Army, awaiting news of Hitler's death. The commanding general of the Reserve Army, Fromm, had been removed from his post and was under arrest in another room. He had been replaced by Colonel General Hoeppner.

An official message came through from Rastenburg that some officers of Hitler's group had been wounded, but nothing was said of Hitler's having been killed. Orders to the field commanders were sent out under the Walküre code name. Fifty teletypes and hundreds of telephones operated busily, sending messages about an SS attack on the Wehrmacht. High SS leaders were ordered arrested. In Paris everything functioned smoothly, and before the Gestapo and the SS knew what was happening they had been arrested on orders of General von Stülpnagel.

But almost immediately difficulties arose in Berlin. The Berlin

Guard Battalion, commanded by a Major Remer, was to play a crucial part in the plot. The conspirators were doubtful of Remer and would have preferred someone more reliable than this Nazi, but they decided that removing him and putting him on furlough as had been done with some other commanders might arouse suspicion. When Major Remer was told that Hitler was dead and received orders to surround government buildings, he was puzzled and called his company commanders to ask their advice. A National Socialist political officer, assigned to the unit for political control, propaganda, and indoctrination purposes, suggested that he consult Goebbels, for whom he had once worked.

They went together to see Goebbels. He connected them by telephone with Rastenburg. Goebbels, as a civilian, could not countermand military orders, but Hitler could. Above all, Hitler could be proved to be alive by means of this phone call. The communication system at Rastenburg was supposed to have been destroyed by one of the conspirators, but he had failed. Hitler talked with Major Remer and ordered him to put down the revolt and shoot as many people as he wished.

Then events moved swiftly to the doom of the men engaged in the conspiracy. General Guderian, Inspector General of Armored Divisions, helped suppress the revolt in Berlin, and he and Major Remer stopped the troops that were pouring in. The Führer's headquarters countermanded the orders of Berlin, and Himmler announced that he was now commander of the Reserve Army. The SS around Berlin were quicker and more ruthless than the Wehrmacht. When one Wehrmacht unit returned to their barracks at Crampnitz they found them burned and their fellows who had remained behind massacred. By 8 P.M. the Berlin Military District Commander, General von Thuengen, who earlier in the day had replaced the Nazi General Kortzfleisch, was wavering, and by nine o'clock control of the city was again in the hands of the Nazis. The Guard Battalion had indeed formed outside the War Ministry as requested, but not as protection to the conspirators.

I waited all day for news, knowing nothing definite. About 5 P.M. the radio announced the failure of the assassination.

Strangely enough, I had no doubt that this was an accurate statement. Soon the telephone rang. Peter Yorck asked me to join them at the War Ministry. I put my Bible in one pocket, my pistol in the other. My wife, fully aware of the significance of the event, accompanied me to the nearest streetcar. We said good-by, knowing that only a miracle could prevent the inevitable unfolding of the tragedy.

But we had not yet given up hope of the miracle. Colonel General Hoeppner at the War Ministry transferred to me the provisional authority over the Reich Ministry of the Church and Education. This obliged me to abstain from the use of arms, except in case of extreme urgency, and to concern myself above all with a humane transition to a new constititional system.

During the next hours we witnessed the complete collapse of the conspiracy. The partial successes of the coup were annulled by the failure of the assassination. The last attempt for German liberation had failed.

The failure to broadcast over the Deutschlandsender had a serious effect on the course of the coup. A civilian who had undertaken to clarify the situation over the radio failed to do so. When nothing happened word was sent to Colonel General Hoeppner to use troops to bring the radio station under our control. Hoeppner promised to use armored vehicles, which had left their station in Zossen near Berlin according to orders and should have been approaching. But for some reason they never arrived in the Bendlerstrasse.

The situation became more and more critical. Suddenly we heard shots in the corridors. Stauffenberg left the room from which he had been directing activities in the military areas throughout the Reich. We took our pistols. But it was hard to determine who was shooting whom. It soon turned out that some officers on the staff of Generals Olbricht and Fromm who had participated in the coup that morning had deserted us, in order to save their lives in face of the approaching SS. These men had tried to disarm their comrades stealthily and shoot them.

The battle was lost. We were overwhelmed and arrested. General Olbricht, Stauffenberg, and some of his closest military colleagues, including Lt. Werner von Haeften, were condemned to death on the spot. Men of the Grossdeutschland Battalion immediately executed them in the courtyard by the light of armored cars. Beck shot himself. Peter Yorck, Fritz von der Schulenburg, Schwerin, Berthold von Stauffenberg—the brother of Claus— Colonel Bernardis of the General Staff, and I were overpowered and handcuffed by a group headed by Skorzeny, the liberator of Mussolini. We too expected to be executed. But a sudden counterorder led to our being taken from the place of execution to the cellars of the Gestapo in the Prinz Albrechtstrasse.

As I look back today I doubt that the situation could have been saved by handling the coup differently or by the use of all available arms and the immediate execution of all high National Socialist leaders who were within reach.

We had done with life, our struggle for freedom was lost. The torment of slow death began. The interrogations were carried out by devilish means.

The day after the coup Neuhaus, an SS leader, read a copy of the warrant for my arrest made out ten years earlier and noted indignantly, "He tried it once before—ten years ago!"

During the months of interrogation I was incriminated even further by statements, of which the Gestapo had learned, made by key men of groups of foreign displaced persons whom I had helped during the war. To this day I do not know how the Gestapo got the information. I cannot tell if it was of any help to me that I made no confession of consequence, even in the face of threats and under torture—modestly called "intense" interrogation—in the Gestapo cellars.

One after another, my Kreisau friends died on the gallows of the Plötzensee prison. The first to be executed was the one closest to me, Count Peter Yorck; then followed Fritz Schulenburg, Schwerin, Adam von Trott and Hans von Haeften, and finally Reichwein and Leber. My turn was to come, but the date of my trial was repeatedly postponed.

Through it all I cherished, in a strange, inner, religious way, the feeling that my path would lead not to death but to life and freedom. The friends in the cells to right and left of me pitied me for what they considered my cruelly fixed idea.

Finally in January of 1945 Moltke, Father Delp, Haubach,

Steltzer, and I were tried before the First Senate of the People's Court. We knew we had no chance. We had to expect sentence of death by hanging, which the prosecuting Oberreichsanwalt had demanded for us. Moltke, Haubach, and Delp died on the gallows. Steltzer, who had also been sentenced to death, escaped death with the help of the Norwegian underground.

Over the protest of the Gestapo, Judge Freisler sentenced me to seven years in prison. Soon afterward the Russians broke across the Oder River. Most of the prisoners of the People's Court were quickly transported to southern Germany. I was sent to Bayreuth.

A few weeks later heavy tanks of the American Army took Bayreuth. A group of political prisoners was to be executed, but some sensible person abstained from carrying out this order. Consequently, thousands of political prisoners of many nationalities were liberated. I walked through the town of Bayreuth, free —but alone. Now I must face the task of carrying out my friends' legacy—to aid the survivors of war and of the Nazi oppression.

EPILOGUE TO CHAPTER IX

The Church Conspiratorial

I N MAY, 1945, a representative of the International Red Cross
came to Bayreuth from Geneva. Surprised that Dr. Gerstenmaier had survived, and shocked over his state of health, he
arranged to take him to Switzerland to recuperate.

In August, 1945, when the Hilfswerk, or the Protestant Relief
Society, was founded, Dr. Gerstenmaier was made its head.
Through the society all the Protestant churches in Germany are
sharing with their limited means in alleviating the want of the
children and young people, the sick, the bombed-out, and the
homeless among the twelve million Germans who were evicted
from the east.

PROLOGUE TO CHAPTER X

Reich Secret

GÜNTHER WEISENBORN was born in the Rhineland in 1902. He was only twenty-six when his first play, *U-Boat S 4*, scored a hit. Since then he has written a number of other successful plays.

The underground organization of which he speaks here was one of the largest and most active in Germany, and its discovery led to the Third Reich's greatest spy trial, known in Gestapo files as "Red Orchestra." Because of the secrecy surrounding the trial little is known about the group even today. It included probably the only American woman who fought for a free Germany.

X

Reich Secret

GÜNTHER WEISENBORN

IN THE spring of 1937, when I could not stand living in Nazi Germany any longer, I emigrated to the United States. I worked as a reporter in New York City. But from many conversations with friends I saw clearly that I ought to return to Germany in order to fight for freedom. I could go back without danger as I was not Jewish and the Nazis had no political record against me. And so after six months in the United States I went back.

Not long after my arrival I met Luftwaffe Lieutenant Harro Schulze-Boysen, a gifted young man with a revolutionary spirit who was a descendant of Admiral Tirpitz. His political inclinations were leftist and he was an unswerving opponent of the Nazis. In 1933 a group of Storm Troopers had taken him to one of their cellars and for three days subjected him to brutal mistreatment. Berlin police chief von Levetzow freed him by sending a police contingent to raid the cellar—which led to Levetzow's dismissal. Schulze-Boysen was in bad shape; one of his kidneys was seriously injured and he had spent three months in the hospital.

Through connections of his family he got a position in the Air Ministry, which was then not so strongly under party influence as in later Nazi years. He had a brilliant gift for languages and spoke Danish, Swedish, Italian, French, English, and Russian. He also had keen political insight; for instance, a year before Stalingrad he predicted that the decisive battle would be fought there because that was where the crucial east-west and north-south lines crossed. Through his engaging personality and influence on the people he met, he quickly succeeded in organizing a group of passionate opponents of Hitler.

For weeks Harro and I searched each other's ideas and views in conversation. When I was ready to participate actively in his group he invited me to come to his home. A few other men were there. I had no idea then that this small band of six men, which had started in 1936, would develop into one of the most extensive and effective resistance organizations.

We kept strict discipline and secrecy. For instance, I never met Arvid Harnack, a nephew of the theologian, who was the other head of the group. He was older than Harro, a scholarly, careful person who held an important position in the Reich Economics Ministry.

Arvid Harnack's wife, Mildred Fish, whom he met while studying in the United States in the 'twenties, was an American born in Milwaukee. She took her doctor's degree in Germany, had translated Edmond's *Drums Along the Mohawk* and Stone's *Lust for Life* into German, and lectured on American literature at the Berlin People's University. When the Harnacks visited Mildred's family in the United States in 1937 they were urged to leave Germany for good. They could not talk about their anti-Nazi work, and some acquaintances, misinterpreting their silence as indicating approval of the Nazis, were critical of them.

Many of the group which formed over the years were young, joyous people, full of energy and enthusiasm. They were scientists, scholars, workers, artists, officers, who fought for peace against the arch warmonger. There was the young doctor John Rittmeister, the defiant and gifted sculptor Kurt Schumacher; a young student, Horst Heilmann; the sinologist Philipp Schaeffer. Holders of widely different political and ideological views found themselves united against the common enemy. There were determined Communists and equally determined opponents of Communism. Some were devout Christians impelled by religious principles, others joined for purely patriotic reasons. But the general trend of political thinking was to the left.

We were divided into a series of subgroups which distributed leaflets in many factories. At times our places of work served as illegal centers for preparing leaflets, procuring addresses, and obtaining materials.

One series of leaflets, called Agis writings, had titles like "What is the Meaning of a Majority?" "How We Were Led into War,"

"Why the War Is Lost," "Appeal to All Callings and Organizations to Resist the Government," "Freedom and Force." Their printing was arranged by the artist Bontjes van Beek. Leaflets of another subgroup were printed by John Graudenz, a former United Press correspondent who also operated a secret radio station. These were left in such places as the U-Bahn or telephone booths. Many were sent to addresses which were selected from the phone book. Of course we took precautions, wore gloves, used different typewriters, and carefully destroyed carbon papers. We also put out a secret paper, first *The Advance Guard* and later *The Inner Front*, which was published biweekly in German, French, Italian, Russian, Czech, and Polish.

We had regular channels of communication with Switzerland, Sweden, and Czechoslovakia. Foreigners forced to work in Germany participated in the group and were organized in "legions." Many of them took part in our conferences and some wrote articles for the secret paper.

We used speeches of foreign statesmen and churchmen or of men like Thomas Mann for leaflets. Sometimes we went out at night on "poster actions," pasting up on walls and buildings posters calling for the end of the war. In 1941, after the war with the Soviet Union started, sixty of the group, protected by officers with pistols ready, went out on one of the largest poster actions, putting up a placard which read

"THE NAZI PARADISE:
War, Hunger, Terror, Misery
How Much Longer?"

For use at night the group also constructed a contraption which looked like a suitcase. When it was set down in the street it stamped some anti-Nazi slogan on the pavement.

We helped the persecuted and oppressed, and collected food and money for Jewish friends. We liberated one man from concentration camp and took him to Switzerland, and conducted two fugitives from the Gestapo abroad in a sailboat.

Our work was both exciting and nerve wracking. About four weeks after I joined, Gisela von Pöllnitz, a member of the group, was arrested. As a precaution Harro, Kurt Schumacher, and I loaded masses of leaflets into our cars that night, to remove them from our apartments to safer places. For a few weeks we lay low; some made plans to flee abroad. Gisela managed to remain silent and the danger passed. She died a short time after that.

It was in the group that I met the girl who in January, 1941, became my wife. Joy had joined in 1938 through Libertas, née Countess Eulenburg, Harro's wife.

I continued my work as free-lance writer. One day early in the war Harro drove me to the huge building of the Reich Broadcasting Company. According to our plan I was to get a job there and within a year should be taking part in the secret conferences of the corporation. How? I would have to find a way. I did get a job in the information section and after a year I was in on the secret conferences. Thus I acquired regular information on secret material from government sources which I passed on to Harro. Other members of the group were also well placed; Carl Helfrich for instance had a post in the Foreign Ministry.

Occasionally I took home copies of the speeches of foreign statesmen, which we received in the Broadcasting Company as secret material. Joy and I copied them and I returned them the next morning. If necessary we translated them. Someone called for our typescript and tens of thousands of copies were printed. Thus Roosevelt's, Stalin's, or Churchill's speeches sometimes circulated in Berlin as quickly as Nazi speeches.

Now and then it was possible to put something over on the Nazis and have it pass off as a mistake. Some of our group directed important military freight trains to wrong destinations. Once the head of a section of the Broadcasting Company gave me a report that 32,000 doctors had been killed in the Soviet Union in one year—Nazi propaganda which was to serve as evidence of whole-sale killing of intellectuals. I added a zero and the news was broadcast that 320,000 Soviet doctors had been killed. I was violently taken to task, and deplored the mistake in dictation. The Moscow and London radio picked up the fantastic statement as further proof of what any listener must have noticed: that the Greater German Broadcasting Station was lying.

About thirty of our group had a meeting on the Wannsee on August 30, 1942. We went out in a number of sailboats, some our own, others borrowed, and sailed around, inconspicuous among hundreds of other boats. Someone played a guitar, someone else a mouth organ. Others cooked lunch in their boat on a small alcohol stove. It was an unworried and joyful Sunday, a happy contrast to the many tense nights of fear and hard work. But at the same time we discussed our work and made further plans. As our boats slowly approached the landing pier none of us had an inkling that arrests of our group would start the next day.

Shortly after our Wannsee meeting Oskar Ingenohl, an acquaintance, told me that a friend of his, a young soldier, had left with him for safekeeping a suitcase containing pamphlets, manuscripts, and political writings. There was something peculiar about it; would I look it over? In case of danger an illegal group would sometimes leave its material with some respectable citizen. This seemed to be the case here. I wondered what sort of group it was. I agreed to ride with him to his apartment, and we opened the suitcase. As I looked at the papers the floor seemed to give way under me. I recognized Harro's handwriting on drafts, and his doctor's thesis. This was the material of our own group—placed in hiding, a sign of danger!

I managed to conceal my panic from Oskar so that he noticed nothing extraordinary in my reactions. We drank coffee and talked about indifferent matters. I advised him to keep the suitcase well hidden, not to speak of it, to show it to no one. He let me take some of the manuscripts along.

I went to a telephone booth and called Harro at the Air Ministry.

"He is away on an official trip."

"When will he be back?"

"That's uncertain."

Arrested. Our chief had been arrested.

I alerted the friends I could reach. Joy was on vacation in Sorenbohm, a little village on the Baltic Sea. I asked her to return as soon as possible, and she came at once. We cleaned out dangerous papers and books from our apartment. With other friends we prepared our statements and checked them against each other to make sure they agreed.

Early on the morning of September 26 a knock at the door

woke us. It was five o'clock and still dark. I opened. Four men in civilian clothes stood there ominously, their hands in their coat pockets.

"Criminal Police."

They distributed themselves over the apartment. One of them checked the radio. Their spokesman was a Gestapo commissar.

"You are both to come with us. Pack a bag; you may be gone some time."

Joy got a small bag.

"Do you think you'll share a cell?" he snorted at her. "Pack two bags." When she tripped over a rug in the excitement he commented, "Fall slowly, you'll enjoy it more."

When we left two of the men remained behind. Two cars were parked on the street. Joy was put in one, I in the other. Some of the house residents were watching behind the curtains.

A large number of arrests had been made. The Gestapo cellar of the Prinz Albrechtstrasse was full of our friends and members of our group—130 in all. I saw former Minister of Education Adolf Grimme, Professor Dr. Werner Krauss, the physicians Elfriede Paul and John Rittmeister; the writers Adam Kuckhoff, Arnold Bauer, Walter Küchenmeister. The numerous women, most of whom were young, were held in the Alexanderplatz. Two of them gave birth to babies in prison. One child was removed to an SS hospital which informed the mother that it had died. The other was taken away after the mother had nursed it for six weeks. Both mothers were executed soon afterward.

Interrogations were conducted by Gestapo Section Four, headed by Panzinger, a high SS leader. Two of our group, John Sieg and Herbert Grasse, committed suicide after torture for fear they might weaken. Even women were beaten and tortured with leg clamps and thumb screws. The Gestapo put stool pigeons in the cells. One of them claimed to be a cousin of Schulze-Boysen. Another was a pretty, red-haired woman named Gertrud Breiter. Libertas Schulze-Boysen wrote in her last letter that she had confided in Gertrud Breiter, who had betrayed everything.

It was very quiet in the cellar where we were held prisoner. The SS guards passed and repassed in the halls on silent rubber soles. Occasionally I heard the cough of a neighbor through the thick walls or the clash of the special steel handcuffs. Sometimes a door opened and a cold voice commanded: "Interrogation . . . Come." Two men hasten through the corridor; the steps die away. In the distance the elevator door clangs shut and there is the hum of the lift ascending. After a long time the steps again —but slower. The cell door clicks open, slams shut. The prisoner is once more alone—with what thoughts?

One afternoon at four the flap on my door falls. The SS guard looks through it and calls in, "You'll be sent for right away—" and then the dread word, "—for interrogation." I sit benumbed. My heart begins to pound. I start feverishly to map out my plan of battle. If he asks so and so? Wants to know this or that? Find the answer. Quickly. They'll call for you right away. It is five o'clock.

I sit with teeth clenched, determined, charged with energy, tense, ready for the struggle. Again and again my thoughts run over all sorts of possibilities. Six o'clock; I get my soup. Afterward a hurried pacing in my cell. My thoughts race in a circle. I get tired. It is eight o'clock. I lie on the cot, ready to jump up. My thoughts begin to be confused. The cell is cold, I am freezing like a dog. I hear the clock strike ten. I am all in.

It's senseless, all this. Eleven o'clock. I am as if paralyzed after this needless waste of energy. I don't care. I lie with eyes open. Twelve o'clock. They won't come now. And if they do come, I don't care. I am tired.

Finally—about 1.30—the keys clatter, the door opens. A pale, malicious-looking SS guard shouts at me, "Come on, up! Interrogation!" I get up groggily and follow him. They don't want a fresh, rested man. One is supposed to have lost his nerve before it starts.

I am taken to the Reich Security Headquarters. I sit down on a chair. The room has all the earmarks of an ordinary office. The man at the desk is sharpening a pencil to a pin point. He seems to relish it. It takes a long time. It is deathly still in the room in which we sit—prisoner and Gestapo commissar. I shall learn more of him later. His name is Habecker and he is one of the torturers. A newspaper article about him tells how he tortured an

Englishman in Dachau. He is short, broadly built, with a baldish head and a Hitler mustache under his sweaty nose. It is the sort of face one describes as the face of a criminal. From its unclean greyness two dirt-colored sharp-shooter's eyes dart at me ominously at times. His thick jaw shows a brutal hardness.

He cuts a cigarette in two, lights it, arranges papers and pencils methodically, takes out a file, and is ready. The chess game opens.

He starts with a criminal's broad, comfortable question: "Now tell me, what sort of company do you keep?"

That night the game is a draw.

Another time the commissar asks if the word "pasting" was used one evening on the telephone. Harro had called me to ask if I would come join in sticking up posters that night. I admit the phone conversation but deny that we spoke of pasting.

Then the commissar reads me a statement of my wife's. She maintains that it was she at the phone, that I was not even in the room. She has said that in order to protect me and to bear the brunt herself. I feel warm and am quiet in happiness for a while before I set the matter straight. The phone call proved means a charge of being accessory and that means a penitentiary sentence. Joy has made up her mind to go to the penitentiary in my stead, to take my burden on her small shoulders!

Again I am led into the room of the commissar, miserable, unshaven, shivering with cold. Four men in civilian clothes sit across from me.

They look at me and I wait in a paralysis of tension, fear, and defiance. And again I tell myself the old rule: "Admit nothing. Don't answer at once. Be careful!"

The heat in the room is suffocating. The radiator at my side almost burns through my overcoat. I breathe softly and quickly and wait, wondering where they will shoot from today.

The question comes from the commissar, Habecker: "Where is Paul Braun?"

Quick as a flash I think what I have said about Paul Braun. I saw him once for a moment, in an inn. I have told them this and it's the truth. So they don't know where he is. They haven't caught him. I know where he is; at least I know the bookshop where he worked. But these men do not know that I know his place of work.

I shrug my shoulders and say, "I don't know."

"Think it over carefully."

"I met him once years ago. I have never seen him since."

Now come either the gradually mounting threats or a question pursuing another line—and they'll suddenly return to this later. My hands are cold and moist, the handcuffs are getting heavy. The heat stifles me.

The commissar bends over and says casually, with a suggestion of hurt innocence:

"Tell us where Braun is, and we'll release your wife at once."

I would do anything to get her free—but not this. The commissar knows all our letters. He knows that each would sacrifice himself for the other. That's the basis of his plan. All four stare at me. I am sick with the heat and excitement. More than ever I am conscious that I am a miserable enervated victim of the Gestapo. Could I mislead them? No, they would only release her after arresting Paul Braun. Misleading them is ruled out.

So I declare with open mien, "You know I would do anything for my wife, but unfortunately I do not know where Paul Braun is."

What now? Will he go into a rage? Will it start again? There are four of them now . . . But nothing like that happens.

One of them takes me into the hall while the other three talk it over. After fifteen minutes comes the release: "Take him down, Philipp!"

The odds were piling up against me. At first only one deposition, made by a young woman, was held against me. While there was only one it was not so bad. Two were necessary for a death sentence. I would get only the penitentiary.

Then one day the blow came. I was incriminated by another statement, made by Kurt Schumacher. Kurt was courageous and brave; it had slipped out inadvertently under the terrible pressure.

I returned to my cell. Now it was all over. What should I do? Perhaps I could die in my own way. When next I got a pair of scissors to cut my nails, I waited for a moment when the guard standing at the door was not so attentive. Quickly and without being noticed I made two slits in the bed sheet. Now I felt better. I could tear off a narrow strip. At last I had a way out: a trump about which no one knew.

One morning the trusty with his customary pleasant smile gave me as usual the broom to sweep out the cell. Sweeping at the open door I got a glimpse into the next cell, No. 8. I saw a blond head—Kurt. He saw me, we smiled. I went back, for the guard was coming.

There was nothing I could do about the first statement against me. The woman could never take it back; she had been executed. But Kurt was living, in the cell next to mine.

I looked at the wall. It was an arm's length in thickness. Kurt had to withdraw his statement; I had to find a way to communicate with him.

That evening toward ten o'clock I was knocking at the wall for my life. Lying on the cot covered by the wool blanket, I tapped at the wall with the end of my pencil. Then I lay still. At any moment the light might go on and the guard look in at me through the judas. I began to tap at regular intervals. Kurt repeated my taps exactly. The sounds were faint as if very distant. I knocked once for a, twice for b, three times for c. He knocked back irregularly. He didn't understand. I repeated. He didn't understand. I repeated. He didn't understand. I repeated a hundred times. He didn't understand.

I wiped off the sweat, and tried to master my despair. He tapped signals which I did not understand; I tapped symbols which he did not understand. We were helpless.

He emphasized some tones, softened others. Was it Morse? I did not know Morse.

The alphabet has twenty-six letters. For every letter I tapped its number in the alphabet: eight taps for h, sixteen for p . . . Different sounds came back which I did not grasp. It was 2 A.M. We had to establish contact. I tapped . for a, .. for b, ... for c. Muffled and remote came the answer, — —. — — —. —.. No meeting of minds.

But the next night I heard it, quite soft but certain: . .. ... Then a definite signal: twenty-two even knocks. I counted with him. That was the letter v. Then five knocks. After that an r, which I counted breathlessly with precision. Then an s, a t, an e, an h, an e: "v e r s t e h e."

"Understand!" I lay under the wool blanket, limp and happy. We had contact from brain to brain, not by mouth but through our hands. Human intelligence had overcome the thick walls of the Gestapo cellar. I was wet with sweat, overwhelmed by the contact. I knocked back one word: "good."

Later I knocked: "You . . . must . . . take . . . back . . . your . . . statement . . ."

He knocked back: "Why?"

"Is . . . second . . . statement . . . against . . . me . . . means . . . death . . . sentence . . ."

"I . . . didn't . . . know . . . take . . . back . . ."

"Thanks . . ."

"Tomorrow . . ."

"What . . . do . . . you . . . need . . . ?"

"Pencil . . ."

"Tomorrow . . . walk . . ."

Suddenly the light went on. The SS guard looked in. I lay still under the blanket. It got dark again. I had tears in my eyes. "Take back!" I shall never forget. The knocks came softly and smoothly through the wall. A number of barely audible sounds, and they meant that I would be saved. That night it was only an idea in the brain of a death candidate, over there in cell No. 8, invisible, minute. Tomorrow it would be converted into words, then it would become a signed statement in the office, and some day it would be there before the court. Thanks for eternity, Kurt.

I broke off part of my pencil and carried it with me during the daily walk. Five others whom I did not know walked with me in a circle around the small courtyard. Back in the hall three of us stood, far apart, waiting a few seconds for the guard. I darted over to cell No. 8, opened the flap, and threw the pencil in. I shall never forget the surprised look in Kurt's blue eyes, his pale face, the hands which lay handcuffed in front of him on the table. Then I closed the flap quietly and stepped back to my place. The guard came around the corner. My heart rose to my throat.

We were locked in our cells.

Not long after this Kurt knocked, "Thanks . . . took . . . back . . . statement."

I was saved. Perhaps.

After eight months in prison I was taken out of the cell. There, with a Gestapo official, stood Joy. Only bars separated us. She told me that she had been released for lack of evidence. She had been interrogated only once. I could not speak for happiness. I went back to my cell and whistled all day in my supreme joy. And then I wrote a letter, a letter to my wife in freedom.

From interrogations we learned that the group of which we had been a part was much larger than most of us had known. About 600 persons had been arrested, of whom some 270 were imprisoned in Berlin. Our part represented only the "inner front." Schulze-Boysen and Harnack had also created an "outer front," a resistance group which was in constant radio communication with foreign countries. Harro had direct contact with Russia. One secret radio station was on a sailboat in the Wannsee and broadcast information for ten minutes at night. The Nazis had become deeply concerned about how easily important secret information reached enemy countries.

It turned out that one of Harro's closest collaborators, Horst Heilmann, who was working in the monitoring service of the Air Ministry, had known that a secret broadcasting station "Choro" was being searched for but had no idea that it was a station of our group. When he found out by accident, he hurried to Harro to warn him, but he came too late. The Gestapo had been looking for us for years, and a wireless message from Brussels was the touch which opened the sluice gates of arrest.

I had been in prison for many months when a Gestapo official came to my cell and read off, very quickly, the charges against me. But I got nothing in writing.

As I was led to the Reich Military Court, a man in a black gown with a bald hawklike head and horn-rimmed spectacles came up to me. "I am your official defense counsel. I know your file. Don't worry unnecessarily. You know that the death penalty is the maximum you can get. I'll see you later."

These were the only words exchanged between us, and this was the total extent of my legal preparation for a trial for my life.

The court room door bore the sign "Secret Session." I entered a large room. All our trials were being handled by the highest military court of the Wehrmacht, because Schulze-Boysen was an officer and a number of other officers had been in the top ranks of the group. Hitler and Göring received daily reports of the trial and classified it "Secret." Anyone talking about it could be prosecuted for revealing a Reich secret.

We six defendants filed in. The judges were two generals, an admiral, and two other officers. On the right was Roeder, one of the senior prosecutors of the Wehrmacht; below him sat the defense.

I asked for defense witnesses. Request refused. The trial lasted half an hour. Roeder asked the death sentence for five of the six.

Death. I had a feeling of relief. At last I would have rest. I looked at the others. They stood pale and firm. When the judges retired we went up to each other, over the protest of the guards, and shook hands for the last time, before being handcuffed.

Next day the court pronounced sentence on me: "Three years in the penitentiary." As only one incriminating statement counted against me I was sentenced for being an accessory. I could not thank Kurt. He had already been executed.

In the past months the scaffold had taken its heavy toll. Harro, still in his early thirties, was in the first group of eleven to be hanged. He had hidden a poem in his cell and told another death candidate about it, who in turn told a comrade who survived. Three and a half years after Harro's death the poem was found in the ruins of the Gestapo building in the Prinz Albrechtstrasse. It ended with this verse:

> Die letzten Argumente
> sind Strang und Fallbeil nicht.
> Und unsre Richter heute
> sind nicht das Weltgericht.*

* The final arguments
Are not the rope or knife.
And those today our judges
sit not on Judgment Day.

Kurt Schumacher wrote some notes with his bit of pencil and left them in a crack of the floor of his cell. They end with the words:

"Man differs from the beast in that he thinks and can act according to his own will. Terrible is the lot of a human flock of sheep which is chased to slaughter and knows not wherefore. But we fought for our cause.

"Handcuffed. November 2, 1942."

Two girls, the twenty-seven-year-old student Ursula Goetze and twenty-one-year-old Eva Maria Buch, incriminated themselves to save others. Eva Maria Buch had translated a French article for *The Inner Front*. In order to protect the author she declared that she had written it, and thereby pronounced her own death sentence. The prison chaplain reported that she died like a saint.

When the state prosecutor asked the death penalty for eleven accused and eight years in prison for Countess Erika von Brockdorf, she broke out in loud laughter. Prosecutor Roeder shouted at her, "You will stop laughing." And he requested a new trial for her which ended in a death sentence and execution.

At Easter in 1942 the sinologist Dr. Philipp Schaeffer had tried to save an old Jewish couple who were committing suicide by gas. When the janitor would not let him batter in the door of the apartment, Philipp used an air-raid rope hanging from the third floor to climb into the second-floor window. The rope broke and he fell to the pavement, suffering a concussion and fractures of the pelvis and thigh. He was arrested in the hospital and charged with being an accessory because he had not reported the activities of his friends to the Gestapo. Before sentence was pronounced he rose with the aid of his crutches and told the court proudly, "Gentlemen, I have been asked why I did not report this matter. I can only reply to that: I am not a police stooge." The sentence was death.

Mildred Harnack was at first sentenced to six years in the penitentiary. The courier who reported that to Hitler brought back his order that she was to be executed. "And I loved Germany so deeply," she said when she was told. Pölchau, the prison chaplain found her immersed in translating some verses of Goethe's, writing on the walls. One verse read:

"All is given by the Gods, the unending ones,
    To those whom they love—they withhold nothing.
    All joys, unendingly,
    All pain, unendingly—they withhold nothing."
She had done with this world and put up a wall around herself
in order to reduce her suffering.

In the nine months before the trial I had been in three prisons
—Prinz Albrechtstrasse, Moabit, and Spandau—later to house
top Nazi war criminals. Now I was sent to the penitentiary in
Luckau, about forty-five miles southeast of Berlin.

I glued paper bags in a cell with a former prison inspector and
a former Minister. The inspector, a blond Saxon, had been behind bars for three years but had not lost his sense of humor. The
Minister was Grimme who had been sentenced with me. He was
extraordinarily good company. When we ran out of bags we
talked, played chess with bits of paper, and hunted bugs. It was
one of my pleasantest times in prison. It did not last long.

Sometimes we heard faint thunder in the distance. Looking
north at night we could see a vague reddish line on the horizon.
Tiny white rays circled against the sky. It looked pretty and
dreamlike. But it was a heavy attack on Berlin and hell was being
let loose there. And there were our fears and our hopes: our wives,
children, relatives, and homes. In the course of weeks we got
letters, and some prisoners were more depressed than usual.

I was put into a dormitory, Ward IV. One Sunday afternoon
about two o'clock the guard who sat eternally at a table there
inspected us. He was annoyed because one prisoner had left his
book lying in his wardrobe with the back to the left instead of to
the right. The culprit was a feeble Dutch boy, a journeyman
baker who spoke only with difficulty. The guard, a heavily built,
excitable official, ordered us all to attention. Wild with rage, he
started swinging his rubber truncheon at the small, screaming
boy, chasing him up and down the ward as if he were trying to
catch a bat. We stood at attention. After half an hour the guard
sat down at his table, panting, and abused the Dutch boy verbally
until he had caught his breath. Then he beat him again till he
lay on the floor bleeding. We stood at attention. There were

forty of us and we could have torn the guard to pieces. We would of course have been killed. In a white heat of fury, we continued to stand at attention. At 4.30 the guard was relieved. He went off in his clean Sunday uniform, his trousers neatly creased. He undoubtedly drank his beer that evening, played Skat, and probably grumbled at home over a vexing day.

Cold, bugs, military discipline, hunger, and hard work were our daily lot. I unloaded coal. "Faster, faster!" I hurt my hand and it became infected. They warned me not to go to the dispensary. I thought I knew better and went. The orderly cut into the pussy wound with a dirty scalpel and pressed. The next day I had blood poisoning. I felt miserable and went back to the dispensary. "Go to the devil, coming with such a trivial matter." But I recovered.

"Whoever gets sick is dead," the prisoners said. Two inmates died a day. We were a thousand. That meant we would die out in one and a half years. But newcomers arrived and the wheel went on turning.

Later on, I worked in a group which reinforced the roadbeds under railroad tracks. The pace was excessive, and we were cold and hungry. But when the guard was not watching I had a chance to give a section hand a letter for my wife. On a certain afternoon at a definite hour she should come to the Rochau rail stop where we boarded the train to go back to the penitentiary.

Late one afternoon I knew this would be the day. I marched back to the railroad stop in the first row. Two people were standing there, a workman and a woman.

She stood, small and graceful, that dreary, silent October day. There was the clap-clap of our wooden clogs and then the "Halt" of the senior guard. "Tools down! At ease!"

My companions murmured quietly, winked at each other, and nodded toward the dame. They had no idea that she was my wife, that she had traveled two days to look at me at this lonely rail stop.

We were enraptured. My blood never beat so hard and never did I despair so bitterly. Now she began to whistle as a lone girl might whistle to herself in boredom. It was one of our own songs which drifted, thin and quivering, across the tracks. I stood as if stunned. When she stopped I continued the melody, softly and barely audible. Paul, the Jehovah's Witness, advised me, "You better stop that."

The senior guard looked around with stony eyes and asked lazily, "Is one of you whistling?"

"No," I said, and added, so that she could hear my voice, "No, Herr Oberwachtmeister!"

Then the train pulled in, a last glance, and we were separated for another year.

Time passed and the end was drawing near. We slaved in the fields, we felled wood. One day an American fighter plane chased a German fighter into the ground—this in the center of Germany. It impressed us.

We worked in a factory that made tarpaper roofing. One of the foremen was a French prisoner named Gaston. He gave us food and was a comrade to us all. He sang while he worked, no matter how heavy the load. When he returned to his camp in the evening he took our letters to mail and he brought us letters and newspapers. We saw from the papers that the war could not go on much longer.

The last morning before the Russians came thirteen political prisoners were handcuffed and taken away in a Gestapo truck. Those of us who were left were to be taken the next day.

We were working on the rubbish pile of Luckau that day. Suddenly a siren began to blow a steady blast. It blew for perhaps ten minutes. Someone called out, "Enemy alert!"

A civilian passed by and shouted at our guard, "Shoot the dogs!" The guard looked tense. We marched back to the penitentiary, the gates locked behind us. A trusty whispered to us, "The Russians are here!"

About seven the next morning we who were not kept in the main cell building heard the wild roar of hundreds of voices. In the yard stood a big Red Army soldier with a sheepskin cap and a machine pistol. The enemy? No, the liberator.

We wept, embraced each other, shouted, and jumped up and down. We shook the soldier's hand and kissed him. The young

Russian laughed. Some soldiers entered the cell building. This was the realm of "The Terrible," the guard who had tormented and beaten us worst. We found him ash grey, pitiful, his lower jaw quivering.

"Here are the keys," he stammered.

"Open up," we roared.

He opened the first cell, and like panthers three men went for his throat. We separated them; he had to open the other cells. Finally the cell building was a witches' sabbath of six hundred men. As I went out of the building I saw nothing more of The Terrible.

Hundreds of raving, emaciated prisoners rushed to the store-rooms, the cellars, and the kitchen. One held a loaf of bread like a baby and bit into it, weeping. Others gulped down margarine, knocked over sauerkraut kegs, stepped over cabbages. Syrup kegs broke open and faces went down to suck up the liquid from the thick puddles. Half a beef hung on a hook from the ceiling. Men jumped on it, held on to it by straddling it with their legs, and hung there like a cluster of bees. Raging with hunger they tore into the raw meat till the beef smacked to the ground.

Order had to be established. The prison gates were kept locked and a Red Army captain told us we could not be discharged at once. So one hour after our liberation a committee of six prisoners, among them myself, took charge of the thousand men in the penitentiary. We cleared the kitchen, organized food distribution, handed out clothing, regulated the daily schedule by bell signals. The worst criminals were controlled by the decent prisoners. And we kept the guards locked up.

We organized a hospital, and as I had had a few semesters of medicine in Bonn, the committee of prisoners put me in charge. Soon I had eighty sick together and several men with some medical training to help. It was the first time anyone had looked after these pitiful creatures. We cleaned up the mess in the dispensary. A Russian soldier took us to an apothecary in town. After his first fright the druggist gave us all we wanted, for a receipt. As we returned with our riches the soldier laughed, lit two cigarettes and put one in my mouth.

Then for the first time I went out with two other political

prisoners. No guard walked behind us. We could stop where we wanted, step up to any show window. We went into a store to get stationery. I was the first at the door. I waited for it to be opened by some guard. Then I remembered that human beings open their own doors. It was a heavenly pleasure to open it myself.

A captain called the political prisoners together and offered us chances to become mayors in the surrounding communities. I was put in charge of four large villages in the neighborhood, got a certificate, a red arm band, and set out.

The first village was empty. The people were still in the forests. Suddenly a few mortars fell,· and I heard machine-gun fire. The war was still on here. I had come too early. I walked off.

I went to the biggest village and asked for the mayor. The Nazi mayor read my certificate carefully and relinquished his office. Then I wrote a summons on official stationery calling the community to meet at the Schützenhaus that evening. I made a speech and had a community council elected. The next day the dead in the fields were interred, the mill was started, and the school was reopened. The herds were collected and dead cattle buried. It was May 3, and the farmers were glad that order was being restored.

For days there were fires in the huge forests about us. They went out on rainy days, but soon one would see the blue smoke rising again here and there. It was the smoke of the Nazi diehards —the Werewolves.

Finally a doctor made his appearance—a former army surgeon with excellent papers. For the most part he treated women. Before long my attention was attracted to his manner of speech and expressions. He said "Dufftrie," for example, instead of "Diptherie."

I had him come to my office and told him, "Someone claims you are not a physician. Where did you study medicine?"

"In Bonn," he replied, and stated when. I had studied there at the same time.

"Who taught anatomy there?"

"Professor Fischer." I knew it was Sobotta.

"Who was the physiologist?"

"I can't remember." I remembered; it was Ebbecke.

When had he taken his Physikum—the pre-clinical examination on anatomy, botany and zoology, physiology, chemistry, etc.? He gave a date.

"Which subjects did you study for the Physikum?"

"Surgery and general medicine."

"What, exactly, were the subjects?"

"Surgery and general medicine."

"You are a swindler." He went white. I examined his wallet; it contained indifferent papers.

I was about to return them when my hand touched a paper in a hidden inner pocket of the wallet. It was an order of the SA to meet in Jagen 11—the number indicating geographical coordinates for forests. I had him taken away under suspicion of being a Werewolf.

After three months of excruciatingly hard work I rode home to Berlin on a crowded locomotive. Our pretty studio apartment at the Wittenbergplatz no longer existed. No one knew where my wife was. I borrowed a bicycle and rode to Potsdam where a sister of hers had lived. Among the many people on the street I saw in front of me a young woman on a bicycle. A premonition made me ring my bell. The woman turned around, pale and serious. It was Joy. She jumped off her bike, I off mine. And then there was nothing but heaven about us. When next we noticed, people were standing around us laughing.

EPILOGUE TO CHAPTER X

Reich Secret

GÜNTHER WEISENBORN's play *Die Illegalen* in which he commemorates this underground group had a long run in Berlin. He has continued writing and for a time was the editor of an American-licensed German magazine and head of the protective society of German authors.

In 1949 the opening performance of another play, *Eulenspiegel*, in Hamburg drew twenty-six curtain calls.

PROLOGUE TO CHAPTER XI

"Therefore Will I Deliver Him"

HEINRICH LIEBRECHT was born just before the turn of the century. Though his parents were Jewish he was raised in the Protestant faith. As a result of profound religious experiences in World War I, in which he served as a volunteer and an officer, he was converted to Catholicism. Following the war he studied law, was appointed a judge, and served voluntarily as a youth counselor. After Hitler came to power he was dismissed from these positions. He entered the office of an American lawyer in Berlin, who was legal advisor to the United States Embassy, and became his colleague and representative.

This chapter is a condensation of the manuscript written in German by Heinrich Liebrecht.

XI

"Therefore Will I Deliver Him"

HEINRICH LIEBRECHT

A S A theater photographer, my fiancée Lies was acquainted with Gentile actors and corresponded with some of them. When the Gestapo searched her apartment in Hamburg, they found these letters and used them as an excuse for a frame-up, charging her with *Rassenschande*—intimate relations with an "Aryan." The proceedings did not lead to conviction because the charges were baseless. But after we were married and settled in Berlin the Hamburg Gestapo sent her deportation orders. That forced us to leave our apartment and made our departure from Germany more urgent. We moved out just in time, for three days after we went into hiding with some friends in July, 1942, the Gestapo came to the apartment. Not finding Lies in, they sealed it.

Although I had been a judge myself, I had long ago abandoned all futile attempts to emigrate legally. We had given a Señor Velasco, a doctor connected with the Chilean Consulate, several thousand marks to help us get out of Germany. He was to deliver forged passports and papers and arrange the trip to Switzerland. But though he had promised many times that he would have the papers ready, he always put us off. At last I gave him the choice of delivering the papers or returning the money. I arranged one final meeting. Velasco did not show up. Our last hope was gone and with it most of the money we had set aside for emergencies.

I wanted to warn others who had put their last hopes in Velasco, so I phoned a former emigration counselor with whom I had been dealing. A voice I did not recognize said that the counselor would be back shortly. I replied that I would be at his office in an hour.

Lies and I took the bus to the Sächsische Strasse in Berlin-Wil-

214

mersdorf. We rang the bell. A man I had never seen before opened the door. "Come in." I hesitated. "You are expected," he said.

When we entered the room we saw four persons with their faces turned to the wall. The man closed the door behind us and announced, "Gestapo." He showed the insignia under his lapel. Lies sobbed.

"Jews?" he asked. I didn't answer immediately. He hit me in the face.

Looking at the four men the thought flashed into my mind, "One man against five!" I jumped on the Gestapo official. He fell on the floor, bearing me with him. "Run!" I shouted to Lies. She stood like a pillar of stone. We rolled on the floor. "Run!" I shouted again. At last Lies moved. He tried to seize her by the skirt, but I tore his hand away. She ran from the room and I heard the door close. She was gone.

The Gestapo official fought like a madman, but now he was lying under me. He shouted to the four Jews, "Get this fellow off me."

The incredible happened. Even though the Gestapo were bent on their destruction, childhood awe and fear of the police won out over their intelligence. They pulled me away from the man.

He locked the door and telephoned for help. Two more Gestapo officials arrived a few minutes later. They beat me with everything they could find and then threw me down the stairs. I was half unconscious when they dragged me into a car. A crowd gathered around.

At the Grolmannstrasse police station they put me under a shower until I was fully conscious again. Then they beat me once more. After that I was taken to the Gestapo office in the Burgstrasse.

"I want to see the Jew who attacks the Gestapo," I heard someone say. I was taken to the section head. He looked me over. "I imagined him differently." "Why," he shouted at me, "you halfpint, how do you dare attack officials? We'll show you!" He struck me with a horsewhip.

I had ceased to feel pain. I was taken to the cellar. New prisoners were coming in all the time; foreign workers were waiting for discharge or transportation. They kept at a respectful distance and looked at me as if I were a man condemned to death.

The door opened. A uniformed SS man took me out and led me deeper into the cellar. He picked up a stick and beat me with it. As I did not scream he did not enjoy it, so he led me back.

I was moved to the prison of the Police Presidium and put in solitary confinement. A prison official came in. "Get yourself some rest, fellow," he said. "You need it. Here is some water." My whole body was swollen and aching. The bloody, puffed-up face I saw mirrored in the window did not look in the least like me.

I thanked God that Lies had escaped. Yet how desolate she must be. And I recalled how some time after Jews were ordered to wear the yellow star, she had burst into tears on coming home and exclaimed, "I can't go on any more." The children in the neighborhood had thrown stones at her. One boy had started it, then a whole group joined in. By now she was probably in hiding with our five-months-old baby, Eva Maria. I wondered if our good friend Konoye, the Japanese symphony conductor, was looking after my mother as he had promised.

My solitude was interrupted the next day. Another prisoner and I were taken on foot across the Alexanderplatz, through the curious crowd, to the Gestapo office in the Burgstrasse. I remember the name plate on the door, "Section 4 D, Markert, Deinert," for I was taken there many times. A blonde young girl was sitting in the office.

Markert made a few playful remarks about my fight. "How many rounds today?" I had to go along with him. "More than ten." He laughed, but his companion cut him short, saying furiously, "Did you bring that Jew here to discuss prize fighting?" "Where's your wife?" he shouted at me.

That was the beginning of the first interrogation. I soon gathered to my satisfaction that they had not caught Lies and that capturing her was only one of their interests. They also wanted to know about the money Velasco had received.

Velasco was obviously working with them, and this whole emigration game was a racket by which various members of the Gestapo were getting rich quickly. It appeared that Velasco had cheated them out of their share of the money. Consequently they had arrested him when we were arrested.

The phone rang and the two men were called away. They told another official to continue the interrogation. He was young, tall, and black-haired, and did not look at all unpleasant. He led me to another wing of the building, where he wrote down my dossier. He asked me about my life and I told him that I had volunteered as a youngster in the first World War, that I became an officer, and had been awarded the Iron Cross First Class for bravery. He seemed to be impressed. He remarked that the Jews he had been interrogating were certainly different from the profiteering, cowardly lot he had been led to expect from his instruction in the Hitler Youth. He appeared puzzled and was interested to hear more. I told this boy how I had lost my favorite brother and several close friends in the war—emphasizing that war was not a field of glory but a slaughter. I described my conversion from a freethinker to an inner faith which brought me into the Catholic Church. I told him of my enthusiasm as a boy for the romanticism of the Wandervögel youth movement, of my studies after the war, of an adventurous trip to Central America in pursuit of a girl I was in love with, and of my legal work. I explained how my desire to emigrate legally had been frustrated when war with the United States began and the American lawyer who was my employer and benefactor suddenly died. And now I had fallen into this trap while trying to find some way to leave the country.

He listened with interest and increasing sympathy. Then he said, "It's a pity about you. How could a lawyer like you be so stupid as to attack an official? You haven't a chance." I asked if he was married and had a child. "Yes." "Then you should understand it!" He was silent.

There was no end to the beatings and interrogations. Once an SS man brought me back to the cell and beat me there. The prison supervisor came and shoved him away from me, telling him, "I am in charge here."

A few days passed. It was evening. I took the plate with cold soup and ate, staring at the grey walls. I felt that my endurance was waning. My chances were over but at least Lies and the baby were saved. Nothing else mattered. I wanted to make this my Last Supper.

I tested the window frame, the strength of my belt, and the towel. A deep voice spoke in me, "Thou shalt not kill." But God would understand. I could not live through another day of this.

I lay down on the cot and thought over my life. There had been more than forty good, eventful years, with happiness and excitement, much work and some success; years warmed by the love of good people and fine friendships. I visualized them and bade them farewell. Then I thanked God for my life.

"Have pity on me, O Lord, in your great righteousness!" I confessed to myself, having no priest.

But I could not find the rest and peace that must prepare the path from life to death. "O Lord, take this life from me," I prayed. "Release me, give me a sign."

Church bells rang in the distance. The rays of the sun slanted more and more; the shadows on the walls lengthened. A last ray of sunshine crept through the window. An inscription carved on the wall suddenly caught the light and became visible. I sat up and deciphered it slowly.

"Have confidence in God and learn to pray again.
He will save you in the greatest distress."

Next morning all was quiet. I felt transformed, confident, with an unconquerable will to endure. After that experience my life continued on a different spiritual plane, which had nothing in common with my corporeal misery.

Once a guard watching me through the judas of the door asked, "What are you doing there all the time?" "I am talking to God," I told him. "Listen, fellow," he snorted, "leave the Old Man out of this. He died long ago."

The interrogations became less frequent. For weeks I was left alone in my cell.

My neighbor in the cell block was a Polish student who had participated in a conspiracy against the Germans. Every evening at dusk we climbed up to a small window connecting our cells, opened it, and talked. Above us was the women's prison. Each cell was occupied by two girls who had belonged to a Jewish youth group. They were charged with participation in burning the Nazi's "Soviet Paradise" exhibit. Occasionally they lowered reading matter to us on their belts. We were happy to get it, as we were not allowed anything of the sort. Often in the evenings they sang rounds. The singing would start in one cell, be picked up in a second, a third, and a fourth above me. One of the girls, younger than the others and their pet, had her eighteenth birthday. She shouted down to me, "I scratched something on the wall." "What?" "I am so young and want to live."

Shortly afterward the girls were all taken away. My suspicions of what had happened to them were confirmed much later when I heard that they were shot.

One day I was taken again to the Gestapo office. I was told that I could improve my almost hopeless situation if I would give information about various persons and matters. They were especially interested in particulars about the business of the American lawyer with whom I had been associated for the last seven years. I gave evasive answers, for under no circumstances did I want to say anything to help the Gestapo.

Then I was put into a prison labor battalion which was building barracks in the Tempelhof section of Berlin. We worked with the regular employees of a contractor. These workers were kind to us, gave us sandwiches, and took messages for members of our family. I was very careful and sent only one message, to a former housekeeper of ours.

I did not enjoy my partial freedom long, for I was sent back to solitary confinement and interrogated once more. Markert tried to get information from me, softly at first and then in his usual harsh tone. I wondered why I had been removed from the labor battalion, and tried to sound him out. "You are to be at our disposal," he declared angrily. "Those prison people think they can do what they want; we'll show them!"

That was the last interrogation. Weeks passed. On September 11, 1942, the cell door opened and the guard told me, "You're released." I didn't understand. "You'll be discharged. Take your things, you can go." I couldn't believe it. Perhaps it was just a trick, perhaps they would kill me now. Or had the influence of my Japanese friend Konoye been effective?

I heard later that the Chilean Embassy had effected Velasco's release from prison. I wondered why I had not been tried, but apparently the whole matter of Gestapo corruption and my fight with the official would have resulted in such loss of face that they decided to keep it all quiet and have me deported.

I was discharged but not free. Markert took me to a former Jewish old-age home in the Hamburgerstrasse. This was the processing center for deportation to the east. The men who, like me, were leaving the next day were kept under arrest in one room of the building, the women in another. There was much confusion, excitement, and milling around. Whoever was not assigned to Theresienstadt wanted to go there, and those who were going there were afraid of the unknown. One doctor claimed that all trains to Theresienstadt would stop in a tunnel where the deportees would be gassed.

That night was full of worries and thoughts of Lies and Eva Maria. Were they still hiding? Should I try to send them a message, so that they would go with me? I was told that I would see my mother, but when?

The next day, September 12, was my birthday. We were processed for deportation. We formed a long line to sign our remaining property away, receive a transport number, and be made ready for our trip.

Behind me was a young woman. When she heard my name she asked, "Do you know Elisabeth Liebrecht?"

"That's my wife." She looked at me and hesitated.

"What is it?"

"I was a nurse in the Jewish hospital. Your wife was brought there. She was unconscious. She had poisoned herself. It was already too late."

Back in the room where we were confined I looked out of the window on the old cemetery. I felt empty and unable to think clearly any more. I scarcely grasped what I had heard.

The preparations for leaving and the busy atmosphere in the room around me made me feel even more lost and alone. I thought of the baby. Would I ever see her again, even if I survived? I must find out where she was. I had to escape.

That afternoon a policeman asked for me. "Two ladies to see you. Make it short; it's not allowed, and I might get into trouble."

I followed him. My mother embraced me. Gertrud Jaffe, an old friend, who like me had been converted to Catholicism, was with her.

"My boy, I wanted to congratulate you on your birthday."

"She is dead," I said.

"You know it?"

I asked about Eva Maria. Gertrud put her finger to her lips. Mother kissed me. "You have to stay strong for her and for me. I have only you, and I'll come with you; not in this transport but in the next."

"Mother, don't. Hide. Konoye will help you."

"No, I have only one desire, to be with you. And when I die you will be there with me."

The policeman interrupted. "I'm sorry, but you'll have to leave now." We had hardly said a word about Lies.

Later the policeman handed me a little package from my mother. Inside was a delicious roll with real butter and a piece of sausage. Suddenly I tasted something strange. Paper? I wanted to spit it out. It was a tiny roll, a twenty mark bill.

The next day about a thousand men and women were loaded into trucks and taken to a freight station in northern Berlin. A lot of police and Gestapo were around. Most of those assigned to Theresienstadt were older or were sent there as a "privilege," because of serious wounds or decorations in World War I, or because they had been leading officials in the Jewish community. We climbed into the obsolete shabby passenger coaches of an incredibly long train. Jewish men and women orderlies helped the old people. The aid service was excellently organized and provided hot soup, traveling rations, and a very useful eating kit and spoon.

The train proceeded slowly via Dresden and arrived the next morning at Bauschowitz, the rail terminal for Theresienstadt. SS troops, Czech police, and the Jewish ghetto guard, who could be recognized by their Czech military caps, were standing on the platform. After the larger pieces of baggage were removed we were formed into columns and marched to Theresienstadt. We saw it about two miles away, a peaceful little town nestled in the hills. The wooded mountains were lovely in the reddish-blue light of dawn.

After processing, during which most of our remaining property was stolen, I was assigned to house Q 312, a small two-story structure which might at one time have accommodated about eight people. There were already seventy in it, and now sixty more were being added. We were put in the attic, where the old people lay on the floor without mattresses or blankets. The house elder was an egotistic, despotic, incompetent fellow, who lacked all compassion.

Suddenly it occurred to me that I had been in Theresienstadt before. Once on an auto tour from Dresden to Prague I had stopped there because I liked the detached dreaminess of the place. The little fortress town looked then as if it had been sleeping for centuries. It was still a garrison town, with a population of eight or ten thousand made up of soldiers, their followers, and some peasants. Now there were probably more than sixty thousand internees. In the center of the town was a large square with a plain church and the buildings of the former city administration and military headquarters. Everything was just the same: the fortress walls, covered with moss; the star-shaped bastions; the old barracks with their thick brick walls surrounding several courtyards.

The Gestapo had taken over the few modern buildings on the market square and had confiscated the Hotel Victoria for their billets. The streets leading from outside to these buildings were lined with barbed wire and wooden fences. This made the whole town look ugly, as well as blocking traffic.

The old walls of the town contained casemates which served as living quarters and storerooms and housed the camp bakery which was operated by internees.

I learned the recent history of the town. Its residents had been evacuated in the summer of 1941 with all their property. They left nothing but two or three pianos and some old junk, but even these few things were welcome to their successors. For most of these a table, chair, or bed was an unattainable luxury. Anyone who found a few rusty nails to make a stool became an envied aristocrat.

I was amazed to find quite a large number of young people in Theresienstadt. We had always thought of it primarily as a camp for older people and war invalids. Most of these young people were Czech Jews, fine, strong, and healthy. They had trusted the false promises of the Gestapo and had volunteered in November and December of 1941 to help construct a ghetto for the "privileged." The one promise that had been kept was that they could bring a lot of baggage. In this way the place had acquired musical instruments, sheet music, and other things which gave Theresienstadt an outward aspect of luxury. Having arrived first, the Czechs held many key positions in the housing and food administrations. Some of them thought of themselves primarily as Czechs, so that our relations with them were not always without problems. Their attitude strengthened my belief that nationalism differed only in degree from Nazism. In its extreme form, chauvinism, it exhibited both the mentality and the methods of the Nazis.

The new life was hardest on the old people. Many had been told in Germany that if they signed their property away they would be sent to an old-age home. Instead they were brought here, to sleep on the floor, shorn of all their familiar possessions. Many of them had no close relatives left, and merely lived on, depressed and listless.

A dysentery epidemic broke out, and many of the older people were affected. The water came from wells, and few of the houses had modern hygienic plumbing. There were only two or three toilets for a hundred inmates, and people had to wait in line, writhing in pain and terribly ashamed if they could not wait long enough. Thousands were so weak that they could not get up, and they literally died in their own excrement.

For many Theresienstadt was only a transit camp. The dreaded transports would eventually take them further east. "Transport" was a word of terror; it paralyzed all life and thinking. One heard the order, "Five thousand people to be processed!" Who would be called—your friend, your mother, your child, yourself?

No one could understand why people were not deported east directly from Germany. Perhaps the reason lay in the inadequate capacity of the gas chambers and crematories. But at that time we knew nothing of these; we only feared the unknown.

Shortly after my arrival I reported for work and was assigned to a group of a hundred men who did odd jobs each day. At my request I was transferred to the cemetery unit. We worked outdoors and outside of the town, where we could see the beautiful countryside and mountains and were away from the depressing misery of the camp.

At first the dead had been buried separately but now they were placed in mass graves. Each day we went out to a large field where the fall flowers were blooming and shoveled deep graves. Around noon the wagons came, heavily loaded with wooden boxes. We had to take the bodies out of the boxes, which were to be used again. That autumn of 1942 there were usually two hundred or more bodies a day to be piled into the graves.

My fellow workers' disgust and horror of the corpses seemed strange to me. To me they were only outer shells from which the soul had gone and become free. But the thin bodies were not a pretty sight. Sometimes the cloth with which they were covered showed traces of dysentery, and occasionally a dried-up limb would hang out of the covering.

The work gave me time to meditate, and the thought of death helped bring me closer to God. I thought of Lies' death, and wondered if I would see Eva Maria again. Her brown hair and her sweet ways had reminded us of a young deer, and we called her "Rehlein," Little Fawn.

I found a number of other converts to Catholicism. Brother Kuhnert, who had been evacuated to Theresienstadt from a Viennese monastery because he was of Jewish descent, read Mass every Sunday morning in the drafty attic of an old house. We stood around him in a semicircle, singing and making responses. Often the rain came through the broken tiles and we shivered from the cold. We felt very close to God in this hour and were conscious of an affinity with the early Christians in Rome and what they must have felt in the catacombs. The attic acquired a consecration through a beautiful baroque crucifix which we found. Later Brother Kuhnert's group joined the Catholic services and community evenings organized by Dr. Donat from Vienna who could make us forget the drabness of the day.

Of course, the Jewish services were also crowded with worshipers who were filled with the desire to be close to God in prayer.

The grave-digging unit did not work on Sundays, mainly because the Czech police supervising us were off duty. The camp itself had Saturday as a day of rest. I did not look forward to the free days, for there was hardly anything one could do except wash laundry and keep one's few possessions in order.

We were moved from the attic to a regular room in the house. The large number of deaths, mostly of old women, had made space for us, but all the rooms were still crowded with excited, noisy, or sick people.

As one of the younger residents of the house I was saddled with the task of carrying the dead out of their rooms. Whoever was about to die was placed in the laundry room. The dead were identified with a slip of paper tied to their feet, and then carried to a small stable. The poor creatures hardly had time to die. Once I was told to take out a dead woman. As I picked her up she groaned. But our hard-boiled house elder had her carried out anyway.

I was constantly possessed by one thought: "If only my mother is not sent to this place!" But one day, a month after I arrived, she was waiting for me in my room when I came back from work, as if she had come on a visit.

I couldn't say a word. "My boy, aren't you at all glad?" she asked, quite taken aback. Tears had long ceased to come to me, but at that moment I had to choke back a deep sobbing. Our defenselessness and helplessness overwhelmed me.

Mother told me more about Lies' suicide and what little she knew of Eva Maria. Our friend Gertrud Jaffe and other Catholics were caring for her. Gertrud had received a deportation order, which at first she took as God's will, but then she became convinced of the senselessness of that idea and went into hiding with the help of Caritas, a Catholic welfare organization. Mother did not know where she was.

After my mother arrived I no longer wanted to be a grave-digger. And the crematory which was being built soon made grave digging unnecessary. The group of which I had been leader was assigned to road construction. This hard work was rewarded by higher food rations: a double lunch ration and more bread, sugar, and a bad-tasting synthetic margarine. We repaired the streets in the town, while another unit mended the roads outside. We worked with the most primitive tools, doing almost everything by hand.

As winter approached I became very sensitive to the cold. In spite of the additional rations the food was not adequate for the work. Mother had somehow made some gloves and a scarf out of old rags, but my clothes were much too light. I was wearing the same trousers I had on when I was arrested in Berlin in the summer. Finally the leader of my group of one hundred, who was favorably disposed toward me, had me transferred to another job to replace a man who had caught typhoid fever.

Four of us carried heavy sacks of potatoes to a small room in the barrack called the Hamburger Kaserne, where about a hundred women, mostly elderly, peeled potatoes from early morning till late evening. At noon and night we carried the peelings to a cellar where hungry people were waiting to search for anything edible among them. The atmosphere in the crowded rooms was stifling. The women sat on hard boards till they could scarcely sit any more and peeled till their hands were sore. Many of the women who had come from comfortable circumstances adjusted better to deprivations than those who had always been poor. But the aim of everyone was to "sluice" a few potatoes to increase their own rations. That in itself made the potato-peeling job attractive. The women showed astonishing imagination and skill at finding hiding places in their clothing or on their bodies, so that they could pass the thorough examination made on leaving the room.

We porters had more to eat, twice the ordinary rations, both for hard work and because we handled food. We also had a good view behind the curtain of hunger into the realm of their majesties the cooks and supply masters, and we often benefited from their plenty, though it might be only bits of food we managed to scrape out of the vats. But even the extra food we got was not adequate, although it usually filled our stomachs. There were no fresh vegetables at all, no real fat except the synthetic margarine. But at least we did not always suffer hunger, and I could bring my mother a little something every day, which helped reduce her food deficiency.

Still, her health was deteriorating steadily. She had had an operation in Berlin and needed a medicine which she could not get here. The small supply she had brought along was taken away from her during the processing. She suffered incessantly from digestive troubles and before long was not able to leave her bed. I tried to distract her by bringing books and friends on my daily visits.

The infirmary room in which Mother lay was not a cheerful place. Most of her roommates thought and spoke a great deal of their respective diseases or of food. The nurse had to look after a large family, and so the sick got less attention. But the woman doctor rose above conditions and cared for Mother with sympathy.

There were periodic examinations for lice, and delousings of those affected. Mother, too, was deloused and transferred to another room where dependable, honest nurses and a Dr. Plautus, who had been noted for his untiring work in his district of Vienna, were in attendance. The doctor was with his patients day and night, ate with them, talked with them, and looked after them as if they had been old friends or close relatives. They were placed together according to their preferences. They started to revive the past and tell of their experiences in better days. Like good housewives, they exchanged cooking recipes and wrote them down for the future.

As time went on the chances of survival increased, provided one were not assigned to the dreaded transports for the east and the Allied victory were not too long delayed. Conditions in the camp improved slightly, even though the Nazis made no concessions. But the ration continued to be too small to support life yet too large to permit death; this was true for all who did not receive packages or heavy workers' rations or benefit from ir-regularities in the food distribution.

A number of young girls had a disease which was diagnosed as encephalitis. There were many skin diseases, and often a little scratch would develop into a serious infection. But the death rate, especially among the children, decreased considerably. In-oculations were given regularly. Sanitary conditions, especially, improved a great deal. An epidemic of typhoid fever which cost many lives, especially among the teen-agers, was stopped soon after it broke out. Hospitals were better equipped, more sick wards were opened, and babies' and children's homes were started. Of course, all these institutions had many defects; ma-terials and medicines were lacking, and some of the hospital at-tendants had little sense of responsibility. But on the whole they functioned as well as could be expected under the circumstances. Among the interned there were plenty of excellent doctors, some of them outstanding specialists. The Gestapo itself made use of them surreptitiously. There were also well-trained nurses, and new ones were being trained in the camp.

In the former military laundry, which was located outside the town, a camp laundry was set up. Although the inmates' clothing was washed infrequently, it was laundered well and hygienically. There were watch repairmen, shoemakers, tailors, orthopedists, as well as barbers in the camp. All these establishments provided useful jobs and helped divert attention from hunger, depression, or strained personal relations.

On special instructions from the Nazis, we had to create a false front for Theresienstadt. Stores were provided with attrac-tive window displays, all of things which could not be bought; and ghetto money was issued which had no purchasing power. The reason for these efforts may have been that the Nazis wanted to make the world believe that they were good to the Jews and had only isolated them. They had taken a film of the camp in 1942, and I heard that they published touched-up photographs in magazines.

Some provision was made for the needs of adolescents. Boys' and girls' homes were organized, often under the expert direction of young educators who devoted themselves wholeheartedly to their task. In spite of the Gestapo's orders, they gave the younger boys and girls at least an elementary schooling, and trained the older boys in agriculture or apprenticed them to learn some manual trade in a repair shop. The young people often organized themselves into cooperative groups, usually with a Zionist leaning.

As early as the fall of 1942 lectures, readings, and music were offered, at first in a guard room and in attics, later often in the attractive city hall. There was a great deal of talent available: well-known singers, musicians, and orchestra directors, actors, and vaudeville artists. Operas and concerts were given: Smetana's *Bartered Bride,* and works of Mozart, Bizet, Verdi, etc. A chorus sang Verdi's *Requiem,* Haydn's *Creation,* and other oratorios. An opera, *Brundibar,* was presented by the children with real scenery. The actors played *Liliom* and *Cyrano de Bergerac,* read *Faust,* and recited Villon's poetry. German young folk gave a splendid performance of Schiller's *Maria Stuart* and Czechs put on an equally fine performance of a fairy tale by Capek.

Most pianists had of necessity changed over to the accordion. Unfortunately one of the first performances by an accordion player in the Hamburger Kaserne ended in punitive action by the Gestapo, because the young people were caught dancing after the official concert and because the Gestapo claimed that the camp blackout was inadequate. In our free time many of us had been enjoying walks in town, both near the walls and to a bastion where we had a beautiful view of valley and hills; but for a good while after this concert no one was allowed to leave his area and the use of light was banned during the dark winter month of February.

Those who wanted sociability could go to the always crowded coffee house. Although nothing was served there but a brown-colored liquid which passed for coffee, one could enjoy the company and admire the drawings on the wall, done in the style of Käthe Kollwitz.

This coffee house was symbolic of the contrasts in the life of Theresienstadt: on the one hand, music and entertainments; on the other heartbreak, hunger, and fear. But recreation played an important part in the fight against the constant depression caused by harsh living conditions and the frequent transports to the east.

The gradual improvement in conditions was in no small measure owing to a young Czech, Edelstein, and his successor. Dr. Eppstein from Berlin, who performed tireless service as camp leaders. Eppstein, a former university professor, was endowed with tremendous energy and was always fair and honest. He was a practicing democrat and enlisted the cooperation of other leading Jews in the Council of Elders. He occasionally conducted small seminars on sociology in which the participants made valuable suggestions on our own sociological problems.

Dr. Leo Baeck, the spiritual leader of German Judaism and a noted scholar, came to Theresienstadt at the same time as Eppstein. Except for honorary membership in the Council of Elders, he held no office in the camp administration. I met Dr. Baeck when I submitted plans to him for an emergency organization in case of a sudden political change in Germany. His prominence grew naturally out of his character, and he derived no benefits from his position as did some of the other leaders. He served the community with his great knowledge, his noble example, and his constant readiness to help. Dr. Baeck was also a farsighted, practical person, interested in all questions of daily life, and a link between those of different religions and ideas. We Catholics honored him especially, and he was a frequent guest at our meetings. When he lectured on philosophic subjects or commented on current problems, his appearance, his personality, the depth of his thought, and the clarity of his expression made an extraordinary impression. Respect and tolerance for his fellow man formed the basis of his ethics.

Tolerance and respect for privacy were badly needed in our circumstances. I often contrasted the loneliness I had experienced in solitary confinement with the equally trying lack of solitude here. There was no place in camp where one could withdraw to meditate or to be for an hour a separate individual. There was no private conversation which was not necessarily overheard by someone else. After the toilets had been replaced by latrines there was no privacy there. When one whistled a tune someone always chimed in, especially if it was by Dvořak or Smetana. Those who should have known better from their own experience were themselves often intolerant. The gaps between the various nationalities were never completely bridged. The division into Germans, Austrians, and Czechs was always evident and the split into national groups became more apparent after the arrival of transports from Holland and Denmark. The Zionists added one more nationalist aspiration to those already existing. There was ample evidence that a community like ours formed under compulsion could not really become a successful community, in spite of the common enemy.

National distinctions played a decisive role in the transports to the east. Every transport was selected according to a quota set either by the camp leadership or by the Nazis. Those who received the little blue slip with the transport order started efforts to be taken off the list, through connections and the protection of influential friends. If they were taken off, someone else had to go in their stead.

Members of the Council of Elders and their families were exempt from transport. The Gestapo had ordered that among the Germans those with high medals from World War I, war invalids, those with Gentile relatives or of mixed Jewish and Gentile ancestry, as well as certain skilled laborers, were to be deferred.

In 1943 there were about three thousand baptized "non-Aryans" in the camp. Our religious services were our source of strength and gave us the will to continue to live. I tried to have my mother share these hours of spiritual experience, to make her lot lighter, for she was consciously preparing herself for death. It was obvious that she was getting weaker every day. The beds to her right and left changed patients constantly and all around her people were dying. But she still showed pleasure when we visited her, especially when we could bring her something or tell her good news. A little violet, which someone had brought me from outside, was my only gift for her last birthday. She took it as if it were a bouquet of orchids.

In the summer of 1943 an attempt was made to reorganize the food distribution in order to ensure a fairer division of the supplies. The potatoes were no longer peeled, and a stricter check was made of the food supply. I was then put into a unit consisting mostly of Czech Jews which transported the foodstuffs to the kitchen and distributing places. We worked long hours and much of our work consisted of carrying heavy loads, but we also received a more generous ration than before, so that I could bring more to my mother.

By September of 1943 I had been in Theresienstadt one year and was well adjusted to my new way of life. One day, when I was dishing out food, someone told me to hurry to the transport section in the Magdeburger Kaserne. I rushed over, partly in hope, partly in fear. I ran up the stairs and opened the door.

Gertrud Jaffe was there. She held out to me a child with large black eyes and chestnut-colored hair.

All I could say was, "I can't believe it."

"Yes, it's your Eva Maria, take her, it's your Little Fawn, and I'm really Gertrud Jaffe, and I brought her with me."

I looked at the child. She resembled Lies and was even more beautiful. I took her in my arms, but she turned away in fright. I felt as if my heart were breaking. "I'm your father, Little Fawn," I whispered to her. She fixed her large eyes on me and tears rolled down her cheeks.

At that time there was infantile paralysis in Theresienstadt, and we could not take her to the infants' home. Besides, it was overfull already. A friend arranged a place for Gertrud and Eva Maria in the attic of one of the houses. Everyone admired the child, and the other occupants of the attic said, "She must stay with us always."

Gertrud was very happy. She overlooked the primitive conditions, the inadequate meals, everything. She saw only the child whom, as she thought, she had saved. "Saved" for Theresienstadt!

Gertrud told me how arrangements for hiding Eva Maria had been made by herself, Grete Wünsch, and the courageous Fräulein Dr. Luckner, of Caritas. Fräulein Luckner had tried to conceal the child's identity and in the end had her adopted by a family named Schmidt who lover her dearly. Archbishop Groeber of Freiburg had paid all expenses. But the Gestapo learned of Caritas' help to Jews and in the spring of 1943 arrested many of its members including Fräulein Luckner and Grete Wünsch. They discovered Eva Maria's hiding place, and agreed not to deport her—to certain death—only on condition that Gertrud come out of hiding. As a return "favor" both were sent to Theresienstadt.

Gertrud and I took the child to her grandmother. She was silent a long while, unable to express the fullness of her heart. Then she said quietly, "Now you have someone belonging to you to take care of when I pass away. Be good to the child, but don't spoil her. Children need care and often demand sacrifices, but they too are happy when they can do good deeds."

Eva Maria was lovely, with large black eyes, long, soft eyelashes, brown curls, and little dimples in her red cheeks. At first we were somewhat shy with each other but gradually the barrier our separation had created was broken down.

Mother grew weaker from day to day. She still saw the child as much as possible, and often when I sat at her bedside told me to go to my daughter. She slept more and more of the time. A lung infection hastened her death. When she whispered one evening, "My boy, the end is coming soon," I knew that she was right, and my words to the contrary did not sound very convincing.

Next morning the nurse called me. It was too late to hurry to the hospital. I walked up the stairs, folded back the sheet and kissed Mother's forehead. Then I sat by her bed praying. The carriers came with a bier. I followed outside. They put the bier on a noisy two-wheeled cart and pushed it through the streets.

Mother was the only non-Jewish person to be buried the next day. The funeral service took place in a room reserved for non-Jewish dead. It was quiet and dignified. I would have liked to hear a few words of memorial spoken by a friend who had known her, for what could any stranger say about her life? It had been full of work and care, the life of a noble person devoted to being a good wife and mother.

I did not wait until the coffin was loaded on the wagon and drawn away. I went to the bastion and looked over the countryside, lying quiet and bright in its October colors.

I returned to my job of carrying sacks. Good fellow workers made the task pleasant, even though it was hard. I had developed a close friendship with Jirko, a man from Prague who pulled a cart with me. Once they hitched another cart to the one we were pulling and we did not notice the prank at first because we were discussing a lecture of Leo Baeck's. From then on we were called the "philosopher horses."

The camp commandant, SS leader Seydel, who had an honorary doctor's degree from a Nazi university, was a frequent guest in the showers and bathrooms when the women and girls were taking their baths. Heindl, his sadistic sergeant, hit people when they did not greet him quickly enough or when the Jewish star was not properly attached to their clothing. And he took care to do away with anyone who learned too much about his practice of furnishing the camp with illegal cigarettes. Raids would be made, and the men taken to a concentration camp in a near-by fortress. Few of them survived.

Another unpleasant, though less dangerous, type of raid was conducted by the German women employees of the Gestapo. These hyenas would search the women's quarters for forbidden things such as sweets, and steal whatever took their fancy. Occasionally they destroyed property from sheer vandalism.

Labor transports to Birkenau were sent off during the Jewish holidays, in the autumn of 1943. No one knew where Birkenau was, but gradually word went around that it lay near Auschwitz in Poland, not far from the German border. We feared more than ever before that the Nazis might take desperate action against us at the end of the war. I was no longer so sure that I would survive and my anxiety over Eva Maria increased. She was not well and had apparently had experiences, or perhaps diseases, that had affected her growth and especially her emotional development. Occasionally she appeared depressed, and her deep thoughtful eyes suggested that she was living an intense inner life of which she could tell us nothing.

Gertrud Jaffe continued to look after her and spoil her as if she were her own child. Everyone loved Eva Maria. More than once, when she was sleeping in the improvised baby carriage in front of the children's home, some admirer took her with her, and we had to look for her.

When I tore a muscle at work and was laid up, Eva Maria visited me and would play on my cot, which made me very happy.

She spoke a terrible mixture of Czech and German. Her visits were never long enough for me, and it was apparent that she too was happy to be with me.

After I was well again the head of our food transportation department was deported and the administration, much against my will, put me in charge. I was quartered in a tiny chamber partitioned off from other rooms, the previous occupant having been sent away on a transport. At last I could have Eva Maria visit me in something like privacy.

She finally regained her health, helped to some extent by packages sent anonymously to her, to Mother, or to me. Little parcels containing sardines arrived from Lisbon, ordered by the American Joint Distribution Committee. The oil in them was very valuable; even the Danes, who were receiving regular food packages from their government and so were well off, appreciated their value and would barter for them. Occasionally a package came for Eva Maria from Germany, prepared by courageous friends probably at great sacrifice.

The parcel post in the camp was a fairly well-organized enterprise which employed many camp inmates. But the mail service was more or less of a farce. The house elders were permitted to distribute post cards at intervals of several weeks. Outgoing mail was pre-censored by the camp administration before the Gestapo censored it. One could tell from the few answers we received that only a fraction of it was sent off. Correspondence abroad was prohibited. Anyone who received the answer certificates of the International Red Cross could use them. But in this case, too, it was said that the Gestapo engaged in some crooked business which led to the intervention of the Red Cross, allegedly with a threat of reprisal against the mail of German prisoners-of-war. It was rumored that a camp commandant, Bergel, had been replaced for that reason. It was the first time we had heard of intervention from the outside.

Early one morning in November everyone was chased from bed and herded out of the town. Only small children and the old and sick were allowed to stay in the camp. We were lined up, according to houses, in swampy meadow in a near-by valley closely guarded by SS and Czech police, and kept standing there till evening. We had grave doubts about our fate, and many feared the worst. The young Czechs considered forcing an entrance into the town or fleeing, and wondered if the Czech police would fire on them. I was worrying about Eva Maria, who was left in the infants' home in the camp. It turned out that this was a roll call held because the Gestapo had discovered that names of people who had escaped were still being kept on the list of inmates. It was pure sadism to let us stand in the cold so long. About two-thirds of the people were over fifty, and many were permanently harmed by twelve hours' exposure without food or adequate clothing.

In the spring of 1944 the Gestapo began a ridiculous and obvious piece of camouflage in anticipation of the visit of a neutral commission. Months before the event work was started with the slogan "Town Beautification." All the streets were carefully repaired; the wooden fences and barbed wire enclosures were removed; most of the houses were fixed up and painted; the streets were named and carved street signs put up. Lawns were planted; a children's pavilion and a music pavilion were built; a theater and a library were installed, and pictures distributed for the barracks.

We were promised that no further transports would be sent, although a contingent of young men was to be detached temporarily. Almost all of these men returned and told of luxurious underground shelters they had been building for the Gestapo in the woods northeast of Berlin.

In the summer, shortly before the arrival of the inspection committee, the Gestapo decided the camp was overcrowded and assembled another transport for Birkenau. Gertrud Jaffe and many of my good friends were on the list. I tried in every way to save Gertrud, and when nothing else was successful I made one last attempt by seeing Eppstein. It failed too. Gertrud did not say good-by to Eva Maria, so that the child would not get excited. We walked together to the processing center. The cattle cars were already waiting. We repeated the mass of the day and said good-by. When the packed train moved out I waved again, though I could not see Gertrud, locked up in the dark cattle car.

The inspection commission arrived. That day our work unit

received white gloves for loading the bread. The meat store, which had never been open to the public, received large pieces of meat to hang in the window. The meals were better that day. In the town square the band played cheerful tunes. Eppstein received a car for the occasion and conducted the commission through town at the head of a column of cars. But it seemed that the camouflage was too thin. One of the delegates, for instance, inquired about the real food conditions. One good result of the visit was that buildings like the pavilion and theater remained for our use.

Dietary deficiencies gradually became more noticeable, for although some could fill their stomachs to appease the gnawing hunger, the diet was unbalanced and lacking in fresh vegetables and fats. Most of us had some deficiency disease, such as skin rashes, night blindness, or intestinal disturbances. The children suffered greatly from lack of the most necessary foods for growth.

Eva Maria's condition deteriorated again, in spite of the loving care of the nurse. She missed Gertrud very much and longed for her. She even refused food, and I was advised to ask Böszi, the head nurse of the infants' home, to take care of her. Böszi was indefatigable, vivacious, and cheerful. When she walked through the sick ward and shook back her black hair with a quick movement of the head, it was as if she, and with her the sick, shook off all sorrow and misery. She was loved for her warm heart and her readiness to help. When I asked if she would look after Eva Maria, she told me that she was already playing mother to one orphan baby. "One is enough under these conditions," she said. "But our Eva Maria, that's different. The child needs a mother who can give her a mother's love."

Böszi looked after the child as if she were her own. Eva Maria's condition was so precarious that she was allowed special additions to her rations. She recovered, and became warmly attached to Böszi.

We heard of the invasion of France and the German retreat in Russia. The news started fresh *Bonques,* the rumors which always traveled through the camp. The optimists expected a collapse soon. Some thought that Nazi and Gestapo higher-ups would use us as hostages to buy their freedom from the Allies. The pessimists were convinced that we would all be liquidated at the last moment before total defeat. Later, the attempted assassination of Hitler made some fear further action against the Jews.

In August the Gestapo came up with another project: a film of Theresienstadt was to be made under the direction of a professional team. Some of the inmates were taken to swim in the Eger River, and had to pretend to be enjoying themselves. An outdoor stage was built in an attractive spot near the town, and the cameramen took shots of an applauding audience which had been told to look happy.

In September there was a sudden change for the worse. First Dr. Eppstein was arrested on the pretense that he had not observed some instruction or other. Then rumors spread of new transports. We could hardly believe it, for the invasion and the shortage of transport facilities had made us more hopeful. One transport after another left: five thousand young men for a labor transport, several thousand a few days later, and so on. The camp was almost empty of young men, but those with deferments, such as war invalids and medal holders, were still there. My unit of a hundred men had shrunk to eleven. We literally slaved, storing quantities of food in the depots of the fortress, safely away from air raids. It was, of course, not kept for us. I developed a rupture from carrying the heavy loads, which were often over two hundred pounds. Böszi was just making preparations for me to undergo an operation when the last act of the Theresienstadt tragedy began.

On October 9 all previously deferred inmates had to march past the camp commandant in single file. Almost all of us were included on the transport list. At first I was anxious that Böszi and Eva Maria be allowed to stay, but Böszi declared she would go wherever Eva Maria and I were going. When we were given the plausible explanation that we would be replacing German labor that had been sent to the front, and thus would continue to live, we were happy to be going together.

Before leaving, Böszi somehow procured me a rupture bandage. We both carried the permitted amount of baggage, fifty kilos apiece. Eva Maria carried a little bed pan and a bag. The SS leader laughed when he saw her walk by.

The dark and crowded train moved through the night. Rumor had it that we were going to work at a storage depot in Riesa in Saxony. But in the morning we could tell that we were going east. The train passed through the Silesian industrial area, past factories with heavily smoking chimneys. Flames shot from the blast furnaces; everything looked busy. Then the train slowed down. We saw the first groups of inmates, mostly women with blue-and-white striped jackets. They were guarded by female SS, with sticks and dogs on leashes. There were acres of barracks and guard towers on both sides of the railway line as far as we could see, barbed wire, and inside an ever-increasing number of emaciated persons. The railway tracks branched out with many freight trains on each side. The train slowed down, the brakes screeched; we stopped.

A horde of prisoners stormed the car. "All out, baggage stays in the car. Get a move on!"

We had arrived at Auschwitz, the notorious camp where perhaps three million human beings were to be killed.

Böszi whispered to me, "No matter what happens, I'll take care of the child." The men were being lined up on one side, the women on the other. I quickly kissed Eva Maria. She looked at me, questioning me with her large black eyes.

"Faster, faster," shouted one of the kapos. I hastily shook Böszi's hand and took my place among the men.

I stood next to two acquaintances from Berlin, the one a high official of the city government, the other a mathematician and philosopher. I could not see Böszi and Eva Maria among the mass of women.

The men had to march past a senior SS officer. He indicated with a movement of his thumb that each was to join a group on the right or on the left. Almost all were on the right side, including my two neighbors. It was my turn. The thumb again pointed to the right. I saw that some of the younger men of my section were on the left. Without fully knowing what it meant I said quietly, "Can't I stay with my comrades on the other side?"

"What were you?" the officer asked brusquely. "Heavy laborer." "Show me your hands." I showed them; they were calloused. He pointed to the left. Only a small group waited there, perhaps 120 men out of the transport of 1,500.

I looked for Böszi and Eva Maria. The whole group of women and children had been marched off.

We were marched to a delousing place. On the way we saw signs everywhere forbidding entrance to this or that area. Inmates begged us for bread, anything to eat.

I thought to myself that I might have been better off if I had stayed with the older people. I asked one of the Polish-Jewish oven stokers in the delousing station where the other men had gone.

"Do you see those buildings behind the green bushes?"

"Yes."

"And the chimneys?" He pointed at some large, brick, factory-like buildings with tall, smoking chimneys.

"That's their place. They call it liquidation."

"And the women and children?"

"We don't know," he answered. "They say that there are children's homes—"

In a large room we had to undress and leave all our belongings, except belt, shoes, and glasses. Our shoes were washed in chlorinated water. The dehumanization process started. All hair was shaved off with dull razors, without use of soap or water. We were taken to a shower, and before we had a chance to dry ourselves some rags which passed for clothes were thrown at us. I received a torn shirt, trousers, and a jacket with a cloth stripe to identify me. We got number tags to hang around our necks. We ceased to be human beings. We were never asked our names or any other information.

We were led to a barrack which had apparently once been a stable. A kapo lectured us on "selection," a medical examination for the purpose of selecting the unfit, for gassing. These included not only those who were exhausted but all with an ailment of any sort. I thought of my rupture, which could easily be noticed, and shuddered.

Suddenly someone shouted, "Attention!" We stood at attention. They selected the twenty strongest men first, apparently for work in mines. Then a civilian from a propeller factory in Friedland in Silesia asked for strong, if possible technically trained, "material." "Try to get to Friedland, that's one of the best camps," someone whispered. The civilian chose only a small number. But he came back later and got more men, among them me. We heard the SS pass out instructions that we were not to be tattooed, and that we should receive warm clothing. All the other Auschwitz inmates had their numbers tattooed on their left arm.

After another delousing we received more ragged clothing. The underwear was made of old Jewish prayer shawls. The clothing had almost no buttons; we used strings and wires instead.

After a long roll call we marched to another barrack. We had one blanket for every five men and slept on the concrete floor. There were approximately five hundred men herded together in this barrack. Only the kapo and his colleagues had a separate room. We lay so tightly packed that no one could move. We were ordered to take off our boots but to see to it that they were not stolen while we were sleeping.

We felt exhausted and without hope. Worry and uncertainty over the fate of our dear ones gnawed at us. I was in misery thinking of Böszi and Eva Maria. Should I assume that they had undergone a degradation like ours? Was this a delay to increase our torment and merely postpone the end? Perhaps the gas chamber was the lesser evil. But I had to continue living at all costs, for if Eva Maria and Böszi survived I must be there for them.

We were awakened early in the morning. All the men except our Friedland transport left the barrack. We had to stand naked for a medical examination. I hid my rupture bandage quickly in my trousers. A Jewish doctor from Berlin examined us thoroughly. My rupture was quite evident but he chose not to notice it.

Later another selection was conducted under the supervision of the notorious SS doctor Mengerle. Again I was able to hide my bandage, but I had little hope that the rupture would be ignored now. But apparently they had not calculated on such boldness as mine. As one of the oldest I was examined again but was retained in the group. A few men were taken out and disappeared. Cold sweat was running down my back when the selection was over.

By now it was noon. Food carriers brought two iron pails containing well-cooked cabbage. The whole group received only a few dishes. As there were no spoons, we licked out of the dishes like dogs. It was the first food we had received in Auschwitz.

More roll calls, more waiting. No one knew when the transport to Friedland would depart. Perhaps it would not leave at all. One of the inmates said that one never knew here what would happen from minute to minute. We saw a few friends brought in earlier transports from Theresienstadt. They had been assigned as skilled workers to some transport, but it was always postponed. We were happy to see each other again. None of them knew anything definite about the women and children.

We did leave that evening, and the train seemed to wander around the country, leaving a carload of men here, a carload of women there. Finally we reached Friedland and marched from the station to a high barbed wire enclosure. A large gate was opened by the SS. I noticed electrically charged wires and guard towers with large searchlights. We marched to the square of a real concentration camp.

An SS leader and a few inmates appeared. The bright lights of the searchlights were focused on us. Each of us received two thin blankets, a dish, and a spoon. We were quartered in one of the five barracks of the camp, which had double-decker bunks and even some tables and benches.

The next day was a day of rest. They registered the new arrivals, and selected a clerk and an orderly for the SS. We were able to make the barracks more livable and received straw mattresses. We were warned against escape, which would lead to the sternest punishment. Then they shaved a wide strip from forehead to neck on our already nearly bare heads. Our numbers were attached to our pants where they could be plainly seen.

We found that shortly before our arrival fifty men had come from Slovakia, where the Jewish persecutions had apparently only recently started in earnest. Three hundred sturdy young Jews from Poland had been at the camp for about six weeks. They had come from the Lodz ghetto camp.

The camp senior was intelligent, considerate, and no more brutal than was necessary for discipline among this mass of men who had been stripped of human dignity and were often demoralized or apathetic. The other inmate leaders, the kapos, were uneducated corporal types, one of them a ruffian, the other two tolerable enough. The kapo from our own group, a Viennese, was quite comradely at first but gradually fitted into his role more and more. Of course the SS furnished the kapos better quarters and gave them enough food.

From the second day on all days were alike. The kapos waked us at 4 A.M. We quickly made our bunks and stood in line at the inadequate latrine and washrooms. We had no soap or towels at first and later received only torn old rags for towels. They were one of the favorite objects of theft.

Then came the early morning rush to clean the barracks. A typical breakfast at first consisted of half a liter of beet soup. After some time we began to get bread too for breakfast. This was followed by a roll call. We had to stand with caps off at attention, waiting till the SS leader arrived and personally counted us. The sick in the dispensary had to lie at attention.

Then we marched to work on the edge of the town, quietly so that as few people as possible would see what miserable creatures we were. Our group at first worked with pick and shovel at a near-by site where two large tunnels had been dynamited into a hill. At noon we went back to the camp for a liter of watery beet soup; in the beginning it still contained some potatoes. Each time we came and went we had another roll call. The SS had an almost morbid fear that someone might escape. In the evening, if we did not have to go back to work again, we often waited from half an hour to an hour in the cold or rain, without gloves or socks, in torn shoes, dead tired and hungry, till the SS leader came to make his count.

In the evening we got the so-called heavy laborers' ration which was intended only for the men working in the propeller factory, where they were most interested in keeping their labor fit. It consisted of extra bread with some sort of spread—perhaps a teaspoonful of marmalade—and sometimes a tiny piece of meat, cheese, or sausage.

Sundays were the worst. We were kept constantly on the go, with roll calls, cleaning, lice examinations, barracks inspection, bailing out the latrines, carrying stones to the open lot or laying them on the muddy paths to the barracks. The only preferred work was potato peeling and cutting up the vegetables; on that job one could at least fill one's stomach.

Very often the water system did not function and water had to be carried in buckets from a well. Some Sundays labor was requisitioned to unload railway cars at the station, or the SS had some personal desire for which the inmates could be chased out of their barracks.

I developed dysentery. One of the two doctors of the camp was kindly disposed toward me and looked after me. It was getting cold, and I was glad when the pick-and-shovel work was suddenly discontinued. We were taken into the propeller factory, where I was trained to run an electric milling machine. Since none of the machines had any protective devices, there were many accidents among the untrained and tired inmates. We had to be careful, as any mistake might be interpreted as sabotage. I doubt that the German Air Force benefited greatly from the propellers on which I worked.

One day in November we got exciting news. A doctor who had been sent to a near-by women's camp to perform an operation reported that he had spoken to women from Theresienstadt. They had told of finding other women from there, and children who had been kept with their mothers. The hope and courage of all the married men revived. I myself was skeptical. Everything, at Auschwitz and here, seemed to indicate that as Enemy No. 1 we were to be worked to death or destroyed.

News of the German drive in the Ardennes depressed us, for every set back delayed our liberation.

Our factory training stopped shortly before Christmas. If the cause was lack of material, it would mean transfer from Friedland. We feared any change because of the uncertainty and the possibility of still worse conditions. We stayed in the camp but longed for work. There was too much time to think and worry. Had someone taken pity on Eva Maria? She was so pretty, people must have been struck by her charm. Perhaps they had not carried out the death order. Böszi surely had done everything possible to save her.

Men who died of exhaustion or after a cold or minor illness were laid in a far corner of the town cemetery. Two young Slovakian Catholics met the Catholic priest during these burials. He showed them sympathy and dared to send them rosaries.

After Christmas the factory instruction was resumed. My feet had swollen and developed infections as a result of malnutrition and dirt, but I continued working, as we were about to be transferred to the operating part of the factory and I feared being considered useless.

Most of the supervisors and foremen were from Hamburg, and apparently inclined politically toward the left. Some showed open sympathy for the inmates and secretly gave us food or tried to ameliorate our inhuman treatment. They had to be careful, for no one could trust the next person and the heads of the factory were Nazis of the worst sort. About half the workers were foreigners: Czechs, Poles, Italians, and French. The French were withdrawn later, for reasons unknown to us. The French, and still more the Italians, were friendly to us, told us news, and talked to us often, in spite of the prohibition by the Gestapo. The Czechs and Poles were not all so well disposed.

My feet got worse, and the doctor tried to stop the spread of the infections. But without medicine there was little he could do. In January, 1945, one foot was so bad that I had to stop working and lie in the dispensary. During the coming months it never got well, but on the advice of my fellow inmate Paul Seligmann I went back to the factory and he got me a sitting job. We feared that if I were considered completely useless I might be liquidated. Some of the exhausted men had already been sent to a "recuperation camp." So, with a paper bandage around my open wound, I dragged myself to the factory. Occasionally, if the SS permitted, I could go to the factory first-aid station. The nurse, Agnes, took good care of my foot. Sometimes she brought me food, and if I was not allowed to go to her she came into the plant and bandaged the foot, or passed by, winked at me, and slipped a bandage into my pocket.

When gangrene threatened to set in the camp doctor cut my foot open with a scalpel, as he had no operating knife. While he cut, we talked about the children, Eva Maria, the chances of living and getting to the United States, and the Americans' magic drug, penicillin, with which they healed all infections.

That January we saw the first German refugees. The trickle

grew into an uninterrupted chain of horse-drawn farm wagons, loaded with personal belongings, kitchen utensils, and furniture. Cows and goats were tied to the wagons or driven along. Occasionally military formations passed, apparently rear-echelon supply units. Exotic-looking creatures rode by on small steppe horses, probably Ukrainians and others who had helped the Nazis.

Before long the first évacués of a concentration camp came along. They looked pitiable, ragged, tired, and starved. Some of them stopped near our camp and we took in about a hundred exhausted and dead, who were lying on a wagon. We found out later that the rest stood all night in the snow, without warm food or a chance to sit or lie down. They were driven on the next morning. Word came that the Russians had liberated Auschwitz, as well as many smaller labor camps like ours. Eva Maria and Böszi might be among the liberated.

The camp was more crowded now, and we slept two to a bunk. Once a month we were marched to a small bathing room. Only twenty men could use it at one time, and about 480 had to wait, shivering, outside. One SS man always made free use of the butt of his gun. Our barracks and bodies were full of lice, and even delousing did not help for long. Once when an inspection of the camp was expected, the sick were given more care and all the inmates were weighed. I weighed ninety pounds.

Our hopes rose when we heard artillery in the distance, but later the sound grew more faint.

Spring was approaching. The first inmates had escaped during the winter, and now two more had gotten away. Yet no special action was taken against us.

By April the front had come close, but still the Russians had not overrun our camp. Breslau was surrounded but was holding out. The Russians had advanced much farther west and were approaching Berlin. We were in a pocket which was held by SS troops, who would surely defend themselves in a last-ditch struggle.

The work in the factory slowed down. We could not imagine where they sent the propellers, for everything was going to pieces and the transportation system was in disorder. Those without work in the factory were sent to dig trenches and build road barriers outside the town. We saw foremen of the factory serving as members of the Volkssturm and Hitler Youth getting military training near our camp.

If we could just live through these last days!

We heard all sorts of news. Berlin was surrounded; no, they were sending aid; some German general had reconquered Bautzen. "Don't rejoice too early," someone said, "the Americans and the Russians will get in each other's hair at the last moment. That's the Germans' last great chance." No one knew what was rumor and what was truth.

The Americans took Leipzig, Karlsbad, Pilsen—then Theresienstadt.

There was snow and rain on the first of May. That evening an early roll call kept us standing for a long time. "Take off your caps! The Führer fell in the Battle of Berlin." Everyone had to be silent. "Caps on."

What did it mean? Very little to us, for whom the world revolved around the single question, "Would we be freed or liquidated?"

The number of German civilians escaping from the front had been increasing steadily. Trains passed filled with refugees, at first in passenger cars, then in freight cars, and later on flatcars. Long trains with artillery and airplane fuselages moved west, away from the front. But where was the front? We could still hear artillery in the distance, but it never seemed to come closer.

SS troops were in the area, fighting to the bitter end. An SS officer came to the camp. Surely, we thought, they will shoot us. We are a living indictment of them. The worst SS guards had left already. There was talk of handing the camp over to the city administration.

On May 8 we got better soup than usual and did not have to work at the trenches. Around noon the next day we had to form on the open lot of the camp. The SS camp sergeant, who had been more decent than most of the SS, was still there. He handed the camp over to three civilians from Friedland who belonged to the antifascist People's Defense.

Our new authorities told us to have patience: we were still in danger, the SS was still strong, and we could not be let out of the camp yet. They would look after our security and welfare.

They left the camp, and we separated quietly. Many embraced each other, but most were serious rather than exuberant. The Friedlanders sent us a loudspeaker and we heard news of the armistice. But the SS troops under General Schoerner were still fighting in our sector.

It got dark. We were given some good soup and each received half a loaf of bread. But food was not important at this exciting time.

"We'll defend ourselves, if necessary," someone said. "There's a machine gun hidden under the boards in the kitchen, and a lot of the Poles have had military training."

"There's nothing we can do if they want to liquidate us," replied another.

Later that evening, just as we were about to lie down, word was passed along in whispers:

"Stay up, await further orders."

There was a feverish uncertainty among us, a mixture of hope and despondency. Then came another whispered instruction:

"Everyone is to leave the camp at midnight. The wire will be cut at one place."

"That's a trap; the dogs want to liquidate us all in the dark."

"Nonsense, the kapos want to escape; they know that the Russians will hang them."

"I am staying here. I don't care if the SS shoots us here or there."

But at midnight all left who could. It was like an order, and we were accustomed to obey.

"Sh-sh, quiet, don't talk, no lights."

Four of us, Paul, Heinz, Peppi, and I, held hands going through the barbed wire. We walked past houses to a field, up a hill into a forest.

"Rest; deploy and sit down."

The sound of steps frightened us. Would the SS find us here? Someone was coming cautiously along the path, we could hear the noise of wheels. Germans with heavily laden baby carriages were fleeing like us into the forest.

Red on the eastern horizon announced the morning. Someone

passed the word, "Be careful, don't make any noise; there are SS units everywhere, especially in the valley."

We were dog-tired and went to sleep. It was broad daylight when we were awakened by the noise of artillery and machine guns.

We had a good view of the valley, and watched the scene of battle as if we were sitting in orchestra seats in a theater. The shooting came closer. Some huge thing was moving along the highway—a tank, a Russian tank. It was knocked out. Another tank came along, followed by armored vehicles and motorcycles cautiously feeling their way down the road. The shooting came closer still. There seemed to be a machine-gun nest near by. Infantry columns advanced through the valley, guns and machine pistols ready, but without cover. They were talking loudly. Gradually the shooting died down. Artillery, cars, small and large horse-drawn vehicles were rolling along the street.

Heinz and I got up. The place where another of our groups had been lying was empty. Heinz reconnoitered and ran back to me breathless, shouting:

"The camp, the camp . . . I saw a red flag!"

We hurried down as quickly as our swollen feet would carry us. The camp gates were wide open, the guard towers deserted; a red flag with hammer and sickle was flying at the entrance. A few shot-up vehicles could be seen and some soldiers, wounded or dead, were lying in the street.

Some of the inmates were already wearing civilian clothes. Others were changing clothes or eating food they had found. The kitchen storeroom had been opened. The staff had left meals on the table untouched. We went to our friends in the infirmary. Nothing had happened to them.

The SS food warehouse was opened. Sacks of cereal, peas, and other foodstuffs lay about the street. Some inmates moved into the SS staff building.

Because the SS had wanted to liquidate the whole camp, the antifascists of the town had passed around word to leave. But the SS had been too busy building barricades and defending themselves. Then the Russians conquered the city and the SS had fled.

At last we were really free!

Our group of four walked to the town. I went into a house behind the railroad embankment. The door was knocked in, cabinets broken open and the contents strewn over the floor. I walked up to the third floor, stepped through a bashed door frame, and went to a wardrobe. The residents of the house must have fled hastily.

I had an uncomfortable feeling. Suddenly I heard someone entering. A woman came up the stairs. She was weeping and horrified by the state of her home. I asked her for clothing and underwear. She was not very generous, but at last I could take off the rags I had been wearing without change for almost eight months.

I walked along the main street to the market square. Russian soldiers moved in columns through the town, took down the street barriers, or halted in the squares. They gave the children and us wheat bread and cake. It was difficult to tell the difference between ranks. They gave the impression of a medieval soldiery with modern arms.

The Russian commandant had handed the town over for plundering because the SS had defended it after the armistice. Everyone, including the inmates of the camp, took part. In a senseless frenzy of theft and destruction stores and houses were broken open and property thrown away when something better was found. I passed a shoe store. It had already been looted, but still I found a pair of shoes for myself. There was food in some houses. I could not resist it, and ate fried potatoes, vegetables, and cake.

Then I went back to the camp. I saw a single inmate, an elderly lawyer from Prague, still in his old clothes. "I can't take other people's property," he said, and gazed uncomprehendingly at the disorder around him.

I went back to town and rang the bell at the rectory. A frightened woman opened the door. There was a strange, quieting atmosphere in the house. The old priest welcomed me heartily. He himself had been in a concentration camp for many months. His house was full of refugees, but he asked me to live and eat there. I declined to stay but was happy to have my meals with him.

So I sat at a table with a white cloth and ate with a knife and a fork. The meal was brought to the table.

The doorbell rang. Drunken Russian soldiers pushed in. They respected the priest but took watches and jewelry from everyone.

Again noise outside. Women were seeking protection in the rectory from rape.

The priest said a prayer. At that moment something awoke in me, and suddenly a stream of tears came—not tears of joy that everything was over, nor tears of mourning, although I felt that I would never see Eva Maria and Böszi again; but tears of painful disappointment. I had imagined the day of liberation as the beginning of a new era, as a symphony of joy with men at last understanding each other. But this day was one of good fortune for some, misfortune and misery for others. I saw that the real liberation of humanity was still to come.

I went to the church. The Mary altar was beautifully decorated with lilies of the valley and soft pink anemones. No one was there. But the church seemed to be full of all those dear to me: Eva Maria, my wife, my mother, Gertrud, Böszi, and all my friends.

I knelt before the altar. I felt quieted. Here was real peace. Here was the beginning and the end, the source of all:

"Mary, thou vessel of incarnate love."

EPILOGUE TO CHAPTER XI

"Therefore Will I Deliver Him"

AFTER liberation Heinrich Liebrecht hunted for Böszi and Eva Maria. He searched in Prague and in Theresienstadt, in hope of finding that they had returned there. There was no trace of them. Probably they had perished in the gas chambers of Auschwitz.

Mr. Liebrecht was made head of a transport from Theresienstadt to a DP camp in Bavaria. Here he had to contend with elements in UNRRA who were not distributing all the allotted rations. In the early part of 1946 he was appointed judge of a district court by local military government. After the denazification law was passed he was made chairman of a denazification board. He was later appointed by the Bavarian Ministry of Denazification to instruct other board chairmen.

In spite of many professional opportunities in Germany, he longed to come to America where his only two surviving close relatives, a sister and a brother, were living and where, as he says, "the constitution regards the freedom of the individual as the most precious possession." So in 1946 he emigrated to the United States. In the spring of 1947 he married a friend and companion from Theresienstadt and the DP camp who had lost her husband in Auschwitz.

Mr. Liebrecht now works as a printing machine operator in New York. He hopes to be able to study social work or become a teacher so that others may benefit from the experience he gained in those years of suffering.

252

PROLOGUE TO CHAPTER XII

For Life and Freedom

FRAU WOLFF joined the German Social Democratic party at the age of seventeen and quickly became one of its leading figures in her native Westphalia. She was a member of the city council of Buchhold and lecturer at an adult education institute. She helped frame the social security program of western Westphalia and the Münster area. From the beginning, back in 1922, she fought the Nazis and was persecuted by them both for being a socialist and for being Jewish.

XII

For Life and Freedom

JEANETTE WOLFF

THE Nazis tried to maintain the pretense of a free election on March 5, 1933, but the flood of their propaganda and the curtailment of campaign activities made thoughtful people aware that it was no longer free. I had been speaking for the Social Democratic party at rallies, both in Buchhold, in Westphalia, where we lived, and elsewhere. Nazi hoodlums often broke up the meetings and threatened me, and on election day the Storm Troopers arrested me.

I was sent to the women's penitentiary in Hamborn, in the Rhineland, and kept there two years in what was called "protective custody because of unrest of the national population." Hermann, my husband, a businessman, was arrested two weeks after I was. Our house and books were confiscated by the Nazis. Fortunately our three young daughters were not harmed, in spite of their belonging to a socialist youth organization, the Red Falcons. From prison I was able to arrange to send the youngest, Käthe, to relatives in Holland, but homesickness drove her back.

After I was freed in 1935 I had to report to the Gestapo every two weeks. My husband was not held long, but he had to give up his business. Until 1938 he was employed by the Victoria Insurance Company. Then he lost that job because no Jews were allowed in responsible positions. He turned to manual labor, digging foundations. I supplemented his earnings by opening a boardinghouse.

Although we were under close surveillance and our apartment was searched from time to time, we managed to work against the Nazis, getting in touch with resistance groups and Catholic or-

254

ganizations in the Rhineland, Westphalia, and the Ruhr, distributing leaflets, and spreading counterpropaganda by word of mouth. Our meetings were camouflaged as lunches or suppers in our *Pension*.

We were able to give our children a good education. Juliane, the eldest, born in 1912, received nurse's training in the Jewish hospital in Frankfurt. Edith, born in 1916, entered the university, but Nazi laws prohibited her from finishing. She later became a nurse. Käthe, born in 1920, was still going to school. After 1938 all three had to do hard menial labor.

On November 9, 1938, the Nazis used the assassination by a Jewish youth of the third secretary of the German Embassy in Paris as pretext for a long-planned mass action against Jews. They burned synagogues, destroyed homes and businesses, desecrated graves and cemeteries, and made mass arrests of Jews all over Germany. Armed Storm Troopers and Hitler Youth broke into our house, beat up our boarders, broke the furniture, and threw things out of the windows. The next day my husband and five of our boarders were arrested. A few days later I heard that they had been taken to Sachsenhausen.

My husband came back after five months, much aged, sick, and broken in spirit. He never told me what had happened in the camp.

Jews had for some time been forbidden to attend plays or movies. Käthe liked the movies and sometimes went. Someone saw her and denounced her to the Nazis. Gestapo officials came, searched the house and arrested her, and put her at first in the Steinwache police prison in Dortmund. Later she was sent to the women's prison in Herne. After five months I was told she was to be released, and the considerate prison director let me talk to her for four hours. Käthe was pale and nervous, and I could hardly recognize her. She had been threatened, beaten, and placed in a dark cell. She told me how Gestapo Commissar Bovensiepen had locked himself in the cell with her for six hours, threatened her with a revolver, beaten her, and tormented her till she screamed aloud and collapsed. He wanted to shoot her, but the prison director who had heard her cries came and stopped him.

That was the last time I saw her. Instead of being released she was sent to Ravensbrück.

Shortly after Käthe's arrest we had to evacuate our house on six hours' notice and go to the "Jew house," about forty kilometers from Dortmund, leaving my husband's eighty-one-year-old mother behind. She was sent to Theresienstadt.

One day in January, 1941, we received a notice from the Gestapo: "You and your family are to report at 8 A.M., January 20, at the Bourse Hall in Dortmund to go on labor assignment to the east." The notice stated exactly what baggage we might take, and that we were allowed ten marks.

In preparation I got myself a pair of heavy boots and carefully fitted double soles in them. In the space between the two soles I hid some diamond rings, a heavy gold bracelet, and two watches. I had no illusions about the risk I was taking, but told myself that I might be able to buy my life with these, or use them to start a new life after the Nazi hell.

For five days and nights about thirteen hundred of us waited in the Bourse Hall. Someone who became hysterical during the night was shot. On the morning of January 25 a long and dismal march brought us to a train standing near the railroad station. Rumors spread that it was going to Riga in Latvia.

We rode five days in the cold train without warm food and tortured by thirst. A few people at a time were permitted to leave each car to get water; and a few minutes were allowed for cleaning ourselves in the snow. Men and women had to perform their toilet on the rail embankment in each other's presence. In the terrible cold hundreds of people froze parts of their bodies and developed gangrenous fingers and toes, and many died after reaching the camp. The Jewish community of Dortmund had collected three carloads of food to tide us over the first days of deportation. The cars were detached from the train in Königsberg. Such baggage as sewing machines, mattresses, and stoves, which we had been permitted to take along, we never saw again.

At the Shirotowa station in Riga German and Latvian SS welcomed us with sticks and rifle butts. Our hand baggage was taken away. It was a beautiful day and a glorious winter sun shone on the untracked snow. The contrast of nature with human brutality hit me hard. The snow covered ground where thousands had been murdered.

The SS drove us to the ghetto. The houses looked as if vandals had visited them. Floors and stairs were littered with broken furniture and china, torn clothing and shoes, plaster and damaged household articles. Toilets and pipes had been smashed. It was obvious that the previous residents had left in great haste just before we came, but we did not at once understand why. We soon heard rumors that they had been killed. Eleven transports of perhaps two thousand people each had been sent to take their place. The older people and some children in our transport who could not walk from the Riga station were put on sleds, and we never saw them again.

There were two ghettos in Riga, each surrounded by barbed wire: one for German Jews, the other for the Latvian Jews who were left from the liquidation that had preceded our arrival. The sectors of the German ghetto were named for the places of origin of the transports: Hanover, Saxony, Bielefeld, Cologne, Kassel, Berlin, and Dortmund.

We tried to make the best of our situation. Juliane and Edith started to work as nurses, Hermann and I were assigned to cleaning up the debris and dirt. Emergency latrines were built by digging ditches which had to be cleaned out every week. Frozen piles of rubbish as high as one's head had to be sorted out, and silver and other valuables which had apparently been hidden there by our predecessors separated and turned over to SS headquarters.

Twenty-four persons of both sexes were crowded together in our three-room apartment. Signs all over the ghetto warned, "Sexual intercourse will be punished with death." We had to keep the doors unlocked so that the SS could inspect at any time.

New transports arrived. There was no space; three and more families were already living in one room. The commandant of the ghetto, Karl Wilhelm Krause, developed a method of finding space which was called *Aktion:* liquidation of a portion of the inhabitants. Sometimes whole transports were taken directly from the station to the Bikernik Forest and shot there. Groups of young men were sent to a place called Salas Pils, where they were given a hunger ration and were literally worked to death, burying thousands of Jews and Russian prisoners of war who had been shot or had died of hunger. A transport of about 1,300 people from Berlin, among them 750 children from the orphan asylum, was sent there, and only 80 sturdy men were kept apart and sent to work in a cement plant. All that arrived in the ghetto was the clothing and the shoes of 750 children and 450 men and women, sometimes smeared with blood.

During the first two weeks we received no food. We looked in the garbage for frozen potato peelings, vegetable refuse, and so forth, and cleaned, cooked, and ate the stuff. We mixed potato peelings with flour and baked them without fat. The stoves were broken and smoked heavily. If an army bread truck driving through the ghetto stopped long enough, we stole bread. When food came it was a starvation ration: 220 grams of mouldy bread —equivalent to four slices a day—and later fish and herring scraps from the smokehouses. Three slices of bread were the only present we could give my husband on his birthday. We were given spoiled scraps of all sorts of vegetables. Juliane and Edith brought food from other parts of town, although that was punishable by death. Friends who had come with us died of hunger and exposure. Most people had lost their will to live; but some among us derived a determination to survive from our faith in socialism.

Everyone longed to be sent on labor assignments outside the camp, in order to get something to eat and to bring back to his family. There were really good labor commands where one was fed and not beaten, especially those for the army. Work on the railroads was desirable because one could exchange clothing for food with the Latvian population. We found useful clothing in the ghetto, and there was a clothes depot which supplied us from time to time. Also many of us had worn three or four layers of garments when we were deported and so had something extra to exchange.

"Barter will be punished by death" read a sign on every fence and many houses; but hunger forced us to take the risk. Many were fortunate enough not to be noticed when checked on return to the ghetto in the evening, and their reward was in the faces of the children waiting near the barrier at the entrance.

The Latvian Jews were very good to us German Jews. Some of them had buried valuables in the ground and could buy food from the Latvian population. They gave it to us for the sick, the weak, and the children.

When the commandant checked at the gate, he whipped and executed violators himself. With an ironic grin he would drive them to the cemetery, make the victims take off part of their clothes and kneel with their backs to him, and shoot them in the neck. Each Saturday was court day. Jews had to execute Jews. The commandant selected a man who had a large family as hangman. If he refused his whole family would be shot. This was the way the photographs were taken for the Nazi illustrated paper which were captioned "This is how Jews execute Jews." When we returned from work on Saturday we sometimes had to pass the "hill of gallows." Anyone who did not look up to the gallows while marching by received a blow under the chin from the SS guard.

The labor commands assigned to the SS were among the worst, and many lost their lives in them. Some SS men demanded pretty girls; a few girls were requested by name and forced to prostitute themselves. The temptation to take food was particularly great in the SS labor commands, for the SS was living in luxury and had supplies of things which other people had not seen for a long time. The SS were both German and Latvian. The Latvians, recruited chiefly from major criminals, were assigned to handle most of the executions, for which their underworld background fitted them well.

I was assigned to a cleaning command of the Waffen-SS, the SS divisions trained for combat. They were billeted in Riga with German Army units, whose quarters we also had to clean. Shortly after the battle in the Warsaw ghetto the German troops that had participated were billeted here. One of them, a staff sergeant in the military police, asked me if I was not from Westphalia like himself. We talked a little and then he said:

"No matter how the war ends, I can't go back to Germany. We were incorporated in the SS and have been assigned as execution troops in occupied countries. Everyone has a right to call us murderers. Even if we win the war I won't be able to forget the screams of 65,000 people murdered in the Warsaw ghetto. At night I hear the whimpering and moaning of men being burnt alive and see the twisted faces of the dead and bodies torn by grenades. I can't go on living."

Next morning we found his body hanging on the window frame of an empty room.

Our family was separated for the first time when Edith was sent to Olaine, a peat-digging camp. Food there was even less adequate, the barracks were full of lice, and the working conditions miserable. They had to dig down a ways before they hit good peat. Sometimes they were standing in water to the hips. Edith fell seriously ill and was sent back to the Riga ghetto to be placed in the infirmary. I wanted to prevent that at all costs for many patients were known to have been liquidated through an injection by the senior Jewish doctor, who was a willing tool of the SS. I made every effort to have Edith nursed in my room, and succeeded. After two weeks she began to recover.

Not long afterward Edith and her husband—whom she had married in the ghetto—were sent to the Kaiserwald concentration camp near Riga, where they were kept two years. Edith was put to work as nurse in the camp hospital. The kapos in charge of the other prisoners at Kaiserwald were professional criminals and pimps released from German penitentiaries, and prostitutes. Having long been regarded as pariahs, many of them became drunk with power and turned into sadists. They were in a privileged position. For instance, they were given as much to eat as the SS. A typical case was a man known as "Mister X," a notorious thief and swindler. He was inordinately strong and was the most feared executioner in Kaiserwald. He would sneak up behind people, and they lay on the ground before they knew what had hit them. To the boys and pretty girls that he wanted for himself he brought food and clothing.

The prostitutes in charge were just as bad. The first transport of forty criminal whores was officially billeted in the women's quarters. Actually they slept in the men's camp, with the kapos, the night of their arrival. Finding thirty-two of our new "superiors" missing, the SS started looking for them, so the kapos put their naked women in the Jewish men's barracks. The SS commandant was not deceived. There were still ten women missing, hidden by their men in the five-hundred-liter cooking kettles. After they crept out their hair was cut as punishment; but they went back to the men's camp the next night.

The Kaiserwald "hospital" served a group of camps: Mühl-graben, Strazdenhof, Lenta, and Jungfernhof. The two SS doctors in charge of the hospital left all the work to prisoners who like Edith were nurses, doctors, and first-aid men. Patients came in mere skeletons. There was no extra sick ration and although the staff scrounged food for them from the SS kitchen, they often could not be kept alive. Dysentery was the prevailing scourge; and the death rate shot up when a typhus epidemic broke out.

Sometimes the hospital was completely cleared by liquidation. The SS ruled that no patient could stay over twenty-one days. The staff frequently changed arrival dates and usually did not report anyone; but the SS made frequent checkups and gave "twenty-five" for withholding the facts. Edith and the others did everything they could to make the last days of the patients a bit easier, but usually the hospital was a place of death rather than of life.

Two beautiful sisters, Annemarie and Margit, from Gelsen-kirchen, who had recovered from typhus, were merely waiting for their last blood test when they were listed for liquidation. They cried bitterly. Edith hid them in the camp, but they were dis-covered by an SS man and as the others had already been trans-ported they were taken away in another vehicle.

All Kaiserwald was based on bestiality. When someone died in the camp, headquarters had to be notified immediately, and a dental technician would appear quickly to remove gold teeth and bridges. Corpses were carried out and stored in an empty pig-sty until a truckload had accumulated; then they would be driven away to be burned or thrown into a mass grave. After a while the SS did not even supply paper sacks to cover the naked-ness of the bodies.

When new inmates arrived they were searched. The men and women in the transports from the ghettoes of Kowno, Schaulen, and Vilna still had considerable amounts of money and jewelry with them, as the Gestapo there had not examined them thoroughly when they were sent off. When money was found on the men they would be badly mistreated, and a few were beaten to death. The women were subjected to gynecological examination conducted by a Jewish inmate doctor in the presence of the SS and the kapos. At this time their hair was shaved off. The men's heads were not shaved except for a tonsure running over the center.

In Riga we worried a great deal about Edith; but at least Hermann, Juliane, and I were still together.

Although Juliane was a nurse she went out on labor command once a week to get more food. One day when she returned Jewish ghetto police found food on her. That and her opposition to the senior Jewish doctor led to her being placed on the transport list for near-by Dünamünde, allegedly to work in a fish cannery. It turned out that most of the five thousand people selected for that transport were over fifty or else sick and weak. They were promised easier work. I asked Hesfer, a German police lieutenant of a contingent stationed at the edge of the ghetto, what this meant. He told me that all were to be liquidated.

For three days I worked frantically to save Juliane. She was young and healthy, she was a nurse and they needed nurses. I even went to the commandant and begged to have her released. After I had made many humiliating attempts, I was told that she was being taken off the list, perhaps as much because of her personal charm as through my efforts.

When the transports to Dünamünde were ready the victims had to give their blankets, food, everything they had to the SS. Then they were loaded on trucks. The trucks were back after only thirty minutes—the length of time it would have taken just to go to Dünamünde. We soon found out what had happened, from the young men who were sent out to pour chemicals over the naked corpses and burn them. Only a few of these men returned to tell of the liquidation of five thousand men and women.

I would have been sent on that liquidation transport too because of my age if I had not asserted that I could do uniform tailoring. I was assigned to work as seamstress at the army hospital administration of the Nazi party in Riga. That was considered essential skilled labor. Hermann had been appointed by the ghetto self-governing body, the Council of Elders, to supervise the sanitation and cleaning up of our district.

Presently Juliane was sent to a near-by construction camp on the Red Düna River. At first she could visit us occasionally on Sundays; then that too was forbidden. Later she was sent to Kaiserwald, and Hermann and I remained in the ghetto. But not long after our arrival we had adopted a lovely little baby girl who was not quite a year and a half old, and she became the sunshine of our life. Her father had been liquidated, and her mother went mad when she found out. Ruth had golden hair and large black eyes. As she grew older she developed a lovely voice and often had to sing for the pleasure of the SS commandant or the Council of Elders.

The Latvian-Jewish ghetto police were the nucleus of a re-sistance group which was training men in the large cellar of the ghetto smithy. The smiths beat the anvils to drown the noise of practice shooting. On October 10, 1943, another *Aktion* took place against these police because the SS had found out that arms had been smuggled in. Forty men were clubbed to death or chased into machine-gun fire. Many defended themselves with their bare fists against the armed SS. The heads of the Jewish ghetto police, Iska Back, Tolja Nathan, and Boris Lifschitz, were said to have knocked down a number of SS men before they collapsed. Those who had to dig the common grave for the forty told us that many of the boys were riddled with machine-gun bullets.

Tolja Nathan was only wounded and managed to escape. He was searched everywhere in the ghetto and Commandant Krause finally found him. Before Nathan died he spoke his mind to Krause:

"You can shoot me, you dog, but first I will tell you what I think of you. You are the greatest pig on God's earth. You took our wives and girls whom you wanted for yourself, you have slaughtered hundreds of men with your own hand and fattened yourself on their property. You took my girl, and I don't know where she is; you may have killed her. But I tell you today, you will die like a dog and with you the whole false and foul Nazi dictatorship. There—now you can shoot me.'

The commandant stood pale and motionless. Then his face became contorted with hate and he emptied his submachine gun into the young man. This took place in the street next to the fence of the ghetto, and hundreds of Latvians saw it. We heard the story from them later.

Early on the morning of November 2, 1943, headquarters issued the following order: "All children up to the age of twelve are to be taken to the Blechplatz by 7.45. They are to have warm clothes and a blanket." Dread gripped the mothers. Up to now they had borne everything. Many of their dear ones had been murdered, died, or been deported, and now they were to give up their children. Some women were on the verge of insanity. Mothers and grandmothers implored the SS men to let them go with the children. They were permitted only if they were unskilled workers. Our Ruth had had her third birthday in October. She had just recovered from a mastoid infection, and I tried at first to report her sick. When this did not work I hid her in the coal cellar of the district.

Then I went to the commandant and begged him at least to let the orphans stay, who had already gone through one separation from their parents. He told me not to worry, they would all be sent to a Red Cross children's home in Germany. When I got back I found Ruth in the apartment again. Someone had discovered her hiding place and sent her back. I did not know what to do to save her.

I packed a little bag for her and a few things for myself. At least I would go with her. We walked to the Blechplatz. Ruth was frightened. An SS man told me I could not go along; I must go on working in the army clothing office. I stayed with Ruth as long as possible. She kept asking, "Mutti, you are going with me, aren't you?" As I left she was imploring one of the SS men, "Dear policeman, I give you my travel bag, there is bread with marmalade in it, you can keep it all. I only want to stay with my Pappi and Mammi."

While the children were being gathered the SS searched the houses and the older and weaker people were brought to the Blechplatz. The hospital was dissolved and the sick were placed in trucks on stretchers. Some had had recent operations. One woman ran away with the clamps of an operation still in her wound; she died a few weeks later of blood poisoning. The crying of the women and children mingled with the shouting and flailing of the SS. About twenty-five hundred in all were taken to the Shirotowa station and loaded into a long train of freight cars, without straw, with only bread to eat, at temperatures below freezing. We never heard what had happened to them. Less than two thousand, mostly skilled workers, were left in the German ghetto. When we returned to our houses we found that the German and Latvian SS had turned everything upside down. They had even taken some of our few belongings. The ghetto was quiet as death, and all sounds of laughing children were gone. Only twenty-five children had been hidden and escaped discovery.

When Hermann came home that evening he shouted in joy, "Thank God, you are still here! Where is Ruth?" I could not answer. I could only shake my head helplessly and weep. Hermann broke down and cried unrestrainedly. I had never seen him weep before.

About two weeks later those of us who were left had to assemble at the Blechplatz. Some were sent to the Strazdenhof camp, where almost all died of malnutrition. Hermann and I in a group of about fourteen hundred were sent to Kaiserwald, which had apparently taken the place of the Riga ghetto as a sort of mother camp. Although we feared the future, we looked forward to seeing Juliane and Edith.

But we did not find them. Worse still, men and women were separated. We had to undress, and SS assistants took everything away from us, our last links with the past in photographs, letters, personal mementos. I tried to save the pictures of my husband and children. When the supervisor spotted me, she slapped me hard in the face. Fortunately I could keep my valuable shoes.

Then we had to stand outside and watch the brute Mister X beat up our menfolk. While I looked on he knocked Hermann down four times. I never learned why.

Many of us were soon transferred to Mühlgraben, an army quartermaster clothing camp near Kaiserwald. I had no chance to look for my daughters before leaving. But I found that Hermann had also been sent to Mühlgraben, so although it was forbidden I visited him the first evening and dressed his wounds.

Our hair was shaved and kept shaved from then on. We looked like different persons and lost all feminine attraction. We covered our heads with a cloth. But Mühlgraben was tolerable compared to Kaiserwald. I was assigned as seamstress to one of the infantry barracks in Riga. We marched three hours to work in the morning and three hours back at night. That was too slow, so they tried taking us part of the way in cement boats, in which we were loaded like cattle. We stood during the whole trip, shivering and suffocating. Even that was too slow, for the clothing office wanted twelve to sixteen hours of work from us; so we were shipped in an antiquated paddle-wheel steamer. When that was still too slow and led to an accident, we were shipped most of the way by railway on open flatcars. Often we did not return to camp before 10 P.M. Then we got our soup and bread, and by the time we could go to sleep it was twelve o'clock. We had to get up again at four.

Mühlgraben was a reception camp for army material coming from the eastern front. We repaired and cleaned carloads of bloody and torn army clothing. The mass of bloody uniforms told us that the war with the USSR could never be won, in spite of all the reports of victory. Our hope of freedom started reviving.

Liquidation continued to threaten us. From time to time the weak were sorted out. If someone looked very thin, or his face showed many folds and wrinkles, or he had a rupture, he would be sent away to Kaiserwald to be liquidated.

We were happy to have saved a few children from the Riga ghetto. But one evening when we returned from work we heard that all children under fourteen, including those who were already working, had been taken away by the SS.

I saw my husband from time to time and could give him some extra food. I did my allotted sewing at the clothing barracks as quickly as possible so that I could sew extra things secretly, like house shoes. Waiting for our train I could exchange them for bread, bacon, or tobacco with the local Latvians.

One day in June, 1944, word spread that Sunday would be a

free day, with no roll call. We were happy thinking that we could sleep till seven o'clock. But we were wakened at six and driven out by the police. The thoughtful ones said "Transport," and took along what they needed. The hopeful ones said "Only counting," and put their coats on. Names of men were called out first, and those called had to form separately. Hermann was among them. When the women were called I was not included. I begged the commandant to put me on the transport list, and he finally exchanged me for a young girl who wanted to stay with her aunt.

We were given striped prison clothing and three days' food ration, and loaded on a ship, the men and women segregated. In Riga Bay we were transferred to a large steamer. We saw other large ships, and realized that the Kaiserwald camps were being evacuated too. I asked Mister X whether my daughters were in the Kaiserwald transport, and he said no. I lay down wearily on one of the crowded cots; then suddenly I felt that I must look for my girls, and sprang up again. I heard a familiar voice. Edith was coming down the steps in a white hospital frock, looking for me.

Life was easier to bear now, with one of our three children with me again, after more than two years' separation. But Juliane was not in this transport. She had been sent to the camp at Spilve.

After being loaded into still other ships—never less crowded— unloaded, and marching ten kilometers, we arrived at Camp Stutthof near Danzig. It was a huge camp, with electrified double barbed wire enclosure and high watchtowers.

It was plain at once that the discipline in Stutthof was severe. Each barrack had its own high barbed wire fence and enclosure, and a partition dividing it into two separate parts. Each building had a capacity of 250, but 900 women were assigned to it. There were 90,000 inmates in the camp from all parts of the world. Four people slept in each bunk and the rest lay on the floor. There were model washrooms though, and clean modern toilets, and we could take a shower every day—although the washrooms were open only for short periods at a time.

The men were separated from us by barbed wire. The first night we heard sounds of beating from their barracks. The next day Edith again saw and spoke to her husband. I did not see Hermann any more. That day all the men were shipped on—we had no idea where. Edith, who worked on the Hollorith machine files of the camp, soon found out: Buchenwald.

Reveille was at 4 A.M. and we had to be outside three minutes after we were awakened. No day passed without someone being beaten. A Polish inmate, the kapo Max Mosulf, known as the hangman of Stutthof, was in charge of the barracks for Jewish women. He literally thrashed us out of our bunks, laughing when he hit well. Nine hundred women shoved through the narrow doorway, fearful of Mosulf and dreading being late. Two women block seniors, Tjura and Djenna, lashed at the struggling mass with their belt buckles or with sticks until some jumped out of the window. Tjura was a beautiful young Russian, and Djenna a Ukrainian whore and drunkard. The two lived in Lesbian relation.

Three days after our arrival kapo Mosulf said to the SS commandant at roll call, so that everyone could hear: "I don't see why they wasted coal on the Jew boats. I could have burnt the whole herd of sows in the crematorium with less coal. It would have been a holiday for me. I could still hang them nicely, one next to another, like birds. How about it, Herr Commandant, then we'll be rid of them?" He had his chance not much later—to hang sixty men in a row.

Roll call sometimes lasted for hours. After it we got ersatz coffee and a piece of bread. If the woman kapo felt like it she struck the cup so that the hot liquid splashed in the holder's face. Some developed bad burns—and could be liquidated. One bowl of coffee was handed to every two persons in the double line. Before we could find a spot to sit down to drink or had time to eat we had to get in formation again. Sometimes roll call lasted all morning. When the sun was hot women collapsed. No one could go to the toilet. At noon we lined up again and every two got a liter of soup. The soup was not bad, but it was just not enough.

Each day we stood roll calls for hours on end. When we were back in the barracks we always had to fear the chicaneries of the block senior. I would have preferred work. In the evening we went through another long roll call.

Night in the barracks had its own kind of torment. Everyone shoved and squeezed to find a place; those on the floor lay on one another; it was impossible to sleep soundly. When one dozed off one got stepped on.

All night long in the barrack where our "leaders," the women block seniors, lived men came and went. One of the kapos, "Handsome Fritz," had a whole harem of block seniors. He had been sentenced twenty-seven times and was a lifer. Though he treated the Jewish women properly and never insulted or beat us, he carried a five-foot whip as symbol of his mastery over us. Every block senior had a stick or something to beat the inmates with. I remember Fritz in black silk shorts and a shining white sleeveless silk shirt, with the muscles of an athlete.

Huge transports arrived from Auschwitz with thousands of women, mostly Hungarian Jews, distinguished by their beauty in spite of their rags. In the shower room one saw how lovely their figures were—some of them girls barely fifteen years old. Mosulf was usually present during the showers. If we did not undress fast enough to suit him he would pour water over us or strike our naked bodies. The women from Auschwitz had numbers tattooed on their left arms. Mosulf would watch and order the numbers he wanted. The chosen ones had to come to him in the evening. Later, when I was on guard duty, I found out why.

I volunteered for night guard because I could not sleep and I had heard that the night guards received an extra bread ration. Also I wanted to know the camp better: it might be useful. A small circle of socialist women was forming, and we tried to stick together as much as possible in order to give each other added strength.

My first night watch was shared with a young woman from Cologne, Edith Scherwonski. It was a beautiful night, with a blue-black sky, and everything was peaceful. For a little while we forgot our surroundings and hummed some sad melodies. We saw shadowy figures enter the barrack opposite, where Mosulf had a room.

Our block senior Djenna was always thirsty, and we had to scrounge denatured alcohol for her from the supplies. A liter of alcohol made her completely drunk. She set off, naked, one night to go to Tjura—but Tjura was with a male kapo. Djenna banged on the door of Tjura's room with a stool and cursed furiously. Everyone in the barrack was frightened. We wanted to get Mosulf, but we were not supposed to see what he was doing or he would kill us. He was occupied in his favorite game, working, naked, with a riding crop, on seven beautiful naked women. When he was done he came and beat Djenna until she collapsed, smeared with blood. The SS had been awakened by the noise and got a view of the nightly activities in the camp.

Every day men and women were selected for the crematorium. Anyone with a rash on her face, or who looked frail, would be sent to the "other" side of the camp, to barrack 2 or 8, to be liquidated. Our block had few older women.

In spite of our night guard duty we got little sleep during the day. If the block senior wished it, we had to go out for each roll call or formation.

A rumor spread one day during formation: "Today we get sweet coffee." Everyone looked forward to it, but only the older and weaker women got it, or those whose faces expressed fear or despair. Some of them were sick immediately after drinking it; others were dizzy. They were taken to the hospital barrack and sent to the crematorium the next day.

Occasionally we all had to run and were timed by a stop watch. We were literally running for our lives; those who arrived last were taken away and liquidated. In spite of my fifty-five years I was usually among the first, but one day the woman next to me got sick and asked me to help her. We fell behind and arrived at the finish line with the stragglers. We were included in a group which was sent to the "other camp" for liquidation. I convinced a Russian block senior that I had got there by mistake and that I worked on the files. "You'll be shot if you're lying," she told me. I waited in front of the barracks till Edith came past with other clerks from the office and I could shout to her. Edith spoke a few words with the kapo, and I was taken out of the death camp. I managed to take out with me a young girl who was well except for a hurt foot.

That was close enough to death for Edith and me, and at the first opportunity we had ourselves included on a transport list.

Probably other places were better than Stutthof. But unfortunately we could not go at once.

One evening when we were working on the Hollorith files Mosulf came into the office with some SS noncommissioned officers. "Choose any one of the Jew-sows you want for the night," he told them. Did they wish to violate their Führer's race laws against Aryans having to do with Jews, we asked? Certainly we could not violate them. Mosulf raged that he'd have us all shot. Fortunately we were able to get the attention of the office SS, and Mosulf and his friends left unsatisfied. It drew his hatred on us, however, and we could see that he was only waiting his opportunity to get even.

One morning one of Mosulf's girl friends came to the office, talked with us, and gave Edith a cigarette. It was passed around so that everyone could have a puff. A young Latvian woman was holding it when Mosulf came in. He asked where it came from and she replied that she got it from Edith. Mosulf shouted at Edith, "You damned Jew-sow, where did you get your cigarette?" When Edith did not answer he shouted again, "If you don't tell where you got the cigarette, you'll be hanged!" Edith still said nothing, thinking he would kill the girl if he found out that she had favored us, of all people. "Betrayal is a word we don't know" was all she would say. Raging with anger, Mosulf struck her on the cheek so that she reeled. "This evening at formation time report to me. I'll give you twenty-five. You know what that means. No one has ever risen after twenty-five from me. Well, are you afraid?" "No," she answered.

I begged every one of the kapos and the heads of the labor units to intervene with Mosulf, but to no avail. The day dragged by. Edith was deaf on the ear where Mosulf had hit her, and had lost two teeth. That evening she reported to Mosulf. We thought her lost, and waited for news that she was dead or in the hospital.

In about an hour she returned. Mosulf had strapped her on his wooden contraption and asked over and over, "Are you afraid?" "Are you going to tell me the name?" She refused again and again, and would not give his friends who looked on the satisfaction of seeing her squirm. After thirty-five minutes he unbuckled her and let her go with a kick: "It's no fun if you're not afraid. At least you're not a coward." Edith was shaking as she told what had happened.

Shortly afterward we had to work all night making out labor command lists. Our own names were put on at our request, and next morning we found ourselves among the 1,700 women who were assigned to a labor camp. Approximately 1,500 of the 1,700 were Hungarians, mostly from Auschwitz. The rest were Czechs, Poles, and Lithuanians. Only 36 were from Germany. The reason for the small number of Germans appeared to be that the SS wanted to prevent German-born women from being sent to the Reich where they would come in contact with the population. Before we left we had to exchange our clothes for other more ragged ones.

I had heard that the inmates of the camp at Spilve where Juliane had been sent would soon be evacuated to Stutthof. No one was ever allowed to write; in fact any kind of communication, even through an intermediary, was always forbidden and punishable with death. So we resorted to writing on many window frames at Stutthof that we had been sent on transport, hoping that Juliane would see or hear of what we had written. We could not give our destination since we did not know it.

We marched off provided with a tin dish and rations for three days. The lucky ones even had a metal spoon. We were guarded by seventy-two heavily armed Lithuanian SS and a German non-commissioned SS officer as transport commander. Our route took us through a forest, and as we heard nothing but abusive language most of us feared that the forest would be our cemetery.

We marched more than twenty kilometers to a small railroad station, where we entered the usual crowded freight cars. When we were transferred to a clean passenger train in Marienburg, East Prussia, with seats for almost everyone, we started breathing easier. It was the first time in four years that we had ridden in such a train or been able to talk freely without guards. Arrived in Argenau, we marched for two hours until we came to an open space in the woods where a small village of plywood barracks had been built. These were "Finnish tents, capacity twelve horses"—or sixty women! They had no floor; we slept on the ground. The outdoor kitchen was equipped with six large vats that held about eighty gallons apiece. There was a supply of potatoes, so that evening we cooked a soup of unpeeled cut potatoes, a treat in comparison with the thin soup we got at Stutthof.

Work groups were set up in the morning and with our spades over our shoulders we went out to dig entrenchments, guarded by armed SS. Our life was tolerable. Our new commandant, Heinz Binding, was a young man and had never run a camp, had no idea how to go about it, and was dependent on our know-how. Only the guards were difficult. The Lithuanian guard commander, an SS noncommissioned officer, told us that in Kowno and Schaulen he had waded hip-deep in Jewish blood and enjoyed it.

Life took its course. We got soup and bread and almost an ounce of margarine or marmalade daily, so that we continued to become more hopeful in spite of our heavy work. Almost every day Wehrmacht soldiers came to the camp, talked with us, and let us describe what we had been through. They were dismayed and said that the German people knew nothing of this. When they saw the guards hit us and shout at us as our food was distributed, they forbade it. It made no difference to the guards, though. I was struck with a rifle butt on the left hip, and was still lame when we were freed.

After about three weeks our trench digging in this area was completed, and we marched ten hours to another barrack camp near Schlüsselmühle, part of a camp for Russian prisoners of war.

Here a Wehrmacht captain from Westphalia came to visit us almost every day and inquired if we were treated decently. The soldiers often gave us bread and always behaved correctly toward us. Our new camp commandant was old and a weakling, and could not keep the SS guard in check. One night when he and drunken guards came into the kitchen where some of us were sleeping and started to shoot around wildly, several Wehrmacht officers came over, took the commandant to task, and promised to report the incident.

As a result, permission was given from Stutthof to move us on. So we came to another forest camp, Korben near Thorn in East Prussia. Here two pumps, one of which was usually out of order, delivered the water for seventeen hundred inmates, the kitchen, and the private apartments of the two commandants, an old one, Wilhelm Anton, and a young one—the same Heinz Binding who had commanded us before. There were no washing facilities for the inmates. A couple of large marmalade buckets scrounged from the kitchen had to serve as basin and tub for sixty women. Yet each one who valued her health washed her whole body daily with cold water. We used a portion of our margarine as skin cream; it was more precious to us that way than spread on the bread. We used margarine and oil in little lamps we fashioned out of hollowed-out potatoes. When we got a small Todt stove we washed our bodies after work, letting the warmth of the stove dry us, for towels of course were scarce. A restaurant and cinema owner from Thorn, Herr Stahnke, was in charge of our food supplies. He was one of the most decent people we ran across in all our time behind wire and he also influenced Commandant Anton favorably.

Winter started in earnest. Rain and snow soaked through the plywood boards. The ground that served for tent floors was just puddles. We dug a wide trench around the tents and piled the earth about the walls. Then we covered the roofs with moss and used fir branches for insulation.

Frozen potatoes, meat from diseased animals, and raw vegetable refuse contributed to stomach and intestinal catarrhs and dysentery. There were infected wounds, frozen limbs, rashes, throat infections, diptheria, and scarlet fever. Through Edith's initiative two tents were set up for the sick, one of them for contagious diseases. But as the winter went on and it got colder disease increased; kidney, bladder, and other internal ailments became more frequent. Some of the sick could not manage to reach the trench latrine any more, and every morning the path had to be cleaned of human excrement.

The Hungarians from Auschwitz were in a peculiar mental state as a result of medical experiments that had been made on them. Many of them were apathetic and had lost all desire to live. They did not care to wash; they ate all sorts of scraps. Weeks and months of dysentery had pared their bodies to the bone, and they were covered with lice.

Of the women and girls, some of them fourteen-year-olds,

who had been taken out of the shower room at Auschwitz and raped by the SS, a number had children. Three of the four babies born in the camp died shortly after birth.

Two Hungarian women, already partly abnormal, tried to commit suicide. They fled to the forest, dug their own graves and tried to beat themselves to death with a spade. They were found and brought back to the camp. After another attempt at flight Commandant Binding shot them—the only time he shot anyone. He did it because at Stutthof, the main camp, fifty hostages were shot for anyone who got away. Apparently he lost his mental balance after killing the two girls. From this time on he drank heavily and did a lot of wild shooting around the camp. Sometimes he selected a target for practice—a chimney, or dishes, and once a keg of marmalade. We could not help laughing then.

After about forty women had died, we received warm clothing from Stutthof. But there were still four to five deaths a day and we had to argue with Commandant Anton, who had been an SS concentration camp guard, each time we wanted a blanket or a paper sack for the dead, for the order from Stutthof was to bury them naked. We did accompany the bodies to burial, say a short prayer, and commemorate them by cutting their initials on a tree.

Edith took the place of a doctor and worked constantly. Every day she checked for lice and cleaned many women's heads. Our hair was growing back, and we took special precautions to keep our heads free of lice. We even received a bit of soap every four weeks, and our food ration was larger and more varied.

Although our Lithuanian SS guards were courageous about beating women, the mere word "partisan" could frighten them. One night when I was on watch in the kitchen I heard shooting. The guard was called out, and Commandant Anton shouted excitedly, "Partisans! Comb the woods!" I saw the little white dog of the guard commander hide in the kitchen. He shivered with every shot and there were many—for the guards were running out, some of them drunk, and shooting in all directions. Then all was quiet and the commandant and the SS went back to their tents. Later that same night Commandant Anton came into the kitchen dead drunk. Now I found out what had happened.

The commander, his adjutant, and some other SS noncoms had been drinking heavily and thrown themselves, still dressed, on their beds. Only the commander had taken off his boots. His little white dog lay at his feet as usual. He must have moved and kicked it. At any rate it bit his foot. Awaking out of his drunken stupor he thought himself attacked, pulled out his pistol, and shot— into the boot of his adjutant. The adjutant, waking from his stupor, fired too; the guard was alarmed, and that is how the "partisan battle" started.

An opportunity offered for Juliane to join us. Forty women were to be brought to our camp from Stutthof. Another woman and I dared ask the commandant to have our daughters included. We gave him their names when he set off for Stutthof. The evening of their expected arrival seemed to drag on endlessly. Finally the truck with the newcomers arrived—but our daughters were not among them. A friend of Juliane's who was in the group told me that Juliane had indeed seen on one of the window frames that we had been sent on transport but did not know that this particular transport would lead her to us. The commandant explained that he was not permitted to go into the women's camp and could not ask for the two girls by name. The failure of our attempt to be reunited was to have grave consequences for Juliane.

In the fall of 1944 Commandant Binding had bought himself a portable radio, and during the day we would hear music coming from the small office tent. He often forgot to have the radio taken away in the evening. We would go to the tent and listen to foreign stations, so we learned a good deal of what was going on. It was particularly interesting to us since we had been cut off from the outer world for so long. We knew that our hour of liberation would strike soon.

A few days before Christmas we were marched to the Birglau station, some four to six kilometers from the camp, to a delousing train of the Wehrmacht. The white snow and clear blue sky were in sharp contrast to the thin sick bodies with sores and boils. After this march in the bitter cold many fell sick and about twenty died from pneumonia and heart ailments.

New Year's Eve despondency gripped us, for our rescue seemed to be coming much more slowly than we hoped. We tried to encourage each other. I made a little speech and said, without fully believing it: "The day of freedom is almost here. This is our last New Year's Eve in bondage."

A few days later we knew that the front was near again, for we could hear bombs exploding.

One evening it was announced, "The camp has to be vacated, we are moving deeper into the Reich." We were given several days' food supply the next morning, and put our few belongings in the small rucksacks many of us had made from rags. We were told, "The Security Service of the SS will pick up the sick and those who cannot walk."

"Tell the women not to stay behind in camp under any circumstances," Commandant Anton told me. "Everyone walk, walk for your lives." We warned the women who had reported themselves unfit to march, and got a number of them to come along. The stronger supported the weak so that no one would remain behind. But we had to leave about 183 women and one child. Ten guards volunteered to stay behind with them. We started our march through the ice and snow, guessing what lay ahead, because some of us had read the secret order from Stutthof: "No prisoner shall be allowed to fall into the hands of the enemy alive when the front comes closer."

Before the tail of the procession was more than a hundred meters from the camp we heard the noise of a machine gun. It was as we had feared: the Security Service had only corpses to fetch. We marched in silence, our hearts heavy, wondering who would be next. We had to avoid the highways, which were crowded with refugees and horses and wagons, and keep to the snow-filled forests. As we tired, the sight of the sixty-two Lithuanian SS guards behind us urged us on. A woman collapsed and before her neighbor could raise her there was a shot. The guard commander said to his men: "Shoot any hag that dawdles." Some eighty-seven women died this way on the eve of liberation, in the four days that we spent walking ninety-six kilometers.

While we were halted briefly on the edge of the town of Bromberg, satisfying our thirst with snow, and moistening our cracked lips, Edith called my attention to the guards, who were hanging their cartridge belts around their shoulders. We moved close enough to hear the guard commander ask Commandant Anton to leave the women to him, he would repeat the Lithuanian treatment and shoot them down in the forest. As they were arguing, an SS noncommissioned officer raced up on his motorcycle.

"Order of Berlin," he reported. "No prisoners to be killed; every camp commandant guarantees with his life for the prisoners assigned to him."

"What did you do with your camp?"

"Let the women go where they wanted. I have only thirty-five left of eight hundred; the others ran away. I want to save myself, that's all I care about."

The guard commander insisted on having the women handed over for shooting—or he would leave with his guard. Commandant Anton shouted at him to clear out with his murderers before he killed him. The Lithuanians departed, and we thought ourselves saved. We spent the night on an estate about thirteen kilometers from Bromberg. Next morning the commandants told Edith to look after the women—and then they disappeared. We heard later that one of them had committed suicide.

Unfortunately some of the Hungarian women went onto the highway against our advice and were seen by a motorized SS man. As a result, that afternoon Security Service men from Bromberg arrived and arranged for a guard of military police and Volkssturm to take over that evening. Our short-lived freedom was over.

Next morning at seven we had to move on. All along the highway we saw the army in flight and dissolution. We were sure that freedom could not be far off; some of the women had already run away. We had no more supplies, not even a piece of bread. We were told we would spend the night at Koronowo on the Brahe River near the Polish border.

The guards permitted the requisitioning of some horses and carriages from abandoned farms, so that the weakest at least could ride. About 7 P.M. we arrived at the penitentiary at Koronowo. We were given hot soup, bread, margarine, and sugar, and the officials, mostly Poles, were very kind to us. One of them told Edith that the Konitz Security Service were to take us in the morning and shoot us in the forest. With some of the prison officials Edith and I sat much of the night wondering what could be done to save us all. We had shrunk from sixteen hundred to less than a thousand.

We planned that if the Security Service came the acting director of the prison would release the political prisoners and arm us all so that we could fight. But we did not have to worry. At 5 A.M. we heard an artillery barrage. At 8.47 the Russians opened the doors of our prison. We were free. We could pay our debt to the prison heads who had planned to help us. They were being placed against the wall to be shot. We told the Russian officer what they had done for us, and they were saved.

Edith was immediately engaged as nurse in the penitentiary hospital which was used as prison camp for Germans and Germanized Poles. I began my years of search for the rest of my family.

Toward the end of 1945 we returned to Germany, thus ending our wanderings and ordeals but continuing our struggle for life and freedom.

EPILOGUE TO CHAPTER XII

For Life and Freedom

FRAU WOLFF learned that her husband was shot on April 21, 1945, on a march from Buchenwald to the Flossenbürg concentration camp. Edith's husband died in Buchenwald. Juliane died at Stutthof. Käthe was never heard of after she was sent to Ravensbrück. Herr Wolff's mother died in the Theresienstadt ghetto.

When Frau Wolff returned to Germany, Polish militia robbed her of the jewelry which she had guarded from the day of her deportation.

She is now devoting herself to denazification work and the democratic reconstruction of Germany, and is in charge of the western Berlin office for victims of the Nazis. She is active in the Social Democratic party and vigorously opposed its forced integration with the Communist party in the Soviet-sponsored Socialist Unity party. As a leading member of the Berlin City Assembly who has received wide recognition for her courageous stand against coercion, she was singled out for a beating by a Communist mob. Next day, released from the hospital, she spoke in an anti-Communist mass meeting, saying, "We shall not stumble and we shall not fall."

PROLOGUE TO CHAPTER XIII

A People Stands Before Its God

L
EO BAECK was born on May 23, 1873, one of eleven children,
in the Prussian town of Lissa where an old and cultured
Jewish community thrived. His father, a rabbi, was the
author of a scholarly work on the history and literature of the
Jewish people. Both parents were descendants of old rabbinical
families from southern Germany. Leo Baeck studied philosophy
and classical philology and received his doctor's degree from the
University of Berlin. Latin became so familiar to him that he and
his daughter corresponded in it. After serving in Oppeln and
Düsseldorf he was appointed rabbi in Berlin in 1912. During
the World War he served for more than four years as chaplain.
The tall rabbi on horseback was a familiar figure riding from
one sector of the front to another. Jewish and Christian soldiers
both welcomed him.

When he was thirty-two his reputation as a scholar was established by the publication of *Das Wesen des Judentums* (*The
Essence of Judaism*), in which he describes the moral law of the
Bible as the culmination of ethical principles, and the message
of Judaism as being of universal and eternal validity. Among his
books are *Wege im Judentum* (*Paths in Judaism*) and *Aus Drei
Jahrtausenden* (*Out of Three Millenniums*), a collection of profound essays on theological and historical subjects. One of these,
on romantic religion, is a classic. Some have been published in
the United States in *The Pharisees and Other Essays*.

Rabbi Baeck was regularly invited as Jewish representative
to many Christian theological conferences. For years he gave
annual lectures at Count Keyserling's "School of Wisdom" in
Darmstadt. He was professor of homiletics and bible commentary
at the Hochschule für die Wissenschaft des Judentums, and
later was appointed its director, a post which he held until the
Nazis dissolved the Academy in 1942.

Dr. Baeck was a sympathetic but exacting teacher. He told one student who delivered a poor practice sermon: "The introduction should have some organic connection with the thought of the sermon. And the body of the sermon should have a relationship to the text. The language should be more easily comprehensible. The sermon should be about half as long. But otherwise it was fine."

Another student who tried to cram all he knew into his sermon drew the comment: "After your sermon the congregation will ask, 'What did he talk about?' or more likely, 'What did he not talk about?' "

It is not surprising that many important offices fell to Rabbi Baeck. He was elected president of the German Rabbis' Association. From 1924 on he was grand master of the Independent Order of B'nai B'rith in Germany. Though not a Zionist himself, he was co-chairman of the Keren Hayesod, the fund for building up a Jewish state in Palestine, and a member of the board of the Jewish Agency for Palestine. He was able to bridge the gaps between orthodox, liberal, and reformed Jewish congregations. Though his own congregations were liberal, he once stated that he would be among the first to raise money for the orthodox rabbinical seminary if it needed help. At the same time he was highly appreciated outside the Jewish community, in national and international intellectual circles.

Rabbi Baeck's reputation for punctuality became proverbial. Once he arrived early at a meeting scheduled for 7 P.M. When 7 o'clock came he was still alone. The latecomers found a sheet of paper with the lines, "Minutes: 7.00, meeting started. 7.02, meeting adjourned."

Another time, when he had to be at his office at 9.30 A.M., he advanced his eight o'clock class at the Academy to 7.45. The students, most of whom had a good ways to travel, asked him to keep the original time. "We'll compromise," he retorted, "and start at 7.52½."

Rabbi Baeck's most challenging task came during the Nazi period when he was head of the National Association of German Jews. He faced with equanimity the incessant prospect of arrest by the Gestapo. Anxiety over this threat to her husband con-

tributed to the death of Frau Nathalie Baeck in March, 1937—
"the hardest blow," for him, "of these hard years." For months
he went daily to the Berlin-Weissensee Cemetery. And each year
near the anniversary of her death he suggested to his students
that they preach a sermon on women.

Although there were numerous invitations to leave Germany,
Rabbi Baeck always insisted that it was his duty to stay and continue his work for German Jewry to the end. Thus he turned
down a call to the Rockdale Temple in Cincinnati. He returned
to Germany each time after accompanying a transport of Jewish
children to England. One of his former students ran into him
in the Babylonian department of the British Museum in July,
1939. The Rabbi explained that he had just brought over another children's transport and only wanted to enjoy a few hours'
relaxation in study before returning to Germany.

"Why don't you stay here with your daughter? She wants you
to use the immigration visa that is offered you—and war is immi-
nent."

"Yes, I know that war is coming soon. But I cannot forsake
my flock."

To his students Dr. Baeck's life is a lesson, for the unassum-
ing simplicity with which he lives what he teaches. "He is an
aristocrat of conscience and conviction. Combining profundity
of thought with kindliness of heart, he comes close to the Jewish
ideal of saintliness."

A colleague, Dr. Max Wiener, observed of his work during the
Nazi years: "No historian will ever be able to do justice to the
fearlessness, outstanding humanity and dignity with which Baeck
on many an occasion moderated and delayed measures of persecution. His efforts gained precious time during which many
individuals were enabled to reach havens of refuge." The following account was drawn from Rabbi Baeck in a series of conversations. It is hard to persuade him to speak of these things, though
he will talk at length of the heroic work of others.

XIII

A People Stands Before Its God

LEO BAECK

IN 1933 there were few who grasped the full significance of
the rise of Hitler, and those few were often considered
pessimists and defeatists. It was especially hard for German
Jews to believe that *Mein Kampf* and the Nazi program were
more than the projections of a deranged rabble rouser. At first
they felt secure in the belief that they were part of the German
people. Many took refuge in the thought of their high degree of
assimilation or pointed to the contributions Jews had made as
patriotic citizens, as in the World War. In no country except
Palestine was the history of the Jews so old. The first Jews settled
in Germany during the Roman period, and Jewish communities
along the Rhine date back to the early Middle Ages.

In 1933 there were about 500,000 Jews in Germany and
200,000 in Austria, in addition to some hundreds of thousands
who were no longer professing Jews or had been baptized. They
had a profound appreciation of German culture, and their cultural contribution in turn was out of proportion to their numbers. Of the originators of the four intellectual revolutions of the
last century—Charles Darwin in the biological sciences, Karl
Marx in economics and political philosophy, Sigmund Freud in
psychology, and Albert Einstein in physics—three were Jews
from the German-speaking world. Among Nobel Prize winners
from Germany have been such Jews as Ehrlich, Haber, Will-
stätter, to name just a few. German Jews have distinguished
themselves in all fields of culture, as Mendelssohn and Mahler
in music, Heine, Werfel, Wassermann, and Zweig in literature.

It was the task of the spiritual leaders of German Judaism to
get ready for what might lie ahead. So I called all the leaders of
Jewish communities to meet in Berlin in March, 1933, to discuss

a program of action. I pointed out that we would be wise to reckon with the possibility of Hitler remaining in power for some time. The two other European dictators, Mussolini and Stalin, had lasted much longer than most people had predicted. We must therefore face the reality of a Nazi-ruled Germany and endeavor to work out a twofold plan: emigration for the young people and the maintenance of the cultural and spiritual life of the remaining Jewish community. That, substantially, came to be our program.

The solidarity of the German Jewish community and their readiness to make sacrifices were admirable. When the Nazis canceled the tax exemption of Jewish institutions such as hospitals and levied taxes retroactively, large sums were raised readily. When tax levies on the congregations had to be tripled the money was paid without stint, even though the Jewish community had only moral authority, not the power of a state to collect taxes.

The leaders of the National Association of German Jews applied themselves tirelessly and selflessly to their difficult tasks, often turning down opportunities for emigration because of their duty. They included Dr. Otto Hirsch, the executive head; Dr. Konrad Cohn and Frau Hanna Karminski who handled welfare, Frau Cora Berliner who dealt with administrative problems; Frau Paula Fürst, in charge of the educational system; Dr. Julius Seligsohn who handled emigration; and Dr. Artur Lilienthal who took care of legal questions. Persons in such exposed positions were of course arrested often and on the slightest pretext. I was arrested five times, but until the Munich Pact the Nazis were sensitive enough to public opinion abroad so that I was never kept in prison long.

In those early years the Jews suffered severely from the propaganda and calumnies by which the Nazis slyly tried to turn all of the German people against them. It depressed them so gravely that something had to be done to raise their spirits. I prepared a prayer which was said in synagogues all over Germany on Kol Nidre, the solemn evening named after the prayer initiating Yom Kippur:

"In this hour every man in Israel stands erect before his Lord, the God of justice and mercy, to open his heart in prayer. Before God we will question our ways and search our deeds, the acts we have done and those we have left undone. We will publicly confess the sins we have committed and beg the Lord to pardon and forgive. Acknowledging our trespasses, individual and communal, let us despise the slanders and calumnies directed against us and our faith. Let us declare them lies, too mean and senseless for our reckoning.

"God is our refuge. Let us trust Him, our source of dignity and pride. Thank the Lord and praise Him for our destiny, for the honor and persistence with which we have endured and survived persecution.

"Our history is the history of the grandeur of the human soul and the dignity of human life. In this day of sorrow and pain, surrounded by infamy and shame, we will turn our eyes to the days of old. From generation to generation God redeemed our fathers, and He will redeem us and our children in the days to come. We bow our heads before God, and remain upright and erect before man. We know our way and we see the road to our goal. At this hour the house of Israel stands before its God. Our prayer is the prayer of all Jews; our faith is the faith of all Jews living on the earth. When we look into the faces of one another, we know who we are; and when we raise our eyes heavenward, we know eternity is within us. For the Guardian of Israel neither slumbers nor sleeps. Mourning and desolation overflow our hearts. Devoutly and with awe let us look into the innermost depths of our souls, and let that which cannot be spoken sink into the silence of meditation."

The Nazis objected to the prayer, particularly to the words "let us despise the slanders and calumnies directed against us and our faith." I was arrested again.

Our success in promoting emigration of children was limited by restrictive immigration laws in most countries. England, which forbade sending groups of children to Palestine, was herself far more generous than any other country and allowed transport after transport of children to come to her own shores. They were received hospitably by Christian and Jewish families alike.

The Nazis could take our property but not our spirit. So far as possible we wanted the individual Jew, when exposed to persecution, to feel that he could find refuge in the protective mantle of the Jewish community. We were determined to carry out the second task we had set ourselves—maintaining Jewish culture to the end, no matter what obstacles we should meet. The Nazis interfered at all turns. Though they were not very successful at first, they became more thorough as time went on. When they excluded Jews from the cultural life of Germany, the artists turned to entertaining Jewish audiences and the synagogues became outstanding cultural centers. When our children were no longer permitted to attend the public schools we established Jewish schools, often without any facilities. It was difficult to find room to house a school. Yet many boys got a better education than they had had before, and no Jewish child went without a good education until June, 1942, when the Nazis forbade their being educated at all. After that checkups were made in homes and possible meeting places to be sure that no clandestine teaching was going on.

Publishing during those years, too, was very active, and one firm, Schocken, contributed greatly to the maintenance of the cultural level. Newspapers such as the *Jüdische Rundschau, the C(entral) V(erein) Zeitung,* and the *Israelitisches Gemeindeblatt* continued publication. We kept on training rabbis and maintained the Academy for the Study of Judaism until I was the sole professor and only two or three students were left. In June, 1942, the Academy too was banned.

It was sometimes difficult to know the right way to meet Nazi policy. A rabbi from Augsburg, where the B'nai B'rith lodge had been suspended by the Gestapo and its property confiscated, suggested that other lodges should forestall a similar fate by disbanding voluntarily, which would save about a million dollars. I felt that it was wiser to keep them and risk the loss of this money than to give in voluntarily to the Nazis. The lodges were in fact allowed to continue for a few years and did good cultural and charitable work. When the Gestapo ordered the dissolution of the national B'nai B'rith in 1937 they again arrested me, as its grand master. In prison they set before me a statement in which I was supposed to agree to cede all B'nai B'rith property to the government. I refused to sign. Thus their act stood as the theft which it was.

I made it a principle to accept no appointments from the Nazis and to do nothing which might help them. But later, when the question arose whether Jewish orderlies should help pick up Jews for deportation, I took the position that it would be better for them to do it, because they could at least be more gentle and helpful than the Gestapo and make the ordeal easier. It was scarcely in our power to oppose the order effectively.

There were two groups in the Berlin population who were distinguished by their opposition to the Nazi persecution of Jews: on one hand, many of the old nobility and civil servants; on the other, the socialist workers. Life would have been even more difficult without the moral support their actions furnished. Sometimes the only way Germans could express their opposition to the Nazis was to be helpful to a Jew. In the last years a countess came to my apartment every Friday and left vegetables which were not on the Jewish ration card. Occasionally I found a bag of fruit at the apartment door left by an anonymous donor. One Sunday in the crowded S-Bahn a man stepped close to me and asked, "Is Tiergarten the next station?" He added in a whisper, "I am from the country. I just put a few eggs in your pocket." Another time a man came up to me on the street and dropped an envelope. As he picked it up he handed it to me, saying, "You dropped this." It was a package of ration stamps.

I knew of instances where people annoyed Jews after they started wearing the star. But the populations of Hamburg and Berlin treated Jews much more decently than those of many other communities, especially in the smaller and more Nazi-imbued towns.

Naturally the little acts of kindness, which often called for considerable courage, lifted our spirits. My most depressed days were when my expectations of various groups in Germany or in other countries were disappointed: when the Jews were boycotted on April 1, 1933, and Catholic and Protestant churches and the chambers of commerce took no counteraction; when Nazi aggression in foreign fields remained unopposed by the European nations most affected; when country after country sent representatives to the Olympic Games in Germany as if concentration camps and persecution were nonexistent. Each sign of weakness of the democracies, as at the time of the Rhineland invasion in 1936 and the Munich Pact, was another blow. The position of the Jews always deteriorated after such events.

In talking with government officials I soon became aware that there were different tendencies among the Nazis—varying from harsh to lenient treatment of Jews. The harsh group was encouraged by successes in Nazi foreign policy. An official of the Ministry of the Interior suggested to me in 1941 that we might strengthen the hands of the lenient group by preparing a history of German Judaism which would indicate its cultural contribution to European civilization. I had the history started by Rabbi Luckas, Fräulein Dr. Ottenheimer, and my two faithful secretaries, Fräulein Glück and Fräulein Nathan. They performed the task so well that the officials asked us to write more.

Deportation started after the beginning of the war. The first transports left Stettin for "the east," as everyone always said, in February of 1940, and others left Baden for Gurs in the Pyrenees that autumn. We had no means of knowing, at first, how badly off the deportees were.

One day a doctor brought me a Danish paper, *Berlingske Tidende,* in which appeared a notice that the Gestapo had established a special Jewish department headed by a high SS officer, Adolf Eichmann. I had read nothing about this in German papers. I knew Eichmann, since as representative of German Jews I had had to see him occasionally. He was a bitter hater of Jews and in the past had always been one of the worst persecutors. His department had been given special powers. It was a bad omen.

The first news from the east that I saw was post cards from Lublin and Warsaw. From them we gathered that the deportees were wretched, that hunger and disease were widespread, and that the Polish Jews were trying to help, in such contacts as they had with the deported and while they themselves still could.

I got the first indication of the scope of Nazi bestiality in the summer of 1941. A Gentile woman told me that she had voluntarily gone along with her Jewish husband when he was deported. In Poland they were separated. She saw hundreds of

Jews crowded into busses which were driven off and came back empty. The rumor that the busses had a gassing mechanism was confirmed by the apparatus attached to all but one of them. This one carried a group to bury those who were gassed; afterward the gravediggers were shot. Similar stories were told by soldiers who came back on furlough. Thus I learned that the lot of Jews shipped east was either slave labor or death. It was still later that I first heard the name Auschwitz mentioned in connection with atrocities.

By the beginning of 1943 only about ten thousand Jews were left in Berlin. So far I had been spared deportation because of my work as head of the National Association of German Jews.

I had always been in the habit of rising early, but for some reason on January 27 I got up earlier than usual. I was fully dressed when the bell rang at quarter of six. Only the Gestapo would come at that hour. My housekeeper let in two men in civilian clothes. One of them addressed me:

"We have orders to take you to Theresienstadt."

I had a few last things to attend to, so I said, "Please wait a little while. I must get ready."

"You must come with us at once."

"You are two and can use force to take me. But if you will wait an hour I will go with you as you wish."

One of them went to make a phone call. He returned and said, "We will wait."

I sat down at my desk and wrote a farewell letter to friends in Lisbon. They would send it to its real destination, my daughter Ruth and her husband in London. Then I made out postal money orders for my gas and electric bills. My housekeeper had packed my bag. I was ready to go.

The Gestapo took me to the collection center at the Grosse Hamburgerstrasse. I was locked up alone in a room. Later I ate my meal alone. Toward evening I was led to another building and again locked in alone.

The next morning I was taken to the Anhalter station where hundreds of unfortunate Jews were boarding a train. I was put into a compartment by myself. Before long the train moved out and I was occupied with my thoughts. Only once was I disturbed. In Dresden an SS man looked in and asked if I wanted water.

Theresienstadt meant much to me even before I saw it. Three sisters of mine had died there, and a fourth died shortly after my arrival.

At first I performed all sorts of chores such as pulling garbage wagons, but after my seventieth birthday that year I was free to minister to the living, the sick, and the dying. Sometimes so many people died that I felt as if I existed in a graveyard.

I had heard of the crowded conditions, but not until I saw with my own eyes did I fully understand what it meant. Bunks were often constructed in four and five decks, with so little space between them that one had to lean far forward when sitting on the edge. Often people did not have enough room to stretch out. It was a luxury to have an opportunity to sit on a chair. The inadequacy of latrines was one of the worst trials. Many had dysentery, and it was most humiliating for these good people to defile themselves when they had to wait. When I too was affected I fasted for three days and was blessed with recovery.

A package came for me not long after I arrived in Theresienstadt. Its contents had been removed and it was really only an empty cardboard box. But it gave me joy in the knowledge that someone had thought of me in exile. I recognized the sender—a Christian friend—by the handwriting, although he had used a fictitious name.

Our greatest delicacies were the tins of sardines which the Joint Distribution Committee sent from time to time.

There was always hunger at Theresienstadt—for intellectual and spiritual as well as physical food. Most of our property was stolen by the SS when we arrived. Hence books were rare and people would give a slice of bread for the loan of a book for two weeks.

There were great scholars there from all the countries of Europe. They joined in giving lectures on many subjects—literature, history, economics, mathematics, philosophy, law, and astronomy. We gradually expanded these into an extensive scheduled lecture program, and ended up with a veritable small university.

Among the scholars was Professor Palache, an orientalist with a wonderful knowledge of the Bible, who came from one of the oldest Sephardic families of Holland, which had almost been wiped out. Professor Brahn, who had been mediator for Westphalia in the Reich Labor Ministry, lectured on philosophy. Eduard Meyers, one of the few to survive, had been professor of international law at Leyden. Oberbaurat Robert Stricker had been one of the original Zionists and a friend of Theodor Herzl. Desider Friedmann, a jurist and once president of the Jewish community in Vienna, had tasted the bitter cup of misery in Dachau and Buchenwald, and was to be killed in Auschwitz.

The first series of lectures on the history of philosophy was given by Professor Maximilian Adler, a classical philologist from Prague; Professor Utitz, a psychologist; and myself. Some seven or eight hundred people jammed into the attic of one of the barracks to hear the opening lecture, which I gave on Plato. In spite of the discomfort, the group attending was still as large when I gave the last lecture of the series, on Kant. Sometimes when we went to some barrack dormitory for a lecture people were so eager to hear that they clustered on the bunks like grapes on a vine.

The SS tolerated the surreptitious lectures but they had an ironclad rule against the education of children. Not even in the worst periods of persecution in the Middle Ages had the Jews failed to receive at least enough schooling to make them literate. And so, although it had to be done secretly and with great caution, our children in Theresienstadt did receive schooling.

Religious services were held wherever and whenever a group felt the desire for it. In the evening or early hours of the morning we maintained our faith and gave strength to all in prayer. In our services we recalled biblical times—the commandments, the prophets, the Messianic idea—and earlier persecutions of the Jews. Thus a community arose out of a mass and we could forget the misery around us.

One day in August of 1943 a fellow inmate came up to me. He introduced himself as a Czech engineer by the name of Grünberg and asked to talk with me alone. He bound me to silence. Then he spoke.

"I have to tell someone. I was waked last night by my best friend whom I have not seen for a long time. I knew that he had not been sent to Theresienstadt, so I asked how he got here. He cut me short, and told me to listen carefully. He had to tell me. I had to know. But first I must promise not to tell anyone else.

"He was half Jewish and had been sent east. He ended up in the huge camp of Auschwitz. Like everyone there he went through a process of selection and was assigned to do slave labor. The others were led away and gassed to death. He knows that definitely; everyone at Auschwitz knows it. He was sent to a labor camp from which he escaped and made his way back to Prague. How had he gotten into Theresienstadt? A Czech policeman outside took a bribe. We talked for a short while and then he left. He was much excited and said he wanted to warn me and save me."

So it was not just a rumor or, as I had hoped, the illusion of a diseased imagination. I went through a hard struggle debating whether it was my duty to convince Grünberg that he must repeat what he had heard before the Council of Elders, of which I was an honorary member. I finally decided that no one should know it. If the Council of Elders were informed the whole camp would know within a few hours. Living in the expectation of death by gassing would only be the harder. And this death was not certain for all: there was selection for slave labor; perhaps not all transports went to Auschwitz. So I came to the grave decision to tell no one.

Rumors of all sorts were constantly spreading through the ghetto, and before long the rumors of Auschwitz spread too. But at least no one knew for certain.

One November day all of us had to walk out of the camp and stand in a field until evening. We did not know what was to happen to us. I was afraid that they would use gas bombs to kill us on the spot. It turned out that they were checking up on account of irregularities in the list of inmates.

That day had seemed the hardest of all to bear; but its anguish

and disappointment were surpassed in the summer of 1944 when
a commission of the International Red Cross came to inspect the
camp. They appeared to be completely taken in by the false
front put up for their benefit. Many of the houses were so overcrowded that a tour through one of them would quickly have
revealed the real state of things. But since the ground floor could
be seen from the street the SS shrewdly ordered two-thirds of the
people living there to move to the upper floors. Flowers were put
in the windows. The commission never bothered to climb one
flight of stairs. Perhaps they knew the real conditions—but it
looked as if they did not want to know the truth. The effect on
our morale was devastating. We felt forgotten and forsaken.

Transports were dreaded, but when they did leave people were
careful not to give the SS satisfaction by creating scenes. I had already learned in Berlin to admire the self-restraint and inner
strength of our people—even when families were torn apart.

The largest transports left Theresienstadt in September and
October of 1944. I should judge that about twenty-five thousand
people were sent east during those two months, and fifteen to
eighteen thousand were left behind. In December and January
Jews of mixed marriages, who up to now had been spared deportation, began to arrive. Many families were being torn
asunder. The complexion of the ghetto changed, for numbers
of the new arrivals had been raised as Protestants and Catholics.

About the middle of January, 1945, I heard of feverish activity
in the town fortifications. Deep tunnels were being dug into
them, allegedly as storerooms. That did not appear likely; their
real purpose could only have been gas chambers. We spread the
word that if the SS ordered any groups to go to these tunnels,
they should lie down—simply lie down—wherever they were.
There were perhaps three hundred SS men attached to Theresienstadt, and it would have taken two of them to carry one of us to
a gas chamber. Fortunately nothing happened, no doubt owing
to the approach of the American and Russian armies.

But disease threatened to wipe us out. As the winter drew to a
close trainloads of people ill with typhus were sent to Theresienstadt. As the cattle cars came in we unloaded those who had died
on the way. In March we trudged knee-deep in mud carrying

the pitiful victims of the disease. In the first week a dozen doctors and more nurses died. We tried to isolate the sick in separate barracks, but the disease spread through those who took care of them.

One day I was told that a typhus patient wanted to see me. I did not recognize her as I approached, she was so emaciated; but when she spoke I realized that it was Dorothea, my grand-niece. She had passed through Auschwitz and been sent to Theresienstadt from a labor camp near Dessau.

Through the connivance of the Czech gendarmes guarding the camp the Czech Jews could often arrange to receive packages from friends. They readily shared their food with the sick; they never turned me down when I asked them for help for the ill.

About this time the Danish Jews were sent back to Denmark. They had always been in a privileged position on account of the packages they received regularly from home.

One day it was announced that anyone who wanted to be included in a transport to Switzerland should sign up. Of course we suspected a trap, but many did sign. Some two or three hundred people left one day—and really went to Switzerland. I understand that the International Red Cross paid the SS several hundred Swiss francs for each person.

In the street one day that spring a Prague doctor came up to me and exclaimed in surprise, "I just heard that you were dying!"

"I did not know of it. You see that I am walking around."

In the next few hours a number of people looked at me as if I were an apparition. The answer to the mystery was that a rabbi from Moravia named Beck had just died; and since the death of Jews of professional rank, such as doctors or rabbis or Justizrats, had to be reported to Berlin, Rabbi Beck's had been reported to the Gestapo office. Weeks later some people still thought it was I who was dead, and were surprised to see me.

I did not understand the full significance of my "death" until one day in April when I was talking to Hofrat Klang in one of the offices where we kept valuables for camp inmates. The door opened and an SS officer entered. It was Eichmann. He was visibly taken aback at seeing me. "Herr Baeck, are you still alive?" He looked me over carefully, as if he did not trust his eyes, and added coldly, "I thought you were dead."

"Herr Eichmann, you are apparently announcing a future occurrence."

"I understand now. A man who is claimed dead lives longer!"

Feeling certain that I had little time left to live, I wasted none with him. I walked to the door, he stepped aside, and I went to my quarters. I gave my wife's and my wedding rings to a friend and asked him to hand them on to my daughter in England. Then I wrote farewell letters, and was ready for what might come.

But other events moved more quickly than the SS. In the next days we heard the sound of artillery. The Russians were not far away.

The SS commandant, Rehm, published a list of ten more men who were to be sent to Switzerland. My name headed it, followed by Dr. Meissner, former Minister of Justice in Czechslovakia, Professor Meyers, Hofrat Klang, and other well-known persons. But to have left then would have been tantamount to desertion, so we said we would stay. Rehm told us we had no choice.

Yet we stayed, and the SS left instead. They started packing, loading cars, and moving out. After a few days only the commandant and a few SS men were left. We were beginning to breathe more easily. But typhus still took a heavy toll of the living.

Then one day toward the end of April a representative of the International Red Cross, Paul Dunand, arrived at Theresienstadt. He had just driven through the combat lines, and he informed me that it could only be a matter of days until we were liberated. He appointed me head of the town. It relieved us greatly to be given sound support with which to combat disaster in these last chaotic days.

I asked M. Dunand about the transports to Switzerland.

"Transports?" he questioned. "There was only one."

"But had a second one of ten men been planned?"

"No, certainly not."

After I had told him about it he observed, "You would have gotten as far as the Bohemian Forest and been shot 'while trying to escape.' "

We had a limited supply of food left and had to ration ourselves strictly. Through the Czech police we heard that an armistice had been concluded; but the battles continued in our sector of the front. On May 12 the Red Army liberated Theresienstadt.

I was asked to go to the Russian commanding officer, who had taken over the house of the SS commandant. When I entered the office a colonel and a dozen officers sitting there rose and each offered me his chair. The colonel said in broken German, "We have come so that we can help you. Help us to help you."

The Russian troops distributed food and aided us in every way possible. The camp was put under quarantine, those sick with typhus were kept strictly isolated, and Red Army doctors and nurses who had been immunized against the disease assisted in medical care.

Then began the task of getting the people out of the camp. Some electrical engineers worked together to build a small broadcasting station. When it was finished we broadcast lists of survivors and asked for transportation to take them back to their countries of origin. Before long busses from Luxembourg and Holland started to arrive. When anyone worried about what would happen to them, someone always remembered the Joint Distribution Committee and cheered them with, "Don't worry, the Joint will help us." And indeed they sent us food, starting with a shipment of rice.

In the latter part of May a young American officer arrived and asked for me. He had a letter for me from Eric Warburg, son of Max Warburg, the great Hamburg banker and philanthropist, who had been instrumental in founding the National Association of German Jews. It was my first news from the outside. The young officer brought delicacies that I had not seen in years, and took a letter for my daughter.

In the first days in June I was called to the Russian commandant. An American officer at the Defense Ministry in Prague, he said, wanted to hand medicines for the camp to me personally. A doctor and I were driven to Prague in a Russian truck. At the Defense Ministry we met Major Patrick Dolan, who gave us some wonder drugs which strengthen the heart. As we were about to leave Major Dolan said quietly:

"You have a special permit to go to England. Tomorrow?"

"No, not now. I am responsible for the many unfortunate persons at Theresienstadt."

He was obviously dismayed. "Ah— Can you have lunch with me?"

At the delicious lunch I explained to him that in a short time my task would be completed. "How much longer?" he asked. "About a month," I replied. Somehow a London newspaper picked up the story and reported that "Rabbi Baeck did not want to come to England."

On Friday, June 29, Major Dolan came directly to the camp. The next day I said good-by to my friends and to the niece, Dr. Nellie Stern, who was to lose her life in a bus accident as she left Theresienstadt. I was feeling weak. The doctor told me I had a slight case of trench fever which would pass away once I got out of the humid atmosphere of the camp—and so it did. On Sunday morning the Russians took me to Prague, and Major Dolan escorted me to the airfield, where a four-motor Fortress was standing. He and his adjutant and I stepped in. The plane crew all gave me something—one handed me candy, another socks, a third pencils.

In Paris the Joint Distribution Committee took care of me, and I had the opportunity to phone Ruth. And on the afternoon of July 5 I landed at a London airport. Ruth had been there for hours, waiting for me as she had waited and hoped all those years.

EPILOGUE TO CHAPTER XIII

A People Stands Before Its God

OUT of perhaps two thousand people who were sent to Theresienstadt on the same transport, Rabbi Baeck is one of three to survive. He is the only one living of eight brothers and sisters who remained in Germany. With his slightly bent, massive figure and snow-white beard, he retains today his youthful resilience and unimpaired brilliance of mind.

Since reaching London he has participated in many conferences in various parts of the world, has lectured at the Hebrew University in Jerusalem, and has been elected president of the World Union for Progressive Judaism, a union of nonorthodox congregations. He has made several trips to the United States: in 1945 to help in the fund raising of the United Jewish Appeal; in 1947–48 at the invitation of the Union of American Hebrew Congregations, when he stayed for several months and gave an address at the inauguration of Nelson Glueck as president of Hebrew Union College, the seminary for rabbis in Cincinnati. President Truman received him and on the anniversary of Lincoln's birthday he said the prayer before the House of Representatives.

In 1949 Dr. Baeck gave a course of lectures at Hebrew Union College. His place of residence remains London and he said when he was about to return there, "You know I am stateless. I want to go back and become a British subject."

Rabbi Joshua Liebman, who has shared the lecture platform on various occasions with Rabbi Baeck, says of him:

"The soul-force of Gandhi, the sacrificial nobility of Albert Schweitzer have been sustaining bread for the hungry spirit of modern man. And on a par with the Hindu martyr and the Christian hero stands the figure of Rabbi Leo Baeck. . . .

"A soul on fire, truly a contemporary of every great saint who has walked the earth, he can be for all of us, as he is to me, the antidote to pessimism and proof that man truly is created in the image and likeness of God." *

A message to mankind has grown out of Rabbi Baeck's experience of man's inhumanity to man:

"The principle of justice is one the whole world over. Justice is like a dike against inhumanity. If a small spot breaks, the whole dike of justice is threatened and the values it protects may be inundated. There is no such thing as doing an injustice to one person. An injustice to one is an injustice to all.

"Real peace must be based on justice, and justice must be the cherished property of every man.

"It is fitting for mankind today to remember the biblical saying, 'Fear not the strong.' To stand for the right is the real strength before God."

* *The Reader's Digest*, July, 1948, "The Most Unforgettable Character I've Met," by Joshua Loth Liebman. Copyright, *The Atlantic Monthly*, June, 1948.

Epilogues

E ach of the epilogues for the three editions published
after the 1949 original edition—in 1966, 1985 and
now in 2003—reflect the editor's desire to share with
the reader his own search for meaning and understanding of often puzzling human behavior: our capacity for
good and evil. These epilogues are included in this edition in the hope that they may help the readers in their
own groping and catharsis.

Epilogue 1966

THIS EPILOGUE to a new printing of *We Survived* is written twenty-one years after the end of the Second World War. For the survivors, defeat of Nazi Germany in 1945 meant an end to persecution, concentration camps, and genocide. It spelled LIFE to those who had been in hiding or who survived confinement by the Nazi regime.

The book is being reprinted because these stories cast light not only on German history. They reveal much about mankind. Charles Poore, who reviewed the original edition of *We Survived* for the *New York Times*, said in 1949: "These stories of men and women under the lash of the totalitarian state show in terms that everyone can understand the meaning of tyranny." They also give insight into human behavior under deep and prolonged stress.

The epilogues at the end of each chapter tell the reader about the places of residence and the jobs, in 1949, of many of the survivors. Since that time some of the heroes of our stories have died: Alice Stein-Landesmann (chapter I), Erich Hopp (chapter V), Moritz Mandelkern (chapter VI), and Leo Baeck (chapter XIII). Lagi Countess Ballestrem-Solf (chapter VII) was in her forties when she succumbed, after much misfortune involving her husband's imprisonment by the Soviet occupation forces.

"A People Stands Before Its God," the chapter by Leo Baeck, now has special value as a primary source, since the Eichmann trials have stimulated a debate as to what might have been the Jewish course of action against the Nazi government.

Eugen Gerstenmaier's chapter (IX) has current significance, as he has for many years been the speaker *(Präsident)* of the German

303

Bundestag and is often mentioned as a leading future candidate of the Christian Democratic Party for the position of chancellor.

The survivors were determined, without exception, to create a better world in which hatred would not lead to slaughter. Knud Christian Knudsen (chapter III) applies his skills as sculptor and publisher to that goal, and he served for years as an official in a society dedicated to Christian and Jewish understanding. Heinrich Liebrecht (chapter XI) was German Consul General and enhanced that position by a dedication to international co-operation. Jeanette Wolff (chapter XII) is one of Germany's most distinguished Social Democrats, and was in the Bundestag for many years. Though nearly eighty and now retired, she is deeply committed to welfare and religious activities in Berlin. Her extraordinary energy and strength epitomize the undaunted spirit of survival and its purposeful approach to life.

Has the new vantage point of 1966, seventeen years after the original publication of *We Survived,* given us deeper insights? Man has continued to be a victim of tyranny, hatred, and war. Tragedy continuing unabated has heightened our sensitivity to some of the conclusions expressed in the original introduction to the book or mentioned by the reviewers in 1949. Three observations are most noteworthy.

First, the consequences of bad government on a people are much more disastrous than we normally believe, just as the effects of good government are more beneficial than most of us realize. German history from 1933 to the present demonstrates this verity. In only twelve years Hitler made a shambles of Europe by gambling the fate of Germany on a course of aggression. His successors—first the occupying forces, then a German government—inherited a Germany bled, a Germany in ruins, a Germany hated. In spite of these handicaps, there emerged quickly a new Germany, albeit divided. West Germany is identified with the Western democratic tradition and there is peace for both Germanies, in partnership with the nations they had once fought. The welfare of the people has been assured—West Germany relatively soon after 1945, East Germany only more recently, still handicapped by its economic and political system.

Hitler was the embodiment of the pathological essence of Germany and its people at that time. "There are times ruled by madness," said Albrecht Haushofer in the wise "Moabit Sonnets," written in prison shortly before he was murdered. Hitler represented this madness. He provided the escape and ecstasy the people sought and needed, but at a terrible price. His image of the world was so completely false that his decisions contained the elements of the deranged. He committed so many irrational acts that the result could be only disaster, death, and misery for all the peoples under German sway, and for the Germans as well. Postwar events have shown again that public welfare in the modern world is not reached by dramatic speeches, grandiose plans, nor military campaigns, but that it comes from good government—free and representative government which draws on the knowledge and wisdom of many.

The second insight has been provoked by a question posed by readers: "How was it possible for a people to behave as it did?" The typical reader, who has only known a normal world, encounters in these pages a weird world, where man hunts man. The time was out of joint in Germany, and political behavior was irrational. We saw what happened to a people whose hopes are denied and whose fears are fed. Pre-Nazi Germany experienced numerous traumatic events, starting with the First World War and continuing through the great world depression and its unemployment, frustration and hunger. These events paved the way for Hitler's rise. The whole world passed through a number of the same occurrences, but a defeated Germany faced so many traumatic events that its political behavior crossed the threshold from realism to irrationality.

We should apply our knowledge of individual or group neurotic or psychotic behavior to the political scene, to peoples or whole generations. Such insights are reflected in significant works on group behavior, but statesmen have yet to apply these new insights to develop skills of diagnosis and policy to the political scene, to nations suffering from stress and catastrophe, or to critical epochs in history.

Third, these autobiographies of man persecuted, of man set against tyranny, are not just a phase of German history. They have universal human significance. Yet mankind has learned little from

these times. Going into hiding, opposing tyranny, escaping to freedom, surviving amidst slaughter has continued to be the fate of
countless people throughout the world. The nations have failed to
protect the individual against arbitrary government, in their own
realm or abroad. As we have seen in recent years, in Germany and
elsewhere, nations have failed to pass adequate judgment against
proven perpetrators of major crimes against humanity. Mankind
suffers from the consequences of national sovereignty, the lack of a
stronger world authority. A world court is needed with jurisdiction
over such crimes. We may defend the contemporary world against
too severe a judgment by saying "strident passions such as hatred
cannot be avoided" or "national sovereignty must be respected and
we cannot interfere." But the judgment of history will accept such
statements only as the pleas of the defendants—plausible but insuf-
ficient to keep our generations from being judged guilty. The
tragedy of this guilt is that the sentence is passed also on the innocent, on the children, on the generations that follow.

Each country should marshal all its moral resources to lift up its
downtrodden, and to find ways to save man from persecution
wherever it may occur. A thousand objections might be advanced as
to why these goals are impossible of realization, but history has
shown that "impossible" is a word of the tired, and that today's
"impossible" is tomorrow's event. *We Survived* will have provided a
lesson when we have learned to consider human life as sacrosanct,
when we have conquered our callousness and have learned to hold
out our hands in love or friendship.

Epilogue 1985

LESSONS FROM THE HOLOCAUST

I T IS exceedingly difficult to deal dispassionately and diagnostically with an event in history that is bound to arouse our deepest emotions. The Holocaust is for us a matter of contemporary history, a history of the times that many of us have survived.

The sad words written in 1948 by Lagi Countess Ballestrem-Solf, a person who opposed the Nazis with great courage, remain valid for today's world.

> I do not want to think of the past because it has lost its meaning. The world has learned nothing from it— neither slaughterers nor victims nor onlookers. Our time is like a dance of death whose uncanny rhythm is understood by few. Everyone whirls confusedly without seeing the abyss.[1]

We must avoid surrendering to the comforting rationalization that only a particular people is capable of committing genocide. This was the prevailing view shortly after the shocking exposure of the death camps and the mass murders organized by the Nazi government. Such naiveté is no longer excusable. If we are to avoid future Holocausts, it is imperative that we study and understand the multiplicity of causes.

By their nature, humans are extraordinarily capable of being either killers or victims. It would be comforting to believe that only perverse sadistic devils could be killers. To be sure, Nazi policies led to a natural selection of persons of minimum or non-existent moral restraints and maximum pathological behavior. But genocide did not just happen. It was deliberately organized by the government. The appointed executioners marshalled the instruments of violence of the state, and plotted in great detail the logistics of death. Obedience, considered to be a supreme virtue in a society with an authoritarian orientation, or in a given situation such as war, can greatly exacerbate the hazard of genocide. For instance Rudolf Hoess, the head of the Auschwitz death camp, perceived himself as a law-abiding citizen who did his duty. When obedience is coupled with an expediential ethic, in which all means are justified by an end, we reach a point of maximum risk for the potential victim. In any deliberation on the role of values we must also ask ourselves to what degree the secularization of our world and abandonment of moral precepts taught by organized religions can facilitate the rationalizations involved in genocidal behavior. Yet we must recognize that although religious faith has served to restrain brutal behavior, organized religions have often served as vehicles for fanaticism leading to genocidal behavior.

Two experiments of recent years have shed some frightening light on dangerous patterns in human behavior. Let us first recall the experiments of Professor Stanley Milgram, Yale University. Conducted in 1960, these experiments were generated by the questions Milgram posed concerning psychosocial characteristics of Germans: Were they different, especially in their willingness to obey authority? Did Germans possess a basic character flaw that brutalized them? To answer his questions, Milgram designed an experiment to test the readiness to obey instructions and orders from a particular authority. A volunteer "teacher" was instructed to administer to a "learner" what the "teacher" was led to believe were electric shocks. The pain from the shocks was simulated by the learner, who had been instructed by Professor Milgram in advance. The teacher had no way of determining if these shocks, which allegedly went up to 450 volts (for wrong answers), might not in fact electrocute the learner. The experiment was designed so that there was genuine reason to believe that when the learner no longer gave evidence of pain as the voltage was escalated, he may in fact be comatose or dead. Some teachers resisted, but not to the extent that they defended the learner-victim against the perpetrator of the "experiment" (or crime?). These are Milgram's conclusions:

The results, as seen and felt in the laboratory ... are disturbing. They raise the possibility that human nature or more specifically the kind of character produced in American democratic society, cannot be counted on to insulate its citizens from brutality and inhumane treatment at the direction of malevolent authority. A substantial portion of people do what they are told to do, irrespective of the content of the act and without limitations of conscience, so long as they perceive that the command comes from a legitimate authority. If, in this study, an anonymous experimenter can successfully command adults to subdue a fifty-year-old man and force on him painful electric shocks against his protests, one can only wonder what government, with its vastly greater authority and prestige, can command of its subjects.[2]

The second experiment, by Professor Philip G. Zimbardo, Stanford University, involved hiring students to simulate a prison situation. He concluded:

At the end of only six days we had to close down our mock prison because what we saw was frightening. It was no longer apparent to most of the subjects (or to us) where reality ended and their roles began. The majority had indeed become prisoners or guards, no longer able to clearly differentiate between role playing and self. There were dramatic changes in virtually every aspect of their behavior, thinking and feeling.[3]

The extraordinary vulnerability of human beings, illustrated by these two experiments, does not suggest a totally undifferentiated conclusion that all human beings are capable of committing mass slaughter under any circumstance. Such a jump in logic is not only wrong, but dangerous. Instead we need to examine the factors which heighten or minimize the hazard. In what context does a particular historical circumstance reach the critical point that leads to genocidal behavior? By contrast, what are the conditions of safety?[4]

Clearly we must recognize that the nature of the particular government is critical. A highly authoritarian and totalitarian state, without restraints on its leaders, creates a much more dangerous context. If, in addition, some leaders at the top of the hierarchy possess deeply flawed personalities they may be able to co-opt similar types into the government. These persons may then force their pathological fantasies to be acted out by their more paranoid followers thereby creating an explosive situation of the type experienced with Hitler in Nazi Germany.

Other critical factors are derived from the study of psychohistory. A generation that has been severely traumatized and brutalized as were the Germans in World War I, and later with the near destruction of the fabric of their society, is at risk when even further affected by successive traumas. The defeat in World War I followed by post-war revolutionary activities, then inflation, then the world depression, and the polarization of values and politics, all in the short span of fifteen years made the situation maximally hazardous. In Germany, events contributed to a widespread surrender to pat ideologies, simplistic solutions, and rationalizations. The result was the exacerbation of pathological tendencies toward scapegoatism. There appears to be a direct correlation between an individual's or a society's pathology and the readiness to escape self-blame through the search for a scapegoat. Many societies have readily identified scapegoats. The Jews were the convenient scapegoats in Europe, and Nazi ideology, with its concept of "belonging" (to the Aryan race), was well served by anti-Semitism.

In the modern era, governments enjoy the technological capability to render mass killing both easier and more remote. Modern warfare engenders horrible genocidal potential, and remoteness from killer to victim makes rationalization easier. A society that legitimizes brutality and codifies the search for scapegoats also creates victims.

When is the scapegoat in danger of being sacrificed—of becoming the victim?

An individual becomes defenseless when stripped of constitutional and legal safeguards. A society that denies humans these safeguards can quickly make them into victims. In the twentieth

century we have had numerous demonstrations of the relative in-
efficacy of individuals or groups of people resisting against the state,
with its ability to marshal all instruments of power.

How do the potential victims survive? Whenever possible they
exercise the option of escaping to another country. If they cannot,
they must try to create a situation in which they are never subjected
to the arbitrariness of the agents of death. Their homes may literally
become their castles—the last tolerable environment. Some have
sought escape through suicide. If the victims are not organized for
defense, then learning how to engage in passive resistance or civil
disobedience can be another tactic, although one of very limited
effectiveness. This option was difficult to conceptualize for Central
and Eastern European Jews, whose orientation to law and order
represented part of their cultural environment. Another weapon in
the victim's arsenal of defense is the marshalling of public opinion,
both within and outside of the state. Yet, we should be under no
illusion that the uninvolved, remote from the scene and with concerns of their own, will rise to the occasion as need demands. For
instance, the ineffectiveness or callousness of response can be ex-
trapolated from the examples provided by the authorities abroad
that had other concerns. Evidence of the Holocaust was received
abroad with both incredulity and apathy.

What is the paradigm of a nation that has maximum potential for
engaging in genocidal behavior? Its government is authoritarian in
nature or in a state of crisis, such as war. Its people, through circumstances arising from consensus or nurtured by propaganda, have
been persuaded that its particular ideology justifies an expediential
ethic in which the end justifies the means. The sense of connection
that humans have with the vital and nourishing symbols of their
cultural traditions are broken down by the expediential ethic.
Psychologically, the culture is likely to be inclined towards overly
severe child-rearing habits, physical punishment, and instruction in
absolute obedience. Its people have been severely traumatized by
recent historical events, and brutalized by war. Timing itself is critical: a war or violent event in itself enhances the expediential ethic and
leads to callousness. The emerging pathologies can be of such sever-
ity that a scapegoat is ultimately identified and stamped as subhu-

man. Then sadism gone rampant results in slaughter—the elimination of the sacrificial scapegoat.

By contrast, what is the paradigm of a nation that is safe for those who could be identified as potential victims? It is a society engaged in the rule of law, a culture in which childrearing habits are supportive of loving and caring relationships. It is a society with high moral principles, a society that teaches the importance of human dignity and worth, a society that is not troubled by deep traumas or subject to brutalization by wars. It is a nation with a positive attitude toward a diversity of views, in which a large number of minorities display well-developed and positive self-identities. Under conditions of hazard, strong minority organizations will prevail if civil disobedience or resistance to arbitrary authority is deemed to safeguard that society's health. Such a society offers the hope of protection against genocide.

I conclude with an exhortation: The study of the Holocaust is not an esoteric or antiquarian subject, but a matter of vital concern to us all. It is a matter that demands constant awareness and alertness. Else, as Santayana said, those who do not learn from their history are condemned to relive it. The past four decades have shown that humans must learn more quickly if there is to be no need to write a future *We Survived*.

NOTES

1. Eric H. Boehm, *We Survived* (New Haven: Yale University Press, 1949; Santa Barbara, CA: Clio Press, 1966), 149.

2. Philip Meyer, "If Hitler Asked You to Electrocute a Stranger, Would You? Probably," reprinted in *Readings in Psychology*, 78–79 (Guilford, CT: Dushkin Publishing Group, 1978), 288.

3. Ibid., 289.

4. I refer readers to two excellent articles by George M. Kren: "The Literature of the Holocaust," *Choice* (January 1979): 1479–90, and "Psychohistorical Interpretations of National Socialism," *German Studies Review*, 1, no. 2 (May 1978): 150–72.

Epilogue 2003

To ASK ONESELF WHAT BECAME OF THE PEOPLE in these preceding stories is a plausible question, evoked when reading biographies that engage our minds and emotions. Readers are reminded that these are episodes of the lives of persons that were interviewed more than five decades earlier, mostly in 1946 and 1947. Some of them were well along in their lives at that time. Over the years Inge Boehm and I stayed in touch with them as much as possible—not always an easy task as they became older, as their health declined and as we were more distant, they living in Europe, we in the United States. Yet as this edition is being prepared, these are some of the persons whose final years we witnessed—cited here in the order of their chapters in this book:

Knud Knudsen (Chapter 3) became a celebrated sculptor. He died in 1996, predeceased by his wife, Doris, and survived by their son, Bjoern. Knudsen was the last to die of the persons whose lives are conveyed in this book.

Valerie Wolffenstein (Chapter 4) continued to work as an artist and had the greatest longevity of all persons of this book; she lived to be 101.

Lagi Countess Ballestrem-Solf (Chapter 7) despaired about the future of the world; she died in the 1950s, still relatively young.

Eugen Gerstenmaier (Chapter 9) stayed active in postwar German politics and served for a time as president of the Bundestag, the German parliament.

Heinrich Liebrecht (Chapter 11) reemigrated from the United States to Germany to join the German consular service; he served in senior positions in several cities in Europe. He and his wife then retired to Freiburg, Germany, where they died, a decade ago, she the second to die, in 1992.

Leo Baeck (Chapter 13) continued in his role as a distinguished

Jewish leader. I met him in 1948 when he was teaching at the Hebrew Union College in Cincinnati, Ohio. The Leo Baeck Institutes that nurture the study of the history and culture of Central European Jewry were named after him. In addition to the Berlin and London institutes by that name, a branch bearing his name is now located in the monumental Jewish Museum, established in recent years in Berlin.

The maps serving as endpapers of this book were drawn by "W. Ralf," a German artist living in Berlin. They identify the locations of some of the sites mentioned in the text.

The faith expressed in the dark days before and during World War II of "the coming victory of democracy" brought forth also the hope for an ultimate victory of humane behavior over evil. In this sense I close this edition of *We Survived* by quoting the uplifting words of David Krieger, president of the Nuclear Age Peace Foundation, from the initial pages of volume 1 of *The Encyclopedia of Genocide:*[1]

[1]From the frontispiece of Israel W. Charny, editor-in-chief, *Encyclopedia of Genocide* (ABC-Clio, 1999).

ON BECOMING HUMAN

To be human is to recognize the cultural perspectives that bind us to the tribe, sect, religion, or nation, and to rise above them. It is to feel the pain of the dispossessed, the downtrodden, the refugee, the starving child, the slave, the victim.

To be human is to break the ties of cultural conformity and group-think, and to use one's own mind. It is to recognize good and evil, and to choose good. It is to consider with the heart. It is to act with conscience.

To be human is to be courageous. It is to choose the path of compassion. It is to sacrifice for what is just. It is to break the silence. It is to be an unrelenting advocate of human decency and dignity.

To be human is to breathe with the rhythm of life, and to recognize our kinship with all forms of life. It is to appreciate every drop of water. It is to feel the warmth of the sun, and to marvel at the beauty and expanse of the night sky. It is to stand in awe of who we are and where we live. It is to see the Earth with the eyes of an astronaut.

To be human is to be aware of our dependence upon the whole of the universe, and of the miracle that we are. It is to open our eyes to the simple and extraordinary beauty that is all about us. It is to live with deep respect for the sacred gift of life. It is to love.

To be human is to seek to find ourselves behind our names. It is to explore the depths and boundaries of our existence. It is to learn from those who have preceded us, and to act with due concern for those who follow us.

To be human is to plant the seeds of peace, and to nurture them. It is to find peace and make peace. It is to help mend the web of life. It is to be healer of the planet.

To be human is to say an unconditional No! to warfare, and particularly to the use of weapons of mass destruction. It is to take a firm stand against all who profit from warfare and its preparation.

To be human is not always to succeed, but it is always to learn. It is to move forward despite the obstacles.

We are all born with the potential to become fully human. How we choose to live will be the measure of our humanness. Civilization does not assure our civility. Nor does being born into the human species assure our humanity. We must each find our own path to becoming human.

About the Author

We *Survived* was one of the first biographic books to address the evils of Nazi Germany and the Holocaust. It reflected Eric H. Boehm's historical quest for answers about a pathological society. He felt that at the outset that initially this quest could be most effectively addressed via a broad range of biographies that covered the relevant experiences.

Boehm's life spans many years as a historian, editor, and publisher. His educational focus shifted from chemistry to history as a consequence of being mentored by Dr. Aileen Dunham, a brilliant professor of history at the College of Wooster in Ohio. From Wooster he received a B.A.(1940), an honorary D.Litt. (1973), and a Distinguished Alumnus Award (1990); from the Fletcher School of Law and Diplomacy an M.A.(1942); and from Yale University a Ph.D.(1952). After a decade of service in the military and government, as an enlisted man, officer, and employee in the U.S. government, Boehm founded the international publishing house of ABC-Clio, Inc., with its exclusively historical emphasis at the outset. He served as its CEO and, later, as chairman (from 1955 to 1982). He was cofounder of the Information Institute and the International Academy at Santa Barbara, whose focuses have been environment, dissemination of information, and education via computer-facilitated distance learning in management. Currently he serves as its chairman of the board. A pioneer in launching computerized databases, Boehm was the first publisher to bring humanities publications into online computer systems. He originated *Historical Abstracts* and other bibliographic services in history, political science, and art history. Representative of his writings on the subjects that deal with this book are "Policy-Making of the Nazi Government" (Ph.D. diss., Yale, 1951); "The Free Germans in Soviet Psychological Warfare," in *A Psychological Warfare Casebook,* edited by

W.E. Daugherty and M. Janowitz (1958); "Hitler's Decision to Attack the Soviet Union: The End of the Grand Design," in *Essays in Russian History: A Collection Dedicated to George Vernadsky* (1964); and "Comment: 'Prevention of Genocide,'" in *Western Society After the Holocaust,* edited by Lyman H. Legters (Westview Press, 1983). Among the honors he received are, with his family, a "Local Heroes" award as community activists (1994), an "Innovator of the Year" award by the Santa Barbara Chamber of Commerce (1996), and two book dedications, one by R.L. Collison (*A History of Foreign-Language Dictionaries,* 1982), the other by L.J. McCrank (*Historical Information Science: An Emerging Unidiscipline,* 2001). In 2003 (at age 85), the year of publication of this edition of *We Survived,* Boehm continues to pursue his historical and biographic quests through the Inge Pauli Institute (website: http://www.Pauli-I.org) named after his late wife. Dedicated to helping people honor their past as a stimulus for moving forward, the Pauli Institute focuses on lessons to be learned from biographic studies of individuals, families or organizations, and teaches related tasks such as preparation of obituaries, establishment of archives, and celebrations of anniversaries.

INDEX

Names indicated by an asterisk are fictitious.

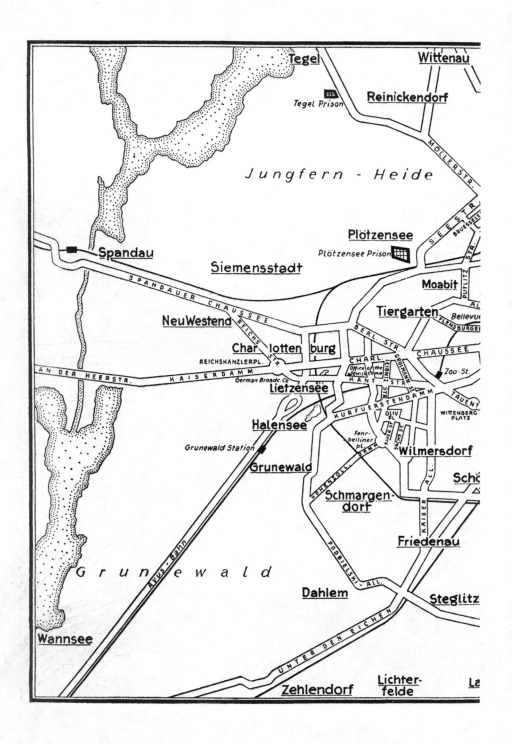

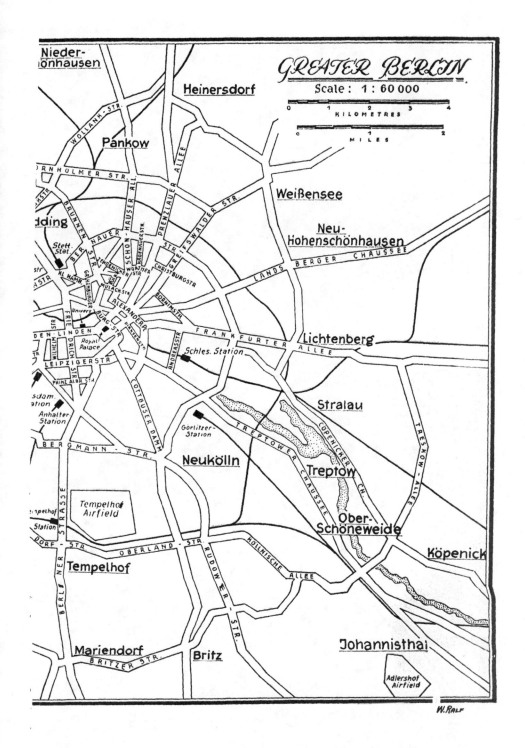